FACING THE DRAGON

How a Desperate Act Pulled One Addict Out of Methamphetamine Hell

DAVID PARNELL

WITH AMY HAMMOND HAGBERG

Health Communications, Inc.
Deerfield Beach, Florida

www.hcibooks.com

Library of Congress Cataloging-in-Publication Data

Parnell, David.
Facing the dragon : how a desperate act pulled one addict out of
   methamphetamine hell / David Parnell with Amy Hammond Hagberg.
      p. cm.
   ISBN-13: 978-0-7573-1523-7
   ISBN-10: 0-7573-1523-2
   1. Ex-drug addicts—United States—Biography.   2. Methamphetamine
abuse—United States.   I. Hagberg, Amy Hammond.   II. Title.
HV5805.P37.A3 2010
362.29'9—dc22
   [B]

                                                      2010034623

Publisher: Health Communications, Inc.
        3201 S.W. 15th Street
        Deerfield Beach, FL 33442–8190

Cover design by Justin Rotkowitz
Interior design and formatting by Lawna Patterson Oldfield

Contents

Acknowledgments

I WISH TO THANK MY COAUTHOR, Amy Hagberg, for her belief in this book and for taking on such a big task that had to be emotionally difficult at times. I also want to thank her for her knowledge of the writing process, all her hours of work, and her dedication.

I'd also like to thank my literary agent, Claire Gerus, for all her work. She embraced this project wholeheartedly and was able to find the perfect publisher in record time.

I wish to thank my wife, Amy, for her continuous love and support and for all the time she spent researching, typing, and coordinating the efforts of Amy Hagberg and myself while still managing our day-to-day lives, which by itself is no easy task.

I am also grateful to Dr. Mary Holley, whose book (*Crystal Meth: They Call It "Ice"*) and research were instrumental in explaining methamphetamine addiction throughout this book.

Vanderbilt University Medical Center physicians Dr. Kevin Hagan, Dr. Addison May, and Dr. Samuel McKenna and their staffs took good care of me and got me to the point of being able to live again, much less write a book. I wish to thank them and also those in the medical records department for making the process of receiving my medical records so painless.

I wish to thank my grandparents, Hale and Oma Williams and Doyle and Edna Parnell, for all their love and care over the years, and my mother, Kay, and my father, David Sr., because without them I wouldn't be here. I am especially thankful for my children—Sarah, David, Rachel, Josiah, Rebekah, Abigail, and Gabriel—for the great inspiration they have given me.

For everyone else across the country who encouraged me to write this book, I extend my heartfelt thanks. At times, I didn't think it was a very good idea and didn't have the enthusiasm to move forward. I am glad I listened to all those voices.

—*David Parnell*

———— ◆ ————

TO MY COAUTHOR, DAVID PARNELL: Thank you for putting up with my nosey questions and constant rewrites. You made me cry, and laugh, and better appreciate those who love me. I am proud of you for sharing your story no matter the consequences. Someday you will be able to grasp the impact you have made on those who are teetering on the edge.

To the love of my life: Being married to a writer, particularly one who specializes in highly emotional subject matter, is no walk in the park. Thank you, Craig, for holding my hand tightly as I walk through the barren valleys and ascend the breathtaking mountaintops. Thank you for encouraging me to sequester myself away, despite the obvious inconvenience to yourself. You are a saint.

To our children, Kaia, Connor, and our new son Josh: Thank you for being proud of me and always emboldening me to reach for the stars. I may be small, and I may never touch them, but I am hopeful all the same.

To my parents, Bud and Joyce Hammond: Thank you for paving the way for me to be who God created me to be. I'm sure you were worried when I cut off my corporate golden handcuffs and stepped into the unknown abyss of writing, but you always told me I could do whatever I set my mind to . . . and you were right!

To my in-laws, Norm and Joyce Hagberg: thank you for opening up your lakeside getaway so I could lock myself in solitary confinement for two months to focus on this book. Your generosity and encouragement will never be forgotten. Someday I hope you figure out where I put everything. My appreciation also extends to the neighbors who interred a dead pheasant, offered a friendly glass of wine, and otherwise made sure I was safe and sound.

To Claire Gerus: Thank you for instantly seeing the purpose and potential of this project and hopping on the phone. I think you had a publishing deal before the ink dried on the proposal. Bravo!

To my editor at HCI Books, Carol Rosenberg: Thank you for your vision and guidance. Your questions and promptings rounded out the book and made it much better. I'm certain editing the work of another editor is a special challenge, so thank you for handling me with grace, and sometimes kid gloves!

To my prayer warriors (you know who you are): This was an emotional assignment. Thank you for lifting me up throughout the duration. I heard your petitions and felt your love every day.

Most importantly, I wish to thank my Father, through whom all things are possible.

—Amy Hammond Hagberg

A Note from Amy Hammond Hagberg

EACH OF US HAS TWO STORIES: one for public dissemination, the other locked away deep inside for self analysis only. In most cases, we allow the world to see but a fraction of who we really are, like an ancient iceberg whose tip feels the sun, but whose massive body lies beneath the surface of a vast, frigid sea. It's a rare thing when somebody shares their most private moments, biggest mistakes, and innermost demons for friends and strangers alike to judge and dissect.

I first met David Parnell when I interviewed him for a small Minnesota newspaper. He was in town to speak at several anti-methamphetamine events in surrounding communities. I was nervous as I walked in the door of a local coffee shop; I worried it would be difficult to focus on our conversation with his obvious disfigurement staring at me across the table. To my surprise, it took just a few minutes to get past his appearance and see the beautiful man behind the mask.

David has an inner glow, a reward for a very hard-fought battle. As he shared his story, I was taken aback by both his humility and his passion for preventing young people from following in his footsteps. We talked for hours, yet I knew instinctively that we had barely brushed the surface.

After more than two years of dialogue, David invited me to come alongside him to write *Facing the Dragon*. This book is the result of more than sixty hours of emotionally draining personal interviews. During the course of our conversations I often sat open-mouthed as David candidly related the events of his childhood and adult life. There were no holds barred, no subject off limits. I am grateful he trusted me enough to tell me things he had never told another living soul.

Our intent was never to produce a shocking tell-all memoir for purely entertainment purposes. *Facing the Dragon* is deliberately disturbing because it is meant to serve as a warning, and as a reminder that seemingly innocuous choices can have devastating —and deadly—consequences. What we do today has a powerful impact on what happens tomorrow in our own lives, but more importantly in the lives of the innocents that surround us.

Few people journey to hell and live to tell about it. David Parnell was clearly spared from eternal torment that bleak February day because he had a special assignment. He is living proof that God is real and that everyone, no matter their mistakes, can be transformed into new creations.

I am honored and humbled to share his incredible story.

A Note from
David Parnell

I WAS A DRUG ADDICT for twenty-three years. Seven of those years were spent abusing methamphetamine. On February 21, 2003, while under the influence of meth, I decided to end my life. I felt like drugs had robbed me of everything, including any last vestiges of hope. I shot myself in the head with a high-powered assault rifle. Miraculously, I survived.

When I woke up in the trauma unit after the shooting, I knew God had kept me alive for a reason—to tell people the truth about drugs. Initially, I had no idea how I was going to do that; I couldn't even talk.

Months progressed, and I learned how to speak again. I began telling my story and that of my family to anyone who would listen. I started speaking at churches and jails, which eventually led to schools, both public and private. I branched out to media outlets and appeared in national newspapers and on television, but it still didn't feel like it was enough. I knew I needed to do more.

For years people have encouraged me to write a book. At first, even though it seemed like the best way to accomplish my mission of warning everyone about the dangers of addiction, I dismissed the idea. I'm not a writer and only graduated high school by chance. I didn't have the faintest idea how to write a book. Beyond that, I wasn't sure anyone would want to read one if I wrote it.

Then one day I met Amy Hagberg, a published author and established speaker, and discovered she shared my vision. The idea of writing a memoir was still daunting, but I had the feeling it was time. With the encouragement of my wife, we decided to give it a shot.

Writing this book was not an easy task. Unless a person has had a fairy-tale life or has a heart of stone, reliving terrible memories and having those memories put on paper for all to see is emotionally difficult, to say the least. There is very little, if anything, in this book that would make for polite conversation. Some things are downright disturbing. I had trouble deciding whether or not some things should be included, but in the end, I decided to bare my soul, because it's the truth. It's reality. It's what so many other addicted people—and, more important, their children—are living through every day, and it is much more common than many people would like to believe.

I knew sharing my story was bound to upset some of the people closest to me, but I couldn't tell it with authenticity without including these things. I struggled with the decision, and I want everyone to know that it wasn't my intention to hurt anyone—only to tell the truth. In some instances, names have been changed to protect the privacy of others or their families.

Addiction doesn't discriminate. It doesn't matter if you come from a highly dysfunctional family and a rough background or from the wealthiest family in town. If you make the wrong choices, the outcome is the same. The dysfunction in my family may have started me on a road destined for addiction and abuse, but the reality is that if I had made better choices along the way my life would have been very different. In the end, I am the one responsible for my reprehensible behavior.

I hope that by writing this book with brutal honesty, I can give people hope. It is my intention to show people that no matter what they've done and how badly they've screwed up, they *can* change and have a good life. They *can* make a good life for their children or future children. They *can* be the ones to break the cycle.

I also hope this book will open the eyes of the nonaddicted population to what is going on around them. There are addicted people in your neighborhoods, churches, and jails who need help. Neglected and abused children everywhere need someone to intervene on their behalf. I hope I motivate people to become more involved and speak for those who cannot. I pray that I help people realize that addiction affects everyone—personally, socially, and/or financially—and we have to put an end to it.

ONE

Between the Devil and the Deep Blue Sea

He who fights too long against dragons
becomes a dragon himself; and if you gaze too long
into the abyss, the abyss will gaze into you.

— Friedrich Nietzsche

STABLE ENOUGH TO TRAVEL, I was loaded into the back of a waiting ambulance for the grueling 170-mile trip to a larger hospital in Nashville. I was in critical condition, teetering on a tightrope between life and death. The paramedic kept a close eye on me, alternating between administering IVs and watching my vital signs. Things were going fine, and then unexpectedly, my heart stopped.

1

I knew instantly I was dead. Yet, rather than feeling fear or panic, I felt an incredible sense of peace—I can hardly put into words how good it felt. One moment I was bleeding on my bedroom floor, my entire body throbbing from the damage I had done to my face, and in an instant the pain was gone and I had been transported to another dimension. I was surprised that I could see my legs; I guess I thought a spirit wouldn't have a body at all. My body was weightless and buoyant; it was like I was ten years old again, but this time I could jump as high as the ceiling. I felt terrific! This had to be heaven.

Out of the inky darkness a woman appeared, flanked by several people on either side of her. She was stunningly beautiful with long, dark, wavy hair, high cheekbones, and a narrow face. She looked very much like a Native American, the type of woman I had always been attracted to. My eyes locked onto her, and I couldn't break my gaze.

"How do you feel?" she asked, smiling broadly.

I felt completely at ease.

"I feel great!" I replied.

I couldn't remember feeling that good in a long time.

No sooner had the words come out than the woman's previously beautiful features contorted, turning dark and sinister. Her lovely face morphed into something revolting and frightening. Her eyes were squinty and penetrating, and she curled her lips and showed her teeth like a snarling animal. Then she hunched over like a beast and growled.

The woman wasn't the only one who had transformed into a demon; the entire group snapped at me like they wanted to rip me apart. I've never been afraid of much on this earth, but that place—especially that woman—frightened me so much I thought

I was going to explode from the inside, like I had a bomb of fear in me. They were so close I could have reached out and touched them, and the closer they got, the more panicked I became. I was gripped by an absolutely indescribable terror.

It wasn't just fear I felt at that moment; it was a profound sense of loneliness. I knew I was separated from God, and I can't begin to explain how desperate I felt. I knew I wasn't in heaven after all; this was most assuredly hell. I don't mean the religious view of a fire-and-brimstone hell; it was more like the outer gates of an inescapable prison. I believe demons come in many different forms, and in my case, Satan's underling came as a beautiful woman, because that was my biggest weakness.

As the woman inched closer I became so frightened I could no longer bear to look at her, and cast my gaze straight up. Having been so focused on the beautiful woman, I hadn't realized how dark it was all around me. It wasn't pitch-black like the dark of night; it was more like a thick, solid black cloud I could literally cut through, a dark abyss. There was a dark, smoky glare around me, like I was onstage in a blackened theater with only a spotlight to illuminate the darkness. I looked up into the inky blackness and screamed with everything I had, "Please, God, help me!" That's when I heard them, the sound of a million souls screaming at the top of their lungs in agony and panic. Their torment was terrifying and sent icy shivers up my spine.

In the blink of an eye I found myself in a completely different place. Everything was bathed in a warm, bright light. I was no longer in the presence of demons, but gazing up at a man who looked like an old patriarch of the Bible. He had solid white hair and a snowy beard, and his mustache was so thick I couldn't see his top lip. His skin was like bronze, reminding me of the Apostle

John's vision of the risen Christ in Revelation 1:15, NKJV: "His feet were like bronze glowing in a furnace, and his voice was like the sound of rushing waters."

The man's most remarkable features were his eyes. They were so piercing I couldn't look away. They were a beautiful warm brown, almost hazel, and he had wrinkles around both of them, like a weathered farmer. I didn't get the sense he was old, though; his were the kind of deep lines one gets from smiling. Still terrified by what I'd just experienced, I stood before the man shaking like a little kid anticipating his punishment. Then he grinned and all the fear left me, replaced by a tremendous sense of calm. I knew then that I was in heaven and was full of gratitude that God had lifted me out of that horrible place.

The next thing I remember is waking up three days later in a hospital bed. I don't know how long I had flatlined in the back of that ambulance—it could've been thirty seconds or it could've been for a minute or two. In eternity there is no sense of time. The experience reminded me of the movie *Contact,* in which actress Jodie Foster climbed into a time machine and went to heaven. When she returned to Earth, she felt like she had spent a week there, when actually she was only in the machine for a few seconds.

My near-death experience proved to me that God is real and so is His enemy. I can't stand the thought of knowing there will be human beings who will spend eternity where I went. I don't want anybody to go to that dark abyss, not even my worst enemy. I've tried my best, but there's no way I can describe how terrifying hell was—I've never felt those emotions before, and I hope I never do again. Please, God, don't let me go back to that place.

I'm always hesitant to share this part of my story, because

people can be skeptical of things they don't understand. When I first started speaking, I shared my experience everywhere I went, but I got such weird responses in churches that I quit. Frankly, I was embarrassed. Those who did believe me thought I had probably met Moses or another prophet, but I know in my heart that I met Jesus Christ that day.

I've even had preachers tell me I was just hallucinating, that I wasn't really in heaven or hell; that it was merely a chemical reaction in my brain when I died. One particular preacher, who is both a police officer and a minister, said he didn't believe me. He operated on facts and evidence, and I had no proof. Believe me, life after death is real.

You can call it whatever you want to, but my family and I know I haven't been the same since I was put into the back of that ambulance. I am a new man.

TWO

Sins of the Father

---

*The words that a father speaks to his children
in the privacy of home are not heard by the world, but,
as in whispering galleries, they are clearly heard
at the end, and by posterity.*

— Jean Paul Richter

YOU CAN GO WAY BACK AND SEE PREACHERS in the Parnell family tree. Great-great-granddad Parnell and his son, my great-granddad, were preachers, as was my granddad and all his brothers. There were uncles, aunts, and cousins, both male and female, who preached the Gospel too. I guess you could say I come from a long line of God-fearing people—to a point, that is.

6

The Cycle Begins

Before my great-granddad Ernest Parnell was a preacher, he was a prizefighter, a rather unlikely metamorphosis. Ernest was a big Irishman, and at six feet four and more than two hundred pounds, he was a real force to be reckoned with. My great-grandmother was a Cherokee Indian. I never met Ernest, but I did meet Grandma Camilla. By the time I met her, she was a heavyset woman full of love and generosity. Every year she sent me something for Christmas.

Ernest was a mean man, especially when things didn't go his way in the boxing ring. His kids always knew when their daddy had lost a fight, because he came home and kicked the door open instead of turning the knob. The family hid when they heard him coming—they were all scared to death of him.

When his son, my granddad Doyle, was about thirteen, his "tough guy" father pulled his punches, stepped out of the ring, and became a Christian. The change in him was like night and day; he no longer fought, quit drinking, and was so on fire for Jesus that he started preaching on street corners. Whether they liked it or not, the whole family was involved in Ernest's evangelism. On a regular basis, he announced to his sons, "Boys, get your guitars—we're going to town to preach."

Ernest made those teenage boys stand on street corners, play their guitars, and do worship music while their dad preached sermons and panhandled to get a little supper money. The boys stood in wonder when people came up to their father and spit on him and he didn't do anything. In days past he would have pummeled them.

Everybody thought the old man was crazy. Sometimes he'd just be standing around when all of a sudden the Spirit would hit him and he'd start whooping, hollering, and jumping up and down on the sidewalk. I'm sure it was a pretty drastic change watching him transition from being a brawler to a street preacher.

Not only did Ernest and Camilla have four boys, they had four girls too. Eventually, the entire brood of evangelists pulled up stakes and traversed the country, preaching the Gospel to the lost. In those early days, the Parnells were kind of like gypsies. To make ends meet they worked as migrant workers, moving from one area to another, following the growing seasons. They might pick cotton or melons or cut tobacco, depending on which crops grew in the areas of the country they were visiting. They picked up a little money holding tent meetings, and somebody would always invite the preacher and his family over for a meal after the revival. The Parnells were desperately poor and survived on big slabs of bologna the government supplied during the Great Depression.

My granddad Doyle Parnell was the oldest of the kids. I remember him telling me stories about his identical twin brothers, Roy and Rex. The twins were built like heavyweight boxing champion Mike Tyson—they stood about five feet eleven, had no necks, and were solid muscle. They were monsters; one of them could bench-press five hundred pounds. Both became Golden Gloves champions in Oklahoma; they didn't take guff from anybody.

Roy and Rex were always punching out somebody. One Sunday morning after the service, the family was invited to a church member's house for dinner. The old farmer gave great-granddad a warning: "Preacher, you'd better watch them boys of yours around that old mule I got out there; that thing will kick 'em and hurt 'em. He's really kind of a wild mule."

Great-granddad Ernest jumped up and said, "You've got a mule out there?" Now it wasn't his twins he was worried about; it was the animal. Sure enough, when he ran outside, he found those boys beating on the poor mule. They had wrapped rags around their hands and were taking turns hitting the defenseless beast between the eyes to see which of them could knock it out first. The mule was already down on its front knees by the time Ernest got out there. The twins did stuff like that all the time. Of course, it embarrassed the heck out of the preacher. Believe it or not, after those boys quit knocking out farm animals, they both became preachers themselves.

Ernest was one of those old guys who wouldn't go to the doctor no matter how sick he was. One day he hurt his leg really bad, but no matter how hard his family begged him to go to the hospital and get it fixed, he just wouldn't do it. Before long, gangrene set in. Doctors told Ernest they needed to amputate his leg to halt the infection, but the stubborn old Irishman adamantly refused.

The infection got into his blood and poisoned him. He became deathly ill and was confined to bed. Visitors said when they walked into his bedroom the smell of that festering wound just about knocked them down. It was the sickening, putrid stench of rotting flesh. Surprisingly, though, when they leaned down to talk to him, they couldn't smell the leg. It was as if God shielded him from the smell. Great-granddad died of gangrene poisoning. It was not an easy way to go.

Next in Line

After his father passed away, Doyle moved his family to a little town called Water Valley, Kentucky. During the week he was a mechanic and taught his boys, David, Joe, and Jerry, how to build hot rods and work on people's cars. Like his daddy before him, Doyle preached at a little Pentecostal church.

Pentecostals are very musical people, and the Parnells were no exception. The whole family played in the worship band: Uncle Joe on drums, Granddad Doyle on the guitar, my dad on the bass, and my grandma and Aunt Glenda on the piano, organ, and electric piano. I think my uncle Jerry was the only kid who wasn't in the band; he had a hard time just playing the radio.

Granddaddy Doyle was a stout, short-haired redneck with a bad temper. A very hard man, he believed it was his Christian duty to whup his kids if they messed up. He'd backhand them and knock them out of their chairs if they said the wrong thing at suppertime. He once whupped my dad so bad he could hardly move for two weeks.

Not only did Granddaddy Doyle beat his boys, he was strict in other ways too. They weren't allowed to play basketball in school because they had to wear short pants, which their father viewed as inappropriate. He did let them play football, though, because that was his favorite sport and they didn't have to show much skin. The kids couldn't do the things their friends did, like dance or go to the movies.

When the kids grew up they had a lot of hard feelings toward their father because of those beatings. They were bitter; their father preached about mercy, love, and forgiveness from the pulpit on Sunday, but was anything but loving during the rest of the week. Doyle didn't believe he was hypocritical at all; in his view the Bible told him to be stern and dish out the discipline. His children disagreed—and rebelled.

Long-haired Country Boy

When the boys got older and had a taste of freedom, they went buck wild. It was as if they were telling their daddy, "We'll show you; we're going to do whatever we want to do." Joe and David became drunks and drug addicts and ran around town getting crazy. Imagine the humiliation. Just to spite his dad, Joe ran off and joined the army and ended up in Vietnam. I understand now why Granddad Doyle left the pulpit and went into evangelism instead. It was tough for him to tell people about God when he couldn't keep his own house in order.

As soon as my dad turned eighteen, he left home to join his uncle Guy, who was playing honky-tonks in Fort Worth, Texas. My dad never went back to church or had anything to do with the faith he was brought up in. Like him, I was told about Jesus by the preaching Parnells. Some of my first memories are of going to church with my mom and my granddad Williams. Mom usually attended Granddaddy Parnell's Pentecostal church, but Granddad was more interested in hearing the Gospel from a variety of perspectives. We visited a bunch of congregations, usually two or three times, but never became members. He and I went to a Mormon church when I was very young, but when Granddad got into an argument with the preacher about some of their doctrines, we moved on. Eventually, we settled in a Baptist church. From the time I was a little guy, all I ever heard about was God, God, God.

I asked Dad once why he didn't go to church. He said he believed in God but had been forced to go to church his entire life. Now that he had a choice, he wouldn't go. Dad made it sound like it was such a terrible thing to make a kid go to church that it

was like torture. There are far worse things than that, believe me.
When I was growing up my father was a drug addict and abusive
to everyone around him. He was so selfish that he'd buy himself
a hamburger and eat it before he got home, even though his kids
were hungry and their feet were hanging out of their worn-out
shoes. He'd take the last little money we had and buy dope or a
beat-up car that didn't even run. Those were his priorities. He was
a fine one to talk about how bad his daddy was.

Before long, Dad was smoking pot heavily. Now this was
around 1960, and marijuana wasn't all that common in those
days. That's where his life of drugs and alcohol started. He was
in total rebellion against God and tried to be the exact opposite
of his father, who didn't lie, steal, drink, or smoke. Dad did all
of these.

After a few years in Fort Worth, Dad moved back to Kentucky.
He ran around with people who stole stuff just for kicks. It wasn't
like thirty years later when Dad did every kind of drug he could
get his hands on and needed to find a way to support his habit.
Dad had a job; in fact, all the guys in his ring of thieves worked.
That's what made it so hard to catch them; the police were looking for people who needed money.

When he was twenty-three, Dad met a pretty nineteen-year-
old named Kay Williams at a dance hall; Kay and a group of her
girlfriends were watching Dad's band perform. It wasn't long
before they got married. I think my mother got more than she
bargained for with him. By this time he was a whiskey alcoholic
and was regularly smoking marijuana. He was mean, violent, and
had a very explosive temper. Not long into the marriage, he
started beating her.

I was born on December 25, 1966. The family was about to sit down for Christmas dinner at my aunt's house when they had to rush my mom to the hospital to give birth. I still kid her that she holds it against me that she missed Christmas dinner.

I was raised in Dukedom, Tennessee, right on the Tennessee/ Kentucky state line, one of the oldest communities in West Tennessee. The town developed on an old stagecoach route back in 1830. It's a tiny, unincorporated town with a population of fewer than five hundred people. Nearly 18 percent of the families live below the poverty line. When I was growing up, there was a bank and a couple of other stores in town, but now all they have is a gas station, a funeral home, and a post office.

When I was one and a half years old, my mom got pregnant with fraternal twins. She was huge; she could literally put her supper plate on her stomach and eat from it like it was a table. When my sisters Mechell and Shantell were born, they were enormous—they both weighed more than eight pounds. It's hard to believe my mother carried more than seventeen pounds of baby inside her! Of course, she didn't have any help from my dad; he missed the birth because he was in prison.

Dad's entire gang, more than a dozen of them, had finally been caught stealing. This wasn't just petty theft we're talking about; they had a thriving livestock-rustling operation. Rustling was something you'd commonly hear about happening back in the 1860s, but this was the 1960s, and these guys were rustling people's cattle. They went out at night and stole hogs and cattle and took the animals down to their private slaughterhouse. Within forty-eight hours the animals were killed and worked into meat, which was then sold so there was no evidence.

The leader of the gang was known as "Scrap Iron" Johnson because he bought old plows and other broken-down equipment from farmers and sold them for scrap iron to make extra cash. I remember Granddaddy Doyle telling me that Scrap Iron was downright scary and the strongest man he had ever seen in his life. When my dad was a kid, Scrap Iron used to visit Doyle's auto repair shop and buy old blown-out motors. Most people need a chain and hoist to extract them, but Scrap Iron could pick up a V-8 engine and set it down in the back of his pickup truck all by himself. I met him many years later, and he was just like my dad and granddad had described him. Even at seventy, you could tell this guy was a bad dude. These were the kinds of guys my dad hung out with.

They say there is no honor among thieves, and that definitely applied in this case. In the end, Scrap Iron's girlfriend ratted out the gang. She had gotten into some trouble with the law, and in exchange for a lighter sentence, she told the police about the rustling operation. Scrap Iron wasn't the kind of guy you wanted to mess with. He told his buddies he was going to kill her: "I won't let that whore walk the streets while I go to prison and sit there the rest of my life." And he meant it. He took a claw hammer and beat that young woman until you couldn't tell who she was, and then, just to make sure she got the message, he shot her in the chest with a 12-gauge shotgun.

Several of his fellow gang members testified against Scrap Iron, saying he had told them he was going to kill his girlfriend, but my dad kept his mouth shut. His friends all thought it was a badge of honor that Dad didn't turn state's evidence, but that's not what motivated him; he was simply scared to death of Scrap Iron. There was no way he was going to tell on a guy who had just beaten his girlfriend to death with a piece of hardware. If Dad could have gotten out of prison without worrying about dying, he probably would have thrown Scrap Iron to the wolves too.

The whole group was sent to prison for a year or two on cattle-rustling charges. Scrap Iron, however, was found guilty of murder and spent two decades in a maximum security facility. My dad served a year in Kentucky State Penitentiary in Eddyville, Kentucky. Back in those days, prison life was pretty rough. He saw two people get killed in a matter of just a year's time. That kind of thing changes a man.

A Vicious Circle

After he was released, Dad went back to running the same old crap, only he was even meaner than before. Like most abusive relationships, the spousal violence didn't start after Mom and Dad walked down the aisle; there were signs of abuse from the very beginning. But after he got out of prison, his level of violence escalated. It wasn't uncommon for him to smack her around and blacken both of her eyes. He frequently committed adultery and didn't care if my mom knew about it. One night he brazenly brought his girlfriend home and proceeded to thrash my mom and shut her in a closet. There's no telling what he and his lover did after that. Hopefully you're seeing a pattern here—my dad was a bad guy.

From the time I was two and a half years old, I lived with my maternal grandparents, Hale and Oma Williams, who lived ten miles up the road from my parents' duplex in town. With my dad's escalating violence, they thought they'd better get me out of there. I only remember staying with my parents twice after moving to the farm with my grandparents, and both incidents had a profound impact on my formative years.

On one occasion I remember Dad choking Mom and then beating her head into the wall until she was unconscious. I screamed at him to stop and jerked on his back pocket trying to pull him away from her, but he backhanded me and knocked me to the floor. The neighbors downstairs heard them fighting and called my grandmother. Grandma showed up a few minutes later with three or four elderly women by her side, all wielding pistols because they were so afraid of my dad.

As a little guy I couldn't understand why these women came to my mom's rescue. But we're talking about the 1960s here, and in those days an abused woman couldn't just pick up the phone and call social services. There were no battered women's shelters or "first call for help" websites. Most of the time, victims of domestic violence didn't even call the police because they were so one-sided against women; many of them were beating their wives too.

That's why my grandmother and her squad of vigilantes came in to rescue her daughter, who was being abused; women had to stick together. Years later I asked my grandmother why she was always the one who came to my mother's aid. She said it was because my granddad was afraid he would kill my dad; that if he ever lost it, there would be no pulling back. Granddad Hale was one of the strongest men in the county, so he wasn't afraid of my dad—he was afraid of himself. That's not to say Hale never intervened. In fact, one time my dad started smacking my mom around right in the back room of her parents' house. Imagine the guts that took. Granddad actually ran him off that day and took a shot over the top of his car.

When I was older, about nine or ten, I used to have flashbacks of my mom's screaming and hollering while my dad beat her up.

In my dreams I was always crying. I actually remember lying in bed in the dark thinking that one day I was going to kill that guy for what he did to my mama. It's frightening to think I had thoughts of murder when I was such a little kid.

Not surprisingly, my parents divorced. I was five at the time, and I vividly remember when my mom and two sisters moved in with me and my grandparents. I didn't see my dad again until I was eleven. Even though we didn't have a relationship, that didn't stop him from being a daddy; he had seven kids with five different wives.

There's no other way to put it—my dad was a lowlife who got off on beating his wives and doing drugs with his kids. Until the day he died, he was nothing but a negative influence on me. His daddy always dreamed his son would be a preacher, but he was sorely disappointed. There's an old proverb that says the nut doesn't fall far from the tree. Well, in my father's case, the tree must have been on a slope, because the nut rolled downhill. The cycle came full circle with me when I became a wife-beating drug addict, too.

THREE

Little Boy Blue

People who treat other people as less than human must not be surprised when the bread they have cast on the waters comes floating back to them, poisoned.

— James Baldwin

EVERY SO OFTEN I SEE a commercial on the History Channel for an upcoming documentary. The film clip shows a little Japanese boy crouched in the mud shaking while an American soldier gives him some water. Whenever I see that footage, my brain flashes back to when I first moved to the farm to live with my grandparents. Grandma Williams told me I was the only kid she had ever seen that shook all the time. I stuttered too; I stumbled on the simplest words. It was almost like shell shock—the abuse I had experienced at the hands of my father filled me with anxiety for years. Even now when I think about those early days, I start to cry.

A Place of Refuge

I loved the farm. Grandma and Granddad Williams had eighty-nine acres in rural Weakley County, Tennessee. Part of it was in tobacco and the rest alternated between wheat, corn, and soybeans. We had all kinds of animals too—cows, horses, pigs, goats, and every kind of bird you can think of. The peacocks were my favorite. It was paradise for a child like me who loved animals. Granddad also tended a huge garden with row upon row of delicious vegetables. Grandma and my aunt Susie did a lot of canning so there would be produce during the winter months.

One of my first memories of life on the farm is sitting in Granddad's lap driving his old tricycle tractor, the kind with two little wheels close together in the front. I felt like a big man when he let me steer. Unfortunately, I wasn't all that good at it. One day, when I was about four, I ran that tractor right into the fence where the hogs were kept and tore it down. *Oh God, I'm in huge trouble*, I thought. I just knew I was going to die. I was used to getting smacked around by my dad for making the tiniest mistakes, so I figured at bare minimum Granddad was going to scream at me. Instead, he started laughing, "Don't worry about it boy—it will be fine." You can't imagine the relief I felt. Granddad Williams became my hero that day.

Hale Williams was a redneck hillbilly farmer. He was tall and lanky with eyeglasses and closely cropped hair. Granddad always had a hat on his head. It wasn't a baseball cap like you see so many farmers wear nowadays; it was more like the kind of dress hat men wore back in the 1920s. His sported a little red feather on the side. He wore that fedora with everything, whether it was bib overalls or the familiar gray button-up shirt and black pants he wore later in life. Of course, he always wore work boots; no self-respecting farmer in those days wore tennis shoes.

Granddad was born in 1903. I don't know where his people came from, but I think he might have been a mix of English and Dutch. Granddad loved his pipe. I can picture him sitting on the front porch puffing away on that fragrant green tobacco in his favorite rocking chair. In all my life I never saw him watch TV, not even the news; he called it the "idiot box."

One of the things I have always admired about farm people is how they stick together. A few times a year we had hog-killing days, and the neighbors came over to help Granddad butcher a hog. Then when it was their time to slaughter, Granddad returned the favor. I sat there with mouthwatering anticipation as they ground the pork into sausage with special spices. It was the best stuff in the world; it was so hot it took two glasses of milk to finish one sausage and biscuit. Those were the days.

The best part of living on the farm usually revolved around eating. During the summer months, Grandma harvested basketfuls of peaches and fixed the most incredible cobbler. You've never tasted anything like it in your life. We rarely got things like Snickers bars or Twinkies; we had homemade pies and cakes. Kids today don't know what they're missing.

In the hot, humid Tennessee summers the boys in my neighborhood had cantaloupe-eating contests. We hit an old man's cantaloupe patch, and he sat back and laughed as we stuffed melon slices into our mouths to see which one of us could eat the most. What sticky messes we were.

My grandparents were just poor share farmers. A few years ago I found one of their old record books and was shocked to see that a typical annual income was only $3,200. In my own family we can hardly survive on that for a month, yet that's what Granddad supported seven or eight of us on for an entire year! Back then farm people were very self-sufficient, so when the Great Depression hit, there was little impact. By today's standards, $3,200 translates into only about $24,000. For a family of eight, that is significantly below the U.S. Department of Health and Human Services 2010 poverty threshold.

We raised nearly everything ourselves; if it didn't come from our own land, we didn't need it. The only things we bought at the store in town were sugar, flour, and salt. We didn't even buy grease; when we killed a hog, the fat was rendered in a big kettle. When Grandma fried fish or chicken, all she had to do was dip into a bucket. Unlike people today who are mortgaged up to their eyeballs, my grandparents didn't believe in credit. With the house paid off and no car payments, $3,200 wasn't that bad.

I actually didn't know we were poor until I went to junior high and saw other kids showing off the stuff their parents had given them or bragging about the vacations they'd taken. They probably didn't get government cheese like we did after Granddad died.

Back in those days divorce wasn't very common, and women rarely raised kids on their own. My deadbeat dad never gave us a nickel; Mom provided for me and my two sisters by working a variety of minimum-wage factory jobs. Government handouts were hard to come by. Even though I was one of the poorest kids in town, I never went hungry, and my hand-me-down clothes were always clean and mended.

Granddad Williams was a workhorse. Other men he grew up with said he was strong as a bull when he was young. They said he could do seventy pull-ups without stopping and then wait five minutes and do seventy more. Of course, they didn't have fancy tractors with CD players and air conditioning back then; more often than not, Granddad used a mule and a plow. In the summer, farming was sweaty business. He toiled from sunup to sundown nearly every day, even when he was under the weather. Like his father before him, he never dreamed of going to the doctor.

One time he was so ill he passed out in the field. When Grandma found her unconscious husband lying in the dirt that day, she got him into the house and called the doctor. Dr. Poe, the physician who delivered me, still made house calls. He took one look at Granddad and told him he needed to stay in bed for at least a week and let the pneumonia run its course. As expected, Granddad disregarded that advice and went out to the field the next day and almost killed himself. When he didn't come home on time, Grandma found him passed out again. This time she made him stay in the house for three or four days, but that's all he could stand.

Being such a hard worker wasn't always a good thing. Granddad's boys thought he was a slave driver who darn near worked them to death. He also took literally the old adage, "Spare the rod and spoil the child"; he delivered some vicious whuppings. My uncles were all terrified of their father, and as soon as they could, the boys left home. When he was just fifteen, Uncle Joseph hopped a freight train bound for St. Louis to seek his fortune. He didn't have hard feelings toward his parents, he just hated farming and wanted to live in the big city and have some fun. Eventually he found his way to California and struck it rich in the garbage business.

To be fair, it's important to understand that Granddad's kids never considered him to be an abusive father. He came from a generation when it was common for parents to whup their kids if they misbehaved. Things are very different today.

My mom's baby sister, Susie, was the youngest of the six kids and still lived at home when I moved in. She was nineteen and worked the second shift as a waitress, and I couldn't wait for her to get home at night. She usually brought me Frosted Flakes, and I would sit up with her well past midnight, have a few bowls of my favorite cereal, and watch Elvis Presley movies with her. I just loved Susie; she was like my girlfriend.

Susie liked to run around town with her girlfriends. I remember those girls getting drunk and then puking in the toilet and bawling and squalling, and I wondered why they would drink if it made them so miserable. I realized when I got older that people like that are called "crying drunks" because alcohol puts them in a sad mood. It just seemed so stupid to me.

Some of the boys she hung around were mean. Johnny was the worst of the bunch. Every time he came near, he threw me across the room into the wall or a piece of furniture. Sometimes I was really hurt. I couldn't stand the guy; I did whatever I could to avoid him, but he always managed to grab me. I was just a little kid—why did he hate me like that? I was too young to understand that it wasn't me; he was just a guy who didn't respect boundaries. Unfortunately, what he probably thought was harmless fun chipped away at my already delicate self-esteem and fueled my anxiety.

Before too long the idyllic life on the farm ended. Granddad went blind because he had such bad cataracts, and he was forced to sell the animals and get out of farming. It was the beginning of a long line of disappointments.

New Pecking Order

I don't think my dad ever really wanted me, and honestly, I'm not sure my mom did either. At least that's how I felt growing up.

I was only five years old when my folks split up. Dad headed to Dyersburg, Tennessee, and my mother packed up the girls and moved in with my grandparents and me. I'm ashamed to admit that I didn't want them there. I was the king of the castle, and for the first time in my young life, I had all the positive attention I craved. I didn't want to share my grandparents' affection with my sisters.

Frankly, Grandma and Susie showed me far more love and affection than my mother ever had. I hardly ever remember her hugging me or saying she loved me. I called my grandmother "Mother" back then, but one day when we were in town and I called her "Mom," she corrected me: "You are going to have to stop doing that now that your mother is with us. I'm not your mother, I'm your grandmother." In my five-year-old mind I felt rejected.

One thing I believe with all my heart is that physical punishment doesn't solve anything. There are other ways to discipline misbehaving children that won't build up bitterness and hatred inside them. I got plenty of spankings from my mother. I can picture her chasing me through the house with a switch trying to get her arms around me. If I managed to get to where Granddad sat in the kitchen, he put his arm around me and said, "Oh no, you're not whupping the boy." He was my salvation, the only thing that kept me sane during those early days. Granddad made me feel loved.

Then one hot summer day, Granddad wasn't there to shield me from my mother's anger. I was about nine at the time and a bunch of kids came over to play with my sisters Mechell and

Shantell. Because I was the oldest, Mom told me not to let the kids get into the water and flood the backyard. After they left, Mom found out they had turned on the hose, so she gave me the worst whupping I'd ever had in my life. She made me pull my pants down around my ankles, bend over a chair, and then she thrashed me with a tree limb. She struck me so hard I had stripes up and down my legs and blood oozed from the lashes. Biting my lip, I pulled my pants back up, walked stoically into the bathroom, and cried behind the closed door. Even my sisters remember that whupping because it was such a bad one.

It wasn't the pain of my wounds I remember most—it was the pain I felt inside. That beating pierced my heart. There were plenty of times I messed up and deserved punishment, but that beating was totally unjustified. I hadn't even been playing with those kids, yet I was the one punished—not my sisters.

As I looked at myself in the bathroom mirror that day, it felt like my heart was going to break. Why was I such a screw-up? Why had I even been born? If God loved me like I'd been told my whole life, why had He brought me into a world in which my dad wouldn't have anything to do with me and my mom acted like she didn't like me? I cried myself to sleep that night, and many nights to come. That incident with the hose will be tattooed in my memory forever; it was the moment I started hating my mom.

Afraid of the Dark

Some kids are afraid of the boogeyman. Some are afraid of spiders or snakes. I was afraid of the dark. It was such a phobia for me that I slept with either my grandmother or Susie every night until I was almost nine years old.

Before my parents got divorced I spent the night at their place a couple of times. During one of those visits I begged and pleaded for my mom to sleep with me, but instead, Dad stuck me in a dark room, shut the door, and wouldn't let me out. There was absolutely no light in that room; not a sliver of light from the moon or a glow from the hallway through the crack in the door. It was pitch-black—I couldn't even see my hand in front of my face. No matter how much I begged, Dad left me in that room all alone. I was only five years old, and I will never forget the paralyzing fear I felt that night.

One night a short time later, my granddad, mom, two sisters, and I went to town to get groceries. When we got home the porch light was out, so we had to walk into the house in total darkness. Living out in the middle of the country, that was kind of scary, especially for a little boy who was afraid of the dark.

Mom and Granddad focused on screwing in a new lightbulb while Mechell, Shantell, and I put the groceries away. We were excited because one of the bags held a special treat: Hostess Ding Dongs, little chocolate cakes with cream filling inside. We weren't used to getting store-bought goodies because Grandma always made homemade desserts.

We couldn't wait to get to the kitchen to open that box. I was the oldest, so I did the honors; I can picture my two sisters standing there waiting while I tore into it. Just as I was getting ready to pull out the first Ding Dong, I heard a noise. Not five feet away, I saw fingers and a yellow sock poking through the pantry door.

"Run, run!" I screamed. We scrambled out of the kitchen and found Mom and Granddad outside. When we all went back to the house, the pantry was wide open and the kitchen door was unlocked. Whoever had broken in was long gone.

Already sensitive from being shut in that dark room by my dad, this episode made me a total wreck. Everybody knew there were no real "men" in the house—just an old blind man and a little boy. But there were certainly plenty of women. We'd had weird Peeping Toms before, but to my knowledge, nobody had ever broken into the house.

One blazing summer day not long after that, Susie was sunbathing in the backyard when she felt something wet on her chest. When she opened her eyes there was a guy standing over her with drool pouring out of his mouth. It was our neighbor Jerry. Poor Jerry was what they called "retarded" back then. He had some serious problems.

I was completely traumatized; I didn't even go to the bathroom by myself for years. The original farmhouse didn't have a bathroom, just an outhouse, but Granddad had built on an addition when his mother had moved in with them years before. She died back in that part of the house, and I was scared to death to use that bathroom. I just knew somebody was going to come get me. Whenever I was in there, Granddad pulled up a chair and sat outside the bathroom door until I was finished. I didn't grow out of that fear until I was a teenager.

You Can't Pick Your Family

There's an old proverb that says "Blood is thicker than water." Sadly, that hasn't always been my experience. Family members caused me more trauma and heartache than strangers ever did.

My aunt Charlotte asked me on her deathbed if I could forgive her for all the things she had done to me. I said I would, but in truth, it has been a pretty tough thing for me to do. Charlotte wasn't a very good woman, but she had a tender heart in some ways. Like me, she loved animals. She and her husband raised cattle, but poor Charlotte just didn't have the heart to send them to market. They were like pets to her, right down to the names she gave them. Many of their cows lived more than twenty years and ended up dying of old age rather than at the stockyards. Aunt Charlotte also cared for strays—primarily the human variety. She bailed her son's friends of out jail and gave them a couple of bucks if they were broke. She helped me out of a jam on more than one occasion. While she certainly had her good moments, most of the time Charlotte was fighting her own demons and took it out on other people.

Charlotte was my mom's older sister and lived next door to us. For years she tried to turn my sisters and me against our own mother. I think it bothered her that we lived with her parents. In truth, Charlotte was the most jealous person I have ever met.

My aunt introduced me to all kinds of bad behaviors. One day Charlotte took me and my cousin Frankie to the grocery store. She sent him in first and told him to steal a toy. When he came back and showed her his prize, she told me it was my turn. I didn't know what to do; I was just a little bitty kid, maybe six or seven years old, and Granddad had always told me one of the worst things a guy could do was steal.

I was shaking like a leaf when I went into that store. I walked up to one of those old spin racks that held little toy cars, pocketed a replica of a Model T, and then walked back out to the waiting car. Charlotte was really proud of me that day, and I felt accepted. I came to enjoy the adrenaline rush of stealing. A year later, my mother caught me shoplifting a toy motorcycle from the local Walmart. I had stuck it in my sock. Mom made me go back to the store manager and confess. It was the second time I'd been caught—the first time I took candy from a little store in town.

In third grade I learned how to smoke cigarettes at Charlotte's house. I thought I was pretty cool standing there with her and the older kids. That was the beginning of a very long, ugly habit. But that's not the only habit Charlotte turned me on to. There was this kid named Tim Rhodes who lived across the street from her. Sometimes Tim came over and my aunt paid us to have cussing contests. For every filthy word we could think of, she gave us a quarter. It is so bizarre to me now. On one hand I loved my aunt Charlotte, and I believe she loved me too. We laughed together, and she did her best to keep my bottomless belly full with her good country cooking. Like most little kids, I just wanted to be loved.

Uncle Dale, my mom's brother, was even worse. He was just plain mean, the type of person who would kill an animal in a heartbeat. If a stray dog came up to him, he hit it in the head with whatever was handy. Dale was a big, overbearing guy, and when he got drunk he liked to fight. Because of that, he had enemies.

Like a lot of guys in their early twenties, my uncle ran in a pack. On one particular night, though, he sat alone in a bar after they had all gone home. Six guys who Dale had obviously ticked off at one time or another jumped him. These guys were already rough, but add in a little moonshine and rile them up enough, and they'd cut your head off or shoot you.

When they grabbed Dale they went after him with a straight-edge razor blade. He broke loose a couple of times and knocked one or two of them down, only to be grabbed again. Then they stretched him out across the pool table and cut him over and over again from the top of his chest clear down to his belly button. They even tried to cut his bicep in two to neutralize Dale's powerful knockout punch. They probably weren't trying to kill him at first—if they'd wanted to do that they would have cut his throat, stabbed him, or punctured his lungs—it was more about torturing him.

The only thing that saved Dale from getting murdered that night was the intervention of a young guy named Lonnie Holms. Lonnie was standing over in the corner watching the whole fight while shooting pool. After getting cut all to pieces, Dale fought his way loose and made it to the back door of the bar. His attackers ran after him, probably to finish him off, but Lonnie stepped between them, held up his pool stick, and said, "He's had enough. If you guys want to go after him, you're going to have to go through me to do it." Already beaten up and worn-out, they probably didn't have the energy to fight Lonnie, too.

Dale escaped to his car and drove himself to the police chief's house. His son had been one of Dale's drinking buddies and had been shot and killed while out hunting with this same group of guys. Dale knew the cop held a grudge. The police chief freaked out when he saw Dale and rushed him to a hospital in Paducah, Kentucky, forty-five minutes away, where he was sewn back together. Dale barely survived.

I found out about this incident from Lonnie. He had a crush on my aunt Susie and came over to our house the morning after the fight, bragging about how he'd saved Dale. I was only seven or eight at the time, and I remember standing in the driveway with my mouth hanging open as Lonnie told the story. I was there when someone brought over a big bucket containing Dale's clothes. They were sitting in three inches of his own blood—that's how much of it had run out of his body.

The attack certainly didn't change Dale for the better; he was still as mean as a snake. Every once in a while he stopped by Granddad's and asked me if I wanted to help him in the watermelon patch or something. One time when I got to his house, my cousin Frankie, Charlotte's son, was there waiting for me. Frankie was five years older and probably fifty to sixty pounds heavier than I was—that's a huge difference in size when one of you is just a ten-year-old. Dale let that boy clobber me. Frankie twisted my arm like he was going to break it and then ground my face into the gravel. I can see myself crying with my mouth open and slobber and snot smeared all over my face. Little bitty pebbles were embedded in my skin and in my mouth.

I begged Uncle Dale to make him stop, but he just laughed and said, "Oh, this will make you tough." He didn't grind his own son's face into the gravel when he had one a few years later, but he sure didn't mind letting it happen to me. Obviously it wasn't about being toughened up, or he would have done it to his own boy. This was all about dislike—maybe it was because I reminded him and Frankie of my dad.

More times than I care to admit, I went home crying and bleeding from being beat up by Frankie and other boys. Surprisingly, Granddad got mad at me instead of Dale: "Every time you go over there with any of them, you're the only one muddy; you're the only one bleeding with dirt in your teeth. Why do you keep going back? What is wrong with you?"

But when you're a kid, you just want somebody to play with. I kept thinking, *Maybe this time they won't do it.* But time after time when I was playing in our yard, the kids next door would holler at me and tell me they were going to play football or something, and I would run right over, forgetting they had pounded me the last time. They thought it was funny how I kept coming back for more. When I was an adult, Dale said he was sorry for what he had done, but by then I was big enough to grind *his* face into the gravel. Dale was one of the toughest men I ever knew in my life. Yet despite the fact that he did some terrible things to me, I wanted to be just like him. As an adult with kids of my own, I have a hard time grasping why.

I still can't understand how my own people, the ones who were supposed to be my family and love me, could do these things. Before I was a teenager, they taught me to lie, steal, smoke, and fight. They ignored, beat, and teased me, and during this period of my life, I was repeatedly sexually molested by a male family member.

The Bible says, "Whoever causes one of these little ones who believe in Me to sin, it would be better for him if a millstone were hung around his neck, and he were drowned in the depth of the sea" (Matthew 18:6, NKJV). I believe we will all be judged harshly in the next life for how we treated people in this one.

Fight or Flight

In May 2002, the Secret Service published a report that examined thirty-two school shootings in the United States. One of the things they learned was that many of the attackers had acted out because they had been bullied. In a small way, I can understand why those shootings took place because I was bullied in school. The anger used to bubble up inside of me until I felt like I was going to burst. Still, no matter how badly a kid is mistreated by his or her classmates, there's no excuse for that kind of violence.

My whole life my granddad taught me to hate a bully, hate a bully, hate a bully. We had two really bad high-school bullies on the school bus that always thumped the little kids. I was only in elementary school, but I figured I could take it better than a kindergartner could, so I got into the middle of it, knowing full well the bullies would take it out on me. And they did; one of them held my arms while the other one punched me in the belly.

Kids can be mean, especially to those who are a little different. My classmates picked on me for all kinds of things; my learning disabilities and stuttering were certainly on the top of the list. They also teased me for being poor and because I was part Native American. My mother's side of the family teased me about that, too. Every time I lost my temper or got mad, they said it was the Indian coming out. They seemed to forget that the Irish had a reputation for having fiery tempers, too.

What hurt the most, though, was what people said about me not having a dad. Everybody had a dad back then. No matter how well I did in sports, or if I had a school function or Future Farmers of America meeting, I never had anyone there to share it with. I remember that real well, the loneliness.

Even members of my family tormented me about not having a dad. When I got older, my uncle and cousin told me my granddad only spent time with me because he felt sorry for me. I didn't have a daddy and had no place else to go. That cut to the core, because as I got older, deep down I didn't know if it was true or not. Maybe Granddad only pretended to love me out of a sense of pity.

I had my face kicked in by other kids many, many times. Sometimes I woke up in the morning after a fight with so much dried blood in my nostrils I couldn't breathe. When I felt threatened by another child, my first instinct was to attack first. It was a defense mechanism. I came out swinging like Uncle Dale and my granddad had taught me. I felt like it was either fight or die. That was the only way I knew how to protect myself. It sounds stupid and childish now, but when I was growing up, the only way I knew how to get respect was to fight, and even though I was pretty good at it, I fought mostly to impress my granddad. I hurt a lot of kids beating them up. I wasn't a bully; I just learned how to take care of myself.

When I was in fourth grade, I got into a fight at the baseball field behind our house with two brothers who were a few years older than me. I punched out one of them and kicked him off an embankment into a briar patch. When I did that, the other one came running at me with a crochet needle that was about eight inches long. I was already bent down looking to see where I had knocked his brother down, so I simply turned around, grabbed a stick, and stabbed that boy in the mouth. The jagged edges on the end ripped his lips to pieces.

My sister saw what happened and ran home to get a glass of ice. I wadded up my shirt and held it against his face to stem the bleeding. Whether I was defending myself or not, I knew I was in big trouble. Mostly I was afraid their parents wouldn't let them play with me anymore.

Another time in fourth grade I beat up a boy named Shane and was taken to the principal's office. Shane had some really big knots on his face and the principal wanted to know what I had hit him with. I had just hit him with my fists, but they didn't believe me. Back in the 1970s, teachers and administrators could beat you with paddles. Even though I hadn't started the fight, I was the one that got a whupping—and it was a bad one. The whole office stuck up for the other kid, partly because his mama was the head of the Boy Scouts. Nobody from my side came to the school to support me—not my mom, my granddad, nobody. I was the boy without a daddy.

I got into a fistfight nearly every week, and it seemed like I was always the one getting blamed. See, after you get into trouble at a young age, anytime you have an altercation with another kid, it's automatically your fault, even if the other guy thumped you in the head first. The principal jumps to conclusions and thinks, *I just had you in my office last week and here you are again!*

My friend Ron told me about a worker who once caught a little boy stealing an apple from a cafeteria. She'd been watching him stuff food in his pockets every day for a week and finally grabbed him by the arm and asked him why he was stealing. The little boy said it was because his mom and dad didn't feed his baby sister and she was starving. He was taking the food home to feed her. That cafeteria employee felt like she was about an inch tall.

Instead of being so harsh on troubled kids and lashing out at them, sometimes we need to step back and determine what's causing their behavior. When everybody thinks the worst of you and nobody defends you, it messes with your psyche. I thought there must be something wrong with me—that *I* was the problem.

But there was nothing wrong with me. My dad was a drug addict, and I was around drinkers all the time who didn't seem to care. If anything, it was my surroundings that were the problem. My learning disability, my speech impediment, my nervousness, and my explosiveness toward other kids came from being traumatized and mistreated. That's not an excuse for why I messed up later in life, but it is an explanation. I thought I was a loser.

The Bottom of the Bell Curve

I was never good at schoolwork; from the minute I stepped into the classroom, the three R's were a struggle. For me, reading was impossible. The teachers thought the problem could be solved by putting me in a speech class. Their reasoning was that it is hard to learn to read or spell properly if you can't pronounce the letters.

My speech class met every day during recess. When everybody else went out to the playground to play dodgeball, four square, or tag, I sat in a colorless classroom sounding out letters. I remember sitting in that room listening to the other kids playing, thinking how unfair life was. I was in that speech class for six years; my stuttering didn't stop until I was twelve.

Even with special tutoring I was always behind in school. Back in the 1970s it wasn't like it is today with 504 plans (part of the Americans with Disabilities Act) and Individualized Education Programs (IEPs). The state didn't pay for paraprofessionals to coach kids like me who had learning disabilities. When you got behind in school that was it—sink or swim. Period. Knowing I couldn't cut it in school did even more damage to my tender self-confidence.

Mom used to chase me around the house trying to get me to do my work. "You've got to do your homework!"

I always ran to the refuge of my grandfather's arms in the kitchen and he would shield me from my mother. "Now, you leave the boy alone, Kay."

"But the boy's got to do his homework!" she'd say, trying to catch her breath, "he's falling behind."

No matter how much she begged or how logical her argument, Granddad wouldn't let her pressure me into learning. "When he wants to get it, he'll get it."

Instead of fighting, Mom always gave in, walking away frustrated. As an adult with school-age kids of my own, I believe that "live and let live philosophy" was a huge mistake. I didn't "get it" until well after my high school graduation, and by then it was too late. I can't really fault Granddad though; he came from an era when education wasn't as important as it is today. Most of his peers dropped out by the eighth grade. After all, you didn't need algebra to plow a field or milk a cow.

I struggled in the classroom, but excelled at anything athletic. When a kid already has some severe self-esteem problems, he over-indulges in what he is good at rather than spending time doing something that makes him feel like a failure. Instead of reading and doing my homework, I played ball until dark every night.

I was always about three years behind in reading and writing. My spelling was the worst. There are a lot of words in the English language that are spelled dramatically different than they sound—like how a "ph" sounds like an "f." Exceptions like that always threw me.

Reading comes naturally to many people, but reading in class was torture for me. For years I prayed to be a better reader, I wanted it so badly. By the time I was in sixth grade and still only reading at the second grade level, my family thought it was time for a tutor. The trouble was they didn't have any money, so they asked one of our neighbors to help.

James Lafuse had graduated from an Ivy League college and had gone to law school, but somewhere along the line he changed. He found God and thought he should no longer be part of the "Establishment." James lived like a hermit in the old house he had grown up in. He had a full beard and long hair, just like an Old Testament prophet.

James said he would teach me how to read better under two conditions: (1) our textbook would be the Bible; and (2) I had to go to church with him. Every Sunday we went to a little bitty Baptist church way out in the country that has since been converted into a house. James drove us in a steam-engine truck that was about the size of a semi. The first time I saw it I said, "What's with the truck, James?"

"Well," he said, "God told me not to drive gasoline vehicles."

It sounded pretty crazy to me, but who knows, maybe God did tell him that. Even though James was eccentric, he was the best guy in the neighborhood: kind, passive, and he never hurt people or animals. James taught me how to read, and that made him a hero in my book.

Now, more than thirty years later, James lives in a barn with no electricity and drives a gasoline-powered vehicle. When he made the switch, I laughed and said mean things like, "I guess God told him gasoline was okay." I feel guilty about that now, because I really loved the guy. He made a huge difference in my life. Not only was I a better reader, I also stopped stuttering.

A Secret's a Secret

Granddad used to call me Uncle Tom because I reminded him of someone he'd known in his youth. I guess it was just his little pet name for me. He gave everyone nicknames. Other people in my family, though, made fun of me for the name.

Some of my fondest childhood memories are of sitting on the armrest of Granddad's favorite chair, playing with my little Hot Wheels cars and talking about the Bible. During one of these conversations, he said, "Uncle Tom, you know I'm not always going to be with you. I'm getting old and one day I'll have to die."

It was like he had a premonition. I started to cry and told him if he ever died, I would take the car and run it off the road. It touched him that I didn't want to live without him. I thought we would always be together. Little did I know that his last days were just around the corner.

When Granddad went in to have his cataracts removed, something suspicious was found on one of his blood tests. Upon further examination, doctors discovered that his body was riddled with cancer. While he got dressed at the hospital, the doctors broke the news to the family. Granddad was so far gone that neither chemotherapy nor radiation would do any good. They figured he had less than a year to live.

I remember standing around listening to the adults talking, just taking it all in. His kids, particularly my aunt Charlotte and my uncle Dale, decided not to tell Granddad he was sick. Their warped logic was that if he knew about the cancer, he would go downhill faster.

The whole conversation was upsetting, because they were talking about how Granddad was going to die. Then out of the blue, Charlotte looked at me and said, "Boy, you'd better not tell him." The other women got after me too, saying Dale would get me if I opened my mouth. So many times I got close to telling Granddad he was sick, but then I remembered that threat. I knew Granddad could no longer protect me.

About a year later Granddad and I were in the kitchen one day with Grandma, Mom, and my sisters. Sitting there smoking his pipe, he said, "Oma, I want all you all to leave. I need to talk to Tom about something." He actually wanted them to go outside, not just to the other room. He didn't want them to hear us at all.

After the women left us, I was nervous, thinking, *What have I done?* Little kids are always guilty of something. Granddad took off his hat and said, "Tom, I've got a knot that's come up on the back of my head. Feel of this." The bump was at the base of his skull right at the top of his neck and was as big around as a golf ball. "Do you feel that?"

"Yeah," I said, "but I don't think it's really nothin'. Your other side's got a little knot too." Of course, the whole time I was thinking, *I know exactly what that is—you've got cancer.*

"I think there's something wrong. I think I'm sick," he said.

"No Granddad, you're not sick. The knot is probably just a little bigger on that side."

I refused to agree with him even though the knot on the left side was about an inch larger. In my heart, I thought if I could convince him he wasn't sick he would get better and this whole thing would go away. I suppose I was trying to convince myself too; I didn't want to lose hope.

Granddad dropped it after that comment; I'm sure he recognized the anxiety in my voice and didn't want to frighten me. "Okay, you can let the women back in now."

Obediently, I opened the kitchen door and motioned them in. "We're finished talking. You can come on back in."

When they asked him what our chat was all about, Granddad said, "Nothing, nothing, I just wanted to talk to him about something. It was between me and David."

The women pestered me about that private conversation several times over the next few days, but I told them I had promised Granddad I would keep it a secret and they finally quit asking. It wasn't until after his funeral that I finally told them what we had talked about that day in the kitchen.

Not long after that day, Granddad went to the hospital again. This time he had a different doctor, one with more integrity than the last one. He was mad that the family had never told Granddad he was dying; after all, he was a grown man and he had a right to know. The doctor told Granddad the bad news, but he already knew in his heart he was sick.

Another Brick in the Wall

By the time I entered junior high, the foundation for a life of substance abuse was being laid brick by brick. I felt alone, rejected, and unloved. Although I wasn't sure Granddad loved me because of some of the things I'd been told by family members, there had never been a question in my mind that he would die for me. Even though he was old and sick, he would have fought a bear to save me. That's the way it was with us. How was I ever going to live without him?

Even though he never complained about it, I knew Granddad was hurting. Those old-timers were tougher than we are today; I get a splinter in my hand and I cry about it for two days.

But Granddad never took a pain pill while that cancer ate holes in his bones. Instead, he medicated himself with alcohol.

Unfortunately, like my father and so many other people in my family, that demon alcohol eventually got ahold of Granddad. His drink of choice was vodka; he drank that stuff straight out of the bottle and chased it with a cracker or a piece of bread to get the taste out of his mouth. He was a hard-core drunk.

Granddad's cataracts prevented him from driving, so whenever Charlotte and her husband went to town, they picked up a bottle at the liquor store for him. When he saw their car pull into the driveway, Granddad sent me next door to fetch his booze. Sometimes I sneaked sips on my way home; other times I took drinks when the bottle was sitting right there next to his chair. He was so messed up he didn't have a clue. My own journey with alcohol began in fourth grade . . . one sip at a time.

As his cancer progressed and the alcohol got a firm grip on him, Granddad became completely psychotic. He morphed into a man I hardly recognized. He became easily enraged and violent, and I grew scared of him. Although he never raised a hand to hurt Grandma, his temper was frightening. One time he threw a slipper across the room and hit her in the shoulder. It made her cry, something I had never seen before.

Grandma Oma was one tough lady; she always had been. Her mama died when she was only six years old, and the household responsibilities fell on her shoulders. She had to cook, clean, and take care of her dad and her six brothers from a very young age. Oma was a tomboy; she liked to climb the old oak trees in their front yard, and when the milkman slowed his buggy to drop off the milk, she threw broken bricks and rocks and hit his horses to make them buck. The milkman said those horses ran half a mile before he could get them to stop, back up, and then do all the stops he had missed. He just wanted to kill that little girl.

Growing up with boys, Grandma learned early on how to take care of herself. In fact, when I was in junior high and had friends over, we used to have arm-wrestling matches. Nobody ever beat my grandmother; she slammed every single one of them.

I knew Granddad hadn't hurt Oma the day he threw that slipper —she started crying because he hurt her feelings. As his drinking got worse, so did their arguing. Sometimes Granddad got so angry he pulled out his .38 revolver and went on shooting rampages throughout the house. He screamed things like "I'll just kill every-body!" as he shot holes in the walls.

It scared us all half to death. We used to hide in the cornfields behind the house when Granddad lost his temper like that. Oftentimes he hollered out the back door, "Tom, where are you, boy? Come here, Tom, I'm not mad at you. You don't have to go out there; it's just those damn women that got on my nerves." I tried to run to him but the women told me to shut up and held me back.

Although he'd physically disciplined his own kids, Granddad Williams had always been sweet and gentle with me. Maybe he'd used up all his anger when he was a younger man, or maybe he was just older and wiser. I think he was nice to me because I'd been dealt such a bad hand early on in my life

Eventually Granddad even turned on me. He only hit me once in his life, and it shocked me. One of my chores on the farm was to help in the garden. One stifling summer day Granddad told me to hoe the garden. By then I was in sixth grade and Granddad and I weren't getting along like we used to because of his drink-ing. So when he told me to go work in the garden, I thought, *I'm not hoeing that f— garden today; it's too hot!*

Instead of doing as I was told, I got on my bicycle and rode the quarter mile down to Greg Wells's house. His parents owned one of those pick-your-own strawberry patches, and I loved play-ing there. About thirty minutes after I got there, a big, brown Ford LTD pulled up and my grandmother got out. My stomach lurched—*Oh crap, I'm in trouble now.*

"Your granddad sent me to come get you. You were supposed to hoe the garden . . . boy, is he upset." Even though he had never whupped me before, that didn't mean I wasn't scared of him. I knew at any moment Granddad could kill me if he set his mind to it.

"Tell him I'll be there in just a minute," I answered. My plan was to ride my bike back really slow. If I was gone a while longer, maybe Granddad would cool down before I got there.

"No," she said, "he told me to get you right now. Load your bike up in the back of the car." I put it in the trunk and got into the car, agonizing over what was going to happen to me. But really, how bad could it be?

When we pulled into the drive, Granddad met us in the front yard. "Boy, I told you to hoe that garden and you didn't do it."

"I just wanted to go down to Greg's for a while and play," I answered.

Granddad was furious. He reached out and grabbed me by the hair. It felt like it was being pulled out by the roots. He slapped me hard with his open hand and then backhanded me. He did that two or three times—*smack, smack, smack, smack, smack!* His hands were so big it felt like they wrapped around my entire head. "Next time I tell you to do something, you'd better do it!"

When it was over, both sides of my face were throbbing and my eardrums were ringing. I ran around to the back of the house and cried my eyes out. It wasn't the pain that hurt so much; it was the shock of it. Granddad had never hit me before; I couldn't believe he hurt me over hoeing the stupid garden. After that, things were never the same between us.

Saying Good-bye

My relationship with my grandfather was strained after the whupping, but I always knew he loved me. It was the cancer and the alcohol that had fueled his rage that day, not me. Despite what happened, he was still my biggest champion. After he found out he was terminally ill, Granddad wrestled with the idea of dying. One of the things that worried him the most was what would happen to me when he was gone. Sitting in our kitchen one day, he said, "You know, you need to find your dad."

Seeing my dad was the last thing I wanted to do. Since my parents had divorced and he'd moved away, my old man hadn't contacted me once. He had never been there for me; why would it be any different now? Granddad wanted me to have a man in my life. Of course, deep down there was a longing for a dad, a buddy I could hang out with. I told Granddad I would do it. Sometimes I wish I could take back the decision to meet him, but what I really wish is that my dad hadn't been a drug addict.

Granddad really suffered at the end. The last few days of his life he languished in a hospital in Fulton, Kentucky. He'd told the family repeatedly that he wanted to die in his own room, but nobody would bring him home. That has always upset me. I hadn't visited him in the hospital often, but something inside told me I needed to go down there one night. I tried to get somebody to drive me there so I could stay overnight with him, but they told me I didn't need to go, that I wouldn't be happy just sitting there. That was the night my granddaddy died—and I wasn't there.

In rural Tennessee, it's a real occasion when somebody passes away. The night before the service, a visitation is held so people can stop by and pay their respects to the deceased and the family. On the day of Granddad's memorial service, the doors at the funeral home opened at about eight in the morning for an hour-long visitation. From the opening hymn to the burial, the event lasted about four hours.

I didn't make it that whole time. One of my cousins from California and I headed over to a restaurant down the block and shot a couple games of pool. The way I was acting, you wouldn't have even known my granddad had passed away. I realize now I was trying to distance myself from what had happened. For the entire twelve years of my life, Granddad had been like a father to me; he was the one who wiped my butt and loved on me. Later on I felt terribly guilty about shooting pool that day. How could I have done that? How could I have played games when my best friend was lying dead in his casket?

We finally left the restaurant and walked back to the funeral home. I tried hard to hold my emotions in check, but I lost it. I started crying and couldn't stop. That's what I had been trying to avoid all day—seeing them shut that lid and knowing that was the last time I would ever see my granddad.

After going to the cemetery, everybody came over to our house for a meal and some conversation. Even though the house was full of people, I felt lost and so alone. I knew my buddy, my protector, was gone. Granddad had always taken up for me, and suddenly I was alone and they could do whatever they wanted to do. I was scared.

FOUR

The Outsider

---

*When people are lonely they stoop
to any companionship.*

— Lew Wallace

IN 1983, ACADEMY AWARD–WINNER Francis Ford Coppola directed the feature film *The Outsiders* about a teenage gang of greasers from the wrong side of the tracks in the 1950s. The group found themselves embroiled in a turf war with a rival gang of more privileged boys. The movie's tagline reads, "They grew up on the outside of society. They weren't looking for a fight. They were looking to belong." That's how I always felt—like an outsider.

On so many levels, I just didn't fit in. Before he died, Granddad Parnell had the entire family registered as official members of the Cherokee Nation. Kids of mixed-race heritage often feel like they don't belong to either group. I was part Native American, but I was also white, and back in the 1960s and '70s, there was some serious prejudice in the South. Even though I'm not dark-skinned and I have blue eyes, some people still made snide remarks about me, especially my mom's side of the family.

Everybody in my house had the same last name except for me. They were Williams. I was a Parnell, which also made me feel like I didn't belong. At school all the kids had two parents, but I was known as the poor boy without a daddy who wore second-hand clothes.

All through my childhood I got pounded by other kids. Then I discovered basketball. It's funny how being good at a sport can raise your popularity quotient. By the time I was in sixth grade, I was already five feet eleven and showed real talent for the sport. From early on, my coach paid for me to go to basketball camp and told me I had a future in college ball. Some parents even told me I was going to play professional ball someday.

Of course, the best part of being gifted on the court was that girls started to notice me. From that point on I always had a girl-friend. It was nice to feel like somebody wanted me, but it didn't matter if I had five or six girlfriends, I was still lost. Deep down, I felt like my mom didn't love me and that I was unworthy of love from everybody else.

Although I was becoming extremely popular at school, I grav-itated toward other kids who were as lost as I was. Most of them came from the other side of the tracks, so to speak, the poor kids. I guess I related to them. The Bible says, "Bad company corrupts good character" (1 Corinthians 15:33, NKJV). I was definitely in bad company.

Back in the Picture

When my granddad realized his cancer was going to kill him, he encouraged me to find my dad so I'd have a male figure in my life. My memories of my dad were not good ones, and the idea of reconnecting with him made me nervous, but I agreed to seek him out so I could put Granddad's mind at ease.

As it turned out, Dad was living only two and a half hours away from us in Memphis. Mom called him and told him I wanted to see him, and they made arrangements for Dad to come pick me up. Dad was like a poster child for an anti-establishment-era hippie. He had long, bushy hair and a Fu Manchu, the kind of mustache that makes a guy look like a badass biker. Dad was really into motorcycles. There were times when he had four or five of them at once.

The funny thing was, my dad had been bald since he was in his early twenties. It was a real curse to him and certainly didn't fit the rock-and-roll image he was trying to portray. To remedy that, Dad wore a toupee when he performed. I remember watching him get ready; on the sides his hair went down past his shoulders, but on the top he was bald as a billiard ball. But nobody was the wiser.

Dad was the bass player in a band called Tiny and the Bandsmen. Naturally, Tiny was a huge woman who weighed more than two hundred pounds. She was the singer, and her husband, Buck, played the guitar. The band wore matching bell-bottom costumes to look like Elvis. When I was as young as twelve years old, I sat in that honky-tonk, sipping soda and watching them play cover tunes like "Good Golly, Miss Molly." They had a great gig as the house band at a bar called Bad Bob's in Memphis. Back in the '70s,

Dad pulled in several hundred dollars a week playing music. That was a lot of money for that time.

My dad had gotten remarried to a woman named Debbie, and they lived in an apartment complex with her little boy from a previous marriage. Debbie was actually Dad's third wife—he was married for about a year before he married my mother.

One morning, after I had been visiting for just a few days, Debbie made me scrambled eggs for breakfast. When you're a kid, you get used to how the woman in your life cooks, and my grandmother was really good. I didn't like Debbie's eggs at all because they were so different from what I was used to. I wouldn't eat them and Dad got so angry he screamed and hollered and flipped out. He just lost it, freaking out about some stupid eggs. I ran and hid under the bed, scared out of my mind, flashbacks of him beating my mom skittering around in my adolescent mind. Eventually he calmed down and came in and talked to me, but I was ready to go home.

My aunt Susie lived thirty miles down the road across the state line in a spot called Bull Frog Corner in Mississippi. After the scrambled egg incident, I begged my dad to let me go home, and he drove me to Susie's. From there I took the Greyhound bus back to my grandparents' farm. I only lasted a week or two at my dad's place when I was supposed to be there most of the summer.

Like Father, Like Son

A rational person might think that the negative experience at my dad's place would make me hesitant to go back again, but I longed for a relationship with a father like other boys had. David Parnell Sr. was definitely not like other fathers.

At the end of my seventh-grade year, I decided to pack up and move in with him. I didn't harbor the illusion that things between the two of us would be any different from the previous year, but my granddad was gone and I felt like I needed to be with a man. It was hard for Dad to say no to me, but truthfully I don't think he really wanted me to live there. After all, if he had really wanted to have a relationship, he would have visited me at some point during the previous ten years of my life, or at the very least paid some child support.

Dad had moved from Memphis to Horn Lake, Mississippi, and rented a little brick house in a subdivision near my aunt Susie. Dad had a special room in that house. Whenever friends came over, he and Debbie took them into that back bedroom, shut the door, and turned on the stereo. I didn't know it then, but they were sitting back there getting high.

My dad seemed more like a kid than a grown man. He told me straight up that he didn't want to be my father; he wanted to be my buddy. One day, Dad and I were kicking back in the living room watching TV when he told me he had something he wanted to show me. I followed him into the back room, and when I walked through the door, the first thing I noticed was a big funny-looking glass cylinder in the middle of the floor. It had to have been at least three feet high with three or four holes bored into the sides. I had no idea what it was, but it sure smelled nasty.

"Have you ever smoked marijuana?" he said.

"Oh yeah, I've smoked it before with Cousin Frankie," I lied.

"Well, do you want to smoke some now?"

"Yeah, I guess.

Dad put some dope into that apparatus, which I came to learn was a water bong (a fancy-looking pipe for smoking marijuana), lit it, and handed it to me. I sucked the smoke into my mouth and blew it out like you would a cigar. In order to get high on marijuana, though, you're supposed to inhale it and hold it for a few seconds to get the smoke into your lungs.

Dad looked at me and laughed. "So you've smoked before, huh? Well, you're not smoking it right—let me teach you how. You need to suck it into your lungs and hold it like this." He took a big hit, inhaled deeply, and blew it out in a long, steady stream. "Now you try it."

He handed the bong back to me and I tried again. This time I choked and thought I was going to cough up a lung, but I kept the smoke down for a few seconds. I felt different right away. Over the years I've heard people say they didn't get high the first time they smoked pot, but when you smoke with an expert who really tutors you in the proper technique, it's a whole different story.

We smoked that stuff for a long time until I was dizzy and completely stoned. It made me feel a little uncomfortable at first, but then I started laughing. Everything tickled me; all I had to do was look at my dad and I busted out laughing.

Marijuana is a common precursor to the abuse of harder drugs. After a while a tolerance is developed and the highs from pot are lessened. Something stronger is needed to produce the same result. Many users think it is a harmless activity. For years I used stupid excuses like, "God put marijuana on this earth. Why can't we smoke it?" God put lots of things on this earth, but that doesn't necessarily mean we're supposed to use them the way we do. Research has shown that marijuana disrupts the activity of a part of the brain called the hippocampus, which can result in memory loss and disorganization. Chronic use causes apathy, learning disabilities, and poor judgment. The human IQ takes a hit as well, irreversibly dropping up to four points. Obviously, pot had impaired my dad's reasoning abilities or he never would have smoked it with me.

After he got me high, Dad told me he wanted to show me something else. "Stand in front of me, take ten real deep breaths, and then hold your arms up."

"Why, what are you going to do," I asked nervously.

"I just want to show you something, you'll really like it."

I obediently stepped in front of my father and started taking breaths. As soon as I exhaled the tenth one, he grabbed me from behind in a giant bear hug and squeezed me hard to cut the oxygen to my brain. I thought he was trying to kill me. I grabbed his arms, trying to fend him off, but it all happened too fast. In seconds, I hit the ground, unconscious.

Self-asphyxiation, or the choking game, is a popular pastime for kids who like to get stoned. The idea is to momentarily stop the flow of blood to the brain to experience light-headedness. This can be achieved by using a rope or a belt, or having somebody push on your chest. Adolescents—and likely some adults as well—have died because they took it too far, or the rope got knotted up and didn't unravel when they let go of it. Cutting off the oxygen that flows to the head causes brain cells to die. It's definitely not something to mess with.

It's hard to believe my own dad made me hyperventilate until I lost consciousness just for his own entertainment. He was so stoned he thought it was hilarious. It scared the crap out of me.

When we walked out of the room, Debbie knew immediately that I was stoned. She was furious with my dad, and said, "What are you doing?" But Dad and I just snickered; we thought everything was funny. Debbie did not.

At first I thought her conscience got the better of her and she thought it wasn't okay to smoke dope with a thirteen-year-old, but it must not have bothered her too much, because before long, the three of us were getting high together on a daily basis. She was a drug user, and wasn't going to let the presence of a kid get in the way of the high.

When I do my educational programs for junior high students, they often ask me why I smoked with my dad when I knew marijuana was a drug. I did it because of my dad. I wanted to be able to hang out with him and his friends. I was tired of getting locked out of the back room and sitting by myself for half the night while they sat in there and laughed and joked around. It made me feel like an outsider. Getting high with dad was all about acceptance—it made me feel like I was a grown-up man who was part of something. I did it because I wanted him to love me.

Believe it or not, I don't blame my dad for any of my problems. A lot of kids, especially younger ones, want to blame their parents for every bad thing that happens to them. But we can't do that, because we all have free will. I chose to smoke marijuana even when I wasn't with my dad.

Once the floodgates were open, Dad and I smoked pot together just about every night. He came home from a night at the bar and we sat around and watched TV in the living room and passed a joint. I never understood why potheads didn't roll a joint for everybody. I wanted my own; I didn't want any stinky breath on mine.

Dad kept his weed on a metal tray under the couch. Honestly, I think part of the reason he introduced me to marijuana in the first place was because he was sick of going into the back room every time he wanted to party.

It wasn't just the weed I was exposed to at Dad's place. Even though the people on my mom's side of the family were all drinkers with rough exteriors, they were really funny when it came to sexual things. Everything was trashy to them. If a comment was even mildly suggestive, my mom jumped all over it. I remember wondering as a teenager how in the world my mom even got married.

My dad, on the other hand, was really into pornography. He had so many dirty magazines that he stacked them up to replace the broken leg at the head of his bed. I would have never, ever, EVER found such a thing at my granddad's house, and there I was, thrown in with a hippie who was constantly getting high and had porn everywhere.

At that age I didn't even know what a naked woman looked like. I remember watching cable TV with Dad and Debbie while we got high and nearly died of embarrassment when a sex scene came on. In those days, R-rated movies were full of sex and violence, closer to a mild X-rated movie today. Mind you, it wasn't hard-core porn, but it was completely inappropriate for a kid my age. Dad and my stepmom were completely okay with me smoking pot and watching that kind of stuff with them.

Most adolescent males already have hormones surging through their bodies; I certainly didn't need encouragement to think about sex. It was on my mind all the time. A young person shouldn't be exposed to the kind of material I was; it only makes things worse. No kid needs to see that kind of stuff.

Debbie worked the night shift as a cocktail waitress. When she and my dad both had to work, they hired a seventeen-year-old girl to babysit little Frankie, who was kindergarten age. She didn't pay any attention to me; I had absolutely no supervision.

There's nothing more dangerous than giving a thirteen-year-old boy the freedom to do whatever he wants—especially if he has already gotten high.

In the evenings I spent a lot of time playing basketball and football with the neighborhood kids. I learned early on how to be accepted by them: I supplied the dope. Oh man, they liked me then; otherwise they acted like they didn't want me around. If I had a little weed, I was the man!

Dad kept his marijuana in his bedroom, and even though he locked it, I had no trouble getting inside. There wasn't a key to the door; Dad just locked it from the inside and then shut it behind him. When he needed to get in he used a butter knife and popped open the door. I quickly learned how to do that too. He was totally clueless that I regularly took little bits out of his ever-present stash.

My father used to tell me war stories about his cattle-rustling days and his experiences in state prison. I was already starting to become wild; I'd been treated differently my whole life, and it had affected me. I think Dad chose to tell me about his misadventures because he wanted me to be in the club, so to speak, and be just like him. He didn't want me to be successful in life because the more I achieved, the more keenly aware he was of his own shortcomings and failures. As long as he kept me at his level, he still felt like the king.

When August came, I registered at Horn Lake Middle School and joined the eighth-grade football team. I'd never played football on a team before, and to be honest, I never liked it that much, but I did it to please my dad. He used to talk about how good he and his brother were when they played football in high school. So naturally, when I moved in with him, I joined the football team, too.

I wasn't a starter in the beginning, but when I finally had a chance to be on the first team, Dad didn't even show up to watch me play. In fact, he dropped me off late so I was benched. Dad never went to one of my games—all he did was pull into the parking lot at the field and drop me off. I joined the team for him, and he never even came to watch me play. I lived with him, but I still didn't have a dad.

I stepped right in at my new school and made a lot of friends. The kids I hung out with weren't football players; I gravitated toward the roughneck kids who were considered the greasers of our time. Most were troubled kids from poor families who were always getting into trouble at school. Of course, the fact that I supplied them with weed didn't hurt my popularity.

Living with my dad was like constantly walking on eggshells. He had a very short fuse, especially when it came to his wife. They got into severe fights all the time, and there was screaming and hollering, cussing, and crying. Whenever they got into it, I tried to leave the house, but sometimes they fought in the middle of the living room and I couldn't get to the front door. On those occasions I stayed in my bedroom until things cooled down.

Dad never hit me; he just got in my face and threatened me. That was enough, because I knew he was capable of really hurting me. He beat his wife, but it was nothing like how he had smacked my mom. Every time Dad lost his temper, I had flashbacks to when he threw my mom around their apartment. I was absolutely terrified of the guy.

Living with Dad and Debbie didn't last long. It wasn't fun like it had been in the beginning; it was stressful. Dad never spent any time with me; the only time we were together was at one in the morning when he got in from the bar and we sat and got high.

There was no relationship. I kept wishing and hoping he would be a regular dad, the kind of dad who would come to my ball games, but he just wasn't built that way. I learned to be happy with what I had and accept our relationship for what it was.

As soon as football season was over, about six weeks into the school year, I asked if I could move back in with Mom. I'd had all I could take in Horn Lake, and my welcome had clearly worn out.

I didn't go back the same kid. I'd been exposed to drugs, drinking, and domestic violence before, but seeing that porn took away another piece of my innocence. I started running around and getting high with kids all over the place. These were the ones other people didn't want to talk to. Most of them either had daddies who were messed up or had their own problems. Other than that, the only things we had in common were our drug use and our feelings of alienation. I felt like an outsider plumb to the end of high school, no matter how popular I became or how many girls I had.

My cousin Frankie next door was already into pot, and I started using with him. At first we got high together a couple times a month on the weekends, but by the time I was fourteen, we progressed to smoking almost every day.

My behavior really tore up my mother and my grandmother. Grandma said something once that I'll never forget: "You were the nicest kid I've ever been around. What happened to you?" She didn't understand how the substances I was using were altering my mind and personality.

On a school vacation, a buddy and I took the Greyhound bus west so we could visit our respective dads. Gary's father lived in West Memphis, which is actually across the river from Memphis in Arkansas.

I spent the first few nights at Gary's house, and then Dad came and picked us up and brought us both to Horn Lake. Gary was also a stoner and thought it was fun to smoke marijuana with my dad. "Man, you're lucky your dad is so cool. I wish my dad was like yours." I guess he was cool—if running around with women and doing drugs with your kid was cool.

I didn't say anything to my friend—I just laughed—but I remember thinking, *I wish my dad was like your dad.* Gary's dad was just a regular dad. I wanted one that would take me places and play ball with me. Why did he get to stay in that nice family neighborhood with a straightlaced dad and I had to go over to the drug house?

By the middle of eighth grade I was becoming really good at basketball. I was already dunking the ball, and my abilities had truly blossomed. My basketball coach, Kenny Hamlet, who later became the principal of Cuba Junior High, paid for me to go to an expensive basketball camp at Murray State University.

Coach Hamlet was one of the most positive influences I've ever had in my life. There were many times I wished he was my dad. I knew he loved me. He followed my basketball career all the way through high school, even though I had moved to another district. In the end, I know I was a disappointment to him.

Chattanooga Changes

Between my eighth and ninth grade years, Dad quit his gig with Tiny and the Bandsmen in Memphis and moved three hundred miles away to the industrial city of Chattanooga, Tennessee, in the Appalachian Mountains. Chattanooga had long struggled with a tarnished reputation for being polluted and economically unstable.

Dad's music career was really lagging, and to pay the rent he put up central heating and air-conditioning units in commercial buildings. That's how he ended up in Chattanooga. The company he worked for sent him to different cities for six months at a time. He became something of a nomad like his father and granddad before him. Every time he moved somewhere new, the first thing he did was hit the bars and find himself a music gig so he could play on the weekends.

After he got settled in Chattanooga, Dad made the five-hour trek to pick me up so we could spend the summer together. By now I was almost fifteen and had established myself as a serious pot smoker. When Dad first got me high, I only smoked with him and Debbie, but when I moved to Chattanooga, I was officially welcomed into his circle of druggies. We sat around and smoked joint after joint, bowl after bowl.

I had my first concert experience with my dad when he drove me to Cleveland to see Ted Nugent. He rolled up a half bag of joints and got some wine and we partied hard. Every time I visited my dad, I got more and more twisted. When I returned home I leveled out a bit, but eventually I was as bad as him.

I ended up with a ton of school clothes that summer. Debbie worked as a cashier at Kmart, and on several occasions she found a way to increase my wardrobe by looking the other way. One time I filled up a basket with clothes and eight-track tapes and brought my haul to her checkout lane.

"You're just supposed to get a pair of pants and a shirt," she complained under her breath.

But I was a stupid kid and thought music was considerably more fun than khaki pants. Besides, what was she going to do, tell me to take it all back?

Debbie rang everything up but only charged me like $1.50 for a pack of gum and a candy bar. I felt bad about doing it, because I hadn't been raised that way. My mother wouldn't have stolen a piece of gum if she was starving. Even though they were wild and drank too much, the Williams clan felt like they still had certain standards. They could curse, drink, and try to kill each other, but they wouldn't have dreamed of stealing or looking at pornography. They thought they were better than that.

My stepmother wasn't the only one ripping off the local Kmart. Druggies hang out with druggies and thieves attract other thieves. The other employees who were her friends liked the easy goods and started going through each other's lines more frequently. You can just about guess what happened with this motley crew; eventually they got caught and were fired—including Debbie.

I wasn't even in high school yet, but I felt like a grown-up because I ran around with my dad's friends and other guys in the apartment complex who were much older than me. Our next-door neighbor was a dope dealer named Brian, and I liked to go over there and smoke with him and his girlfriend. He had been paralyzed from the chest down and was confined to a wheelchair.

One day they had a proposition for me: "We'll give you a bag of weed if you break into the guy's apartment downstairs and steal the racing carburetor he has."

I was nervous. I didn't want to do it, and I knew I shouldn't do it, but I felt like they wouldn't like me if I didn't. Besides, I was tired of relying on my dad for marijuana. I wanted a bag of my own. So, like an idiot, I agreed.

Breaking in was a breeze. I felt like the big man on campus when I returned with the carburetor and everyone patted me on the back and congratulated me. Brian introduced me to all kinds

of new people and told them what a great guy I was. Then we all
packed into his handicap van and brought the carburetor to the
guys we had stolen it for.

We did drugs there all night, and I tried Quaaludes for the first
time. I didn't even know what they were, but I popped them all
the same. Quaalude was the name for methaqualone, a hypnotic
drug that was used in the 1960s and 1970s as a sedative and
muscle relaxant for the treatment of insomnia. "Ludes" made the
user feel euphoric and mellow by slowing down their heart rate
and respiration. They were also an aphrodisiac, so they were very
popular at parties. In 1984 the key ingredient needed to produce
Quaaludes was banned, which fundamentally took the drug off
the street.

A few days later, when I was sitting at Brian's getting high with
a bunch of guys, a uniformed police officer walked by the plate
glass window and knocked on it. Startled, I jumped up and ran
through the kitchen to go out the back door to safety.

They all started laughing and shouted, "Come back in here
and sit down, David. It's okay." They went over to the door,
opened it, and let the cop right in. He bought a bag of marijuana
and left. I was very naive and couldn't believe that kind of stuff
happened.

I also hung out with some kids my own age who lived in the
complex. Being a kid who was always seeking approval, I couldn't
keep my brave feat of burglary to myself, and I bragged to one of
the boys. It turns out the carburetor was worth quite a bit of
money, probably four hundred dollars back in the early '80s, and
its rightful owner wanted it back. He put out a fifty-dollar reward
for information on who had broken into his place. My little
buddy ratted me out for the cash.

The next thing I knew, two detectives were knocking on my dad's door. Dad was at work, so it was just me and Debbie at home. Not surprisingly, I denied having anything to do with the theft. When Dad got back he just about had a heart attack because his apartment was full of dope. He acted like he was going to kill me and jerked me around quite a bit that day. I confessed to ripping off the carburetor and told him Brian had put me up to it in return for half an ounce of marijuana.

He should have said, "Look what they've done to my son," but it wasn't like that. Dad didn't give a crap about me; he was upset because the heat had been brought down on him. The detectives thought he was the thief, not me.

"You had better go down there right now and tell them if they don't give you back the f— carburetor, I am going to go down and clean out their whole apartment."

So I went over and told Brian and his girlfriend what had happened. "My dad will hurt you guys if you don't get that carburetor back." And he would have too; it would have been a bad thing for them.

By later that night they had retrieved the carburetor and returned it to its rightful owner. They knew the party was over. Fortunately, nobody was prosecuted.

After that I didn't hang around those guys anymore. As a matter of fact, I was locked in the apartment for the rest of the summer. I got high with Dad and Debbie, but I wasn't allowed to leave. Even though his carburetor had been returned, the guy I stole it from put a bounty on me and paid off a kid to teach me a lesson with an aluminum baseball bat.

That would've been a great time to send me home, but Dad didn't want to be inconvenienced. He and Debbie were getting ready to move to Brownsville, Tennessee, to follow his job, so I helped them pack up their belongings. As soon as they moved into their new place, Dad took me home. I never lived with my dad again until I was an adult. Then I was like a dog returning to its vomit.

New Kid on the Block

Many people can pinpoint a time in their lives that was a defining moment. Mine was ninth grade. In many ways the events of that year left imprints on my life and changed me forever.

I went home and started the ninth grade with more experience under my belt. Cuba High School had shut down years earlier so the students were bussed six miles to archrival Sedalia High.

During the first week of school, we had picture day. Everybody went to the gymnasium to wait their turn to have their picture taken for the yearbook. I sat in the bleachers next to my brand-new girlfriend. Sitting in front of us was a huge black kid, at least six feet two and two hundred pounds. He kept turning around and throwing scraps of paper in my face and cussing at me.

When I was at my old junior high, I was the best player on our basketball team. The black kid, whose name was Ricky, played for Sedalia's team, and we used to mix it up on the court. Beyond that competitiveness, I think he was jealous of me because I was the new kid on the block. He wanted to fight.

After a while I'd had enough and stood up. I was scared of him because he was so huge, but I never let on. That guy never landed a punch; I just busted him all to pieces. Although we were right in the middle of the gym, nobody—not even the teacher—tried to stop us. I punched that big guy in the face over and over again until he backed up and didn't want any more of me. I hit him so hard in the eye that I broke a blood vessel, and it stayed bloodshot for the entire year. He couldn't have his picture taken that day because his face was so messed up. Ironically, three years earlier I had been beaten up on picture day.

Pounding that guy propelled me to a whole new level of popularity. It shocked everybody how a skinny kid like me could fight. Being the South, racism still ran rampant. There were only a few blacks in our school, and they weren't terribly popular. Ricky was a really good kid, and we became friends after that.

I was the only freshman to make the varsity basketball team that year, which swelled my popularity even more, especially with the girls. I came into what I thought was my manhood in ninth grade, but I know now that I was just a kid.

It happened when I spent the night at my friend Richie's house. His parents had split up and he was at his mama's house. His sister, Missy, was staying with their daddy. We found out she had a girlfriend over, so he and I walked for miles in three inches of snow to go see them. My feet were about frozen right off.

The four of us went out to the old barn, and when Richie hooked up with the girlfriend, it seemed only appropriate that his sister and I make out too. My first sexual experience was in a barn like an animal. When it was all over, Richie and I trudged back in the snow to his mom's house. Sex wasn't at all what I had fantasized it would be.

Sleeping with that girl was traumatizing. She knew far more about sex than I did. Even though we were the same age, Missy had been sexually active with older boys and knew how it was supposed to be done. She told the kids in school that I didn't know what I was doing, which was absolutely true. It was all very embarrassing and humiliating to me. I wish I hadn't done it.

A Wolf in Sheep's Clothing

Bill Floyd had been my bus driver since the time I was in fifth grade. The two of us didn't like each other much, and then all of a sudden, when I had achieved some notoriety on the basketball court, Bill wanted to be my buddy. Before long he was training me. He was really into ball; he'd actually played in the army during the war, and his brother was a big-time college player in the 1950s. Together they had won the state championship in high school.

Almost every Thursday night I went with him and played basketball with the guys in an old-timer's league. The players were all between sixty and eighty, and to a kid it was funny to watch. Some of them could barely walk, let alone run, and a few of them had to shoot free throws granny-style from between their legs. It made me feel like a superstar!

Those old guys sure tried though. Sometimes they scrimmaged with high school girls' teams. Of course, they wouldn't let me play; that wouldn't have been right. Instead I sat on the sidelines, and Bill and I would stick around and work on some things since the gym had already been rented out. He ran me through all kinds of drills and helped me develop my shot. Bill also brought me over to his house and made me protein drinks with goat's milk and raw eggs. It was like he was my personal trainer.

Then Bill dropped a bombshell. "I grow pot. I've got a plant growing in my yard and I'd like to sell it." I'd wondered why his eyes had always been so red, but he said he never smoked and I never smoked with him. Imagine: he was a sixty-year-old man with grown children.

Always the big shot, I said, "I'll sell it for you, Bill." It was one big setup—the training, everything. Bill had been playing me all along.

So in the space of only two years, I had taken a giant leap from being an innocent twelve-year-old when my granddad died to being a dope dealer. Much of the pot was sold to the seniors at my high school. Deep down they didn't really like me—I was just a kid after all—but they couldn't treat me badly or I wouldn't sell them any pot.

I never bought a bag of marijuana from Bill where I handed him the money and he handed me the bag. He was much sneakier than that. He gave me instructions like it was *Mission Impossible* and I was Tom Cruise:

> This is your mission, should you choose to accept it:
> Go to the gravel road where the bridge runs over the little creek.
> Look under the bridge for a coffee can.
> Take the bag out of the can and put the money in it.
> Make sure you are not followed.
> These instructions will self-destruct in ten seconds.

In Bill's mind he thought he was being slick. If something ever happened, he could deny having given me the pot. What he was forgetting, though, is that the police didn't really care about "plausible deniability." Selling drugs to a kid was pretty serious business. I was a mule for Bill Floyd all through ninth grade. I thought he was my buddy, but he was no friend of mine. He just used me.

Bill was a pedophile; I remember how he asked the girls to bend over so he could look in the rearview mirror at their boobs and have the girls rub them on his shoulder. He also stroked his elbow between their legs. He liked to talk nasty about girls around me and plant vulgar thoughts in my mind. He was a filthy, disgusting old man.

My bus driver, pseudo-athletic trainer, and small-time drug dealer ended up getting caught a few years later for giving weed to teenage girls. He didn't go to jail, but he never drove a bus again. He's just another one of the people who was a terrible influence on me.

The Accident

In the fall of ninth grade I had my first of many brushes with death. My buddy Chuck's girlfriend had borrowed her sick grand-dad's pickup truck, and while she was sleeping one morning, Chuck took it. He picked me and another kid up and we opted to shoot pool and take a joyride instead of going to school.

The three of us had a grand time. Chuck was driving, I was in the middle, and Tim was riding shotgun. After we went to the restaurant and shot some stick, we drove around the countryside. Chuck wanted to show off in this new 1982 Ford pickup, so he was driving like a wild man. As he was driving down one road going 85–90 mph, Timmy and I both told him, "Slow the truck down, man, you're not going to make this curve."

Chuck just laughed, went into the curve, and slipped off the road. Panicked, he jerked the wheel, the truck slid sideways, and the tire pulled off the rim. The first time the truck flipped, I saw a flash as the windshield shattered, and I grabbed the steering wheel and hung on for dear life. I shut my eyes and could feel the truck going over another time. On the third rotation it came to rest on its side and threw Chuck and me out of the vehicle.

When I opened my eyes I was looking straight up into the sky in the middle of the road. I felt something hit me, and I realized Chuck had one leg pinned under mine, and the other was splayed over the top of me. Chuck's body was in the middle of a massive convulsion. Thinking my friend was dead, I jumped up; in health class we had learned that muscles contract when somebody dies.

I walked up to the truck and found Timmy crawling out the bottom through the driver's side window. He was bleeding all over the place. "Chuck is dead, Timmy." We looked over and saw our friend doing the fish flop.

Ironically, when I looked down the road, I saw my mother and my grandmother coming toward me. They had been visiting their friend Betty Hodges, and we had wrecked right by her driveway in the middle of the country. My aunt Charlotte actually owned the property where the truck had landed.

The women had heard the force of the crash and came running out to see what happened. Of course, when I saw them I freaked—I was supposed to be in school—so I ran across the field and hid behind a barn. I had glass embedded in my hands from the windshield, so as I crouched in the weeds like a coward, I focused my attention on picking it out. I knew at some point I was going to have to go to the hospital and suffer the agony of having them scrubbed, but I thought it would be better to get out as much as I could while my hands were numb.

The excitement of the wreck drew half the town, and before long ambulances arrived, loaded up my friends, and took them to the hospital. I just lay there in the weeds wishing they would all hurry up and leave. My plan was to walk the three miles back home and hope nobody was the wiser.

Bewildered, Nick Matts, the owner of the restaurant, looked at my mom and grandma and said, "Where's David? He and those boys were just shooting pool up in town. Oh my God, David may be under the truck!"

With that, my mother let out a bloodcurdling scream and ran down the road toward the pickup. When they figured out I wasn't underneath it they started looking everywhere, assuming I had wandered off.

I was about fifty yards away and couldn't hear much of the conversation, but I finally figured out that my mom was calling my name. *Oh no, she knows I'm here!* I thought. Even though I was almost fifteen, I still had a fear of my mom and vividly remembered past whuppings with the switch. I just knew this was going to be bad. *Please don't let them see me!*

All of a sudden I heard the sound of my aunt's old blue diesel pickup truck come barreling across that field. I held my breath as it went right past me and then exhaled hard when I thought I was in the clear. Then the brake lights came on and the truck slid on the grass. Charlotte had spotted me.

I was a nervous wreck. Over the years I had seen confrontations like this turn physical on many occasions, and my adrenaline shot sky high. When they came up to me, Mom and Charlotte alternated between hollering and hugging me.

Chuck and Timmy were hurt, but fortunately not too seriously. Other than sustaining a bruised hip and having my hands torn up by the glass, I was perfectly fine. To this day I think God was looking out for me and that one of his angels had grabbed me and dropped me down just hard enough to show me what a knucklehead I was. The force of the impact had thrown me thirty feet and deposited me on the highway, yet I barely had a scratch. I figured I would hurt more from the whupping I was bound to get than as a result of the crash.

It didn't take long for the school to find out about the accident. The principal really wanted me on the basketball team, but he had no choice but to suspend me for three days. My English teacher didn't cut me any slack either. I missed a test while I was gone and failed the class.

In most schools, you can't play sports if you don't get passing grades. My report card had been full of F's all through junior high, but I had passed anyway. I think it was because of the ball. I did a little bit better in high school, but that's because a bunch of girls did my homework for me.

I'd tried hard to pass English so I could pass the year. And I was right on the verge; I would have passed if I hadn't been kicked out of school and gotten zeroes. That put me over the edge. I knew I had no one but myself to blame.

That joyride cost me my varsity jersey, and I got kicked off the team. So instead of being a varsity player, I got wasted and watched the games from the bleachers. It was a huge disappointment; the only thing in life I ever thought I was good at was basketball. Now they wouldn't let me play because I was dumb, at least that's how I felt. Like I didn't hate school enough already. My downward spiral accelerated.

I Saw the Light

By the time Christmas break rolled around, my behavior was going from bad to worse. I was smoking dope and drinking all the time, I was constantly getting into fights at school and at home, and the one thing I had to make me feel good about myself—basketball—was over.

My uncle Larry, who lived in California, often brought his family to visit during the holidays. Like most of my relatives on the Williams side of the family, Larry had been a drinker when he was younger, but he had become a Christian and turned his life around. He gave up his friends, burned his *Playboy* magazines, and started going to church.

I'd always liked Larry. He and I often spent time chatting, but that Christmas break we spent even more time together than other years. One night Larry and I stayed up until after 3:00 AM talking about God at the kitchen table. He took out his Bible and told me how Christ could change my life. Now, I'd been taught about Jesus my whole life, but faith is like embers in a barbecue grill. If you don't feed those embers a little fire, they eventually get cold and go out. So even though the truth had been burned into my heart, it had been years since I'd paid any attention to God. My coals had gone out.

I gave my life to Jesus sitting in the kitchen with Uncle Larry. After we prayed I got up and headed to my room. I took all my eight-track tapes—AC/DC, Ted Nugent, and Nazareth—put them in a burn barrel, threw in some garbage, and lit it on fire. I swear the flames shot out of that barrel six feet into the air, much higher than they should have. Something weird was going on. Larry thought so too.

Every night for the rest of holiday break, Larry and I talked about God. It was an amazing experience. I didn't smoke any pot and I stayed away from my cousin Frankie and my friends from school. I just hung out with Uncle Larry.

On the first day back at school I couldn't wait to tell my pothead buddies I was a born-again Christian. In my naïveté I thought they would want to be one too. I knew which ones would give me flak about my newfound faith, but I certainly didn't expect the ones who went to church to ridicule me. "You? You've got to be kidding. You, the wild one?" They didn't take me seriously at all. Parnell the Bible Thumper was a joke all over school.

My religious breakthrough only lasted a few weeks. The truth is I was a coward and backed down. If I had been strong and withstood the mocking and the temptation, who knows how many kids I could have impacted during those years in high school. Instead I was weak.

It had taken me years to climb the social ladder and build up my reputation and gain acceptance. In one fell swoop I had slummed right back to the bottom. I was the lowest of the low. Within two or three weeks I was back to selling pot for Bill and getting high with my friends. My Bible was back on the shelf.

Bigger and Better Things

My mom went through hell watching me spiral out of control. I was flunking school, got kicked off the basketball team, and when I came home at night, I smelled like booze. I shut myself in my room and played songs like "Highway to Hell." Mom and I had huge arguments and she cussed and said terribly cruel things. "You're nothing but a bum." "You're just like your daddy." "You're never going to amount to anything." "I wish you had never been born." What she said hurt, but not enough to change my ways.

As soon as the school year was over, I went straight out to stay with my dad. He had moved from Tennessee to Tulsa, Oklahoma, with Debbie and her son, Frankie, and was living with Granddad Parnell and the whole clan. Mom had arranged for me to go to summer school at a large school in Tulsa to make up my English credit; it was the only way I could move on to tenth grade.

The Parnells lived on what they called "the property." They called it that because Granddad and his four brothers had all gone in and bought a large piece of property together. It was a compound of sorts; there were a few acres, and each of the families had their own home. There was also a cooperative shop where they could work on their RVs. At any given time, half of them wouldn't be there because they were traveling evangelists. It was a sight to see when the motor homes all pulled in.

Life with the Parnells was much calmer than anywhere else I had ever lived. It was a really stable environment where we had meals at a certain time, and I helped Granddad work around the place. When the family was around, Dad had to be slyer about his drug and alcohol use.

It was one of my better summers growing up, but I still couldn't wait for the month-long summer school to be over so I could get home. By that time I had established myself in Tennessee and didn't want to waste my whole summer hanging around with my old man. I certainly no longer needed him to get high. He was lame; it was way more fun to get high with people my own age.

Back home, I spent a lot of time at the park, where they had summer softball leagues. I could have played, but I didn't care about softball. I was all about basketball and tried to get pickup games going on the court. If nobody wanted to play, I just practiced by myself.

One night I was down there dunking the ball when a farmer I knew named John Billingsby came over to talk to me. I went to grade school with his son, but I hadn't seen him in years.

"Dave, you're really good at ball. My boys go to a little high school over in Palmersville, and they could really use you out there. Those guys really suck. You could make a huge difference."

Palmersville was a little country school twenty miles away. There were only about three hundred kids from kindergarten through twelfth grade. Sedalia High School, where I'd gone the previous year, was much larger.

I told John my whole sob story, how I wasn't very good at school and how I'd made the varsity team but flunked out. I didn't know if I was going to be able to play on the team in the fall, but I was going to try a little harder in my classes and hope for the best. The truth was I didn't want to go anywhere else and have another failure.

But John was a persuasive one. "You know what? You wouldn't even have to pass over there. I'm telling you, they ain't seen nothin' like you. You wouldn't have to worry about grades if you played for Palmersville."

Immediately my ears perked up. "No kidding? In that case, I'll think about it and let you know." A few weeks later, my mom drove me to Palmersville and registered me for tenth grade.

John wasn't lying; I never took an English class again the rest of high school. I never took American History or any other required subject with the rest of the class either. Instead, my basketball coach personally "taught" me with two other students. I use that word loosely because there really wasn't any instructing going on. When it was time for class, Coach handed me a basketball and sent me to the gym. Kids who didn't like basketball were pretty pissed off about that. They were in the classroom studying for an hour while I was in the gym shooting baskets.

When I had been in the "class" for a semester, the coach said, "It's time for me to put out the grade for the first six weeks. What do you think—about 86 percent?"

I hadn't even cracked a book and he was offering me a B plus! "Well, you know you don't want to get too high because they'll pull me out of your class, but we don't want to go too low either."

"You're right, 86 percent is perfect. Not too high and not too low."

The same thing happened with American History, except he didn't even ask my opinion. I think I got a 90 percent (I was better in that class). I never did a term paper or the other stuff a normal high school student would have been required to do. I will say, however, that I took typing class and passed biology, shop class, and agriculture all on my own.

If I had it to do all over again, I would have tried harder in school. I couldn't learn then because people like my granddad said, "You can't make a horse drink, you can just lead him to water." He never backed up my mother when I was in grade school and she wanted to make me sit down and study.

When I got older I was so far behind I couldn't catch up, which made me lose interest and confidence. School officials also knew I had learning issues, but back then they didn't know what to do about them. I was simply identified as a "slow" learner and passed through the system. Later in life, when I was married and had a kid of my own, I had to get up at four in the morning to go to my factory job. You can bet I realized the value of an education then.

Palmersville High School was great. I had a new girlfriend, good grades, and was a starter on their basketball team when I was just a sophomore. The schools I had been at before were full of good athletes and were highly competitive, but most of the guys on the Pirates basketball team weren't very competitive.

I played guard and center, and I was the only one on the team who could dunk the ball. So I was responsible for dribbling the ball up the floor, but I also had to stay under the goal because I jumped and rebounded so well.

The Pirates hadn't won a game in I don't know how many years, but we won four or five games my first year there; that was just huge. The next season we were over five hundred, and my senior year we placed fourth in the district.

Our victories also had a direct impact on the school's bottom line. Palmersville went from being a school that had maybe half a dozen spectators in the stands to one that made money in tickets and concessions. Everybody liked me at Palmersville, and the parents and students all cheered for me when I ran onto the court. Everything worked out great for everybody; so what if I could barely read?

Not only was I busy shaking it up on the basketball court, I found some other, more private pursuits to keep me busy. I was much wilder than the other boys in my class, but it seemed like most of the girls were as wild as me. Guys would say things like, "Oh, you don't want to be with her; she's a whore. She's slept around a couple of times." I came from a school where many of the kids were sexually active, and I didn't think anything about that kind of stuff.

I slept around a lot in high school, trying to fill the emptiness and loneliness in my life. But no matter how many times I had sex, I was consumed by insecurities and a lack of self-confidence.

Guys like to think sleeping around makes them cool, but there is no kid equipped for that. When you have recreational sex, you bring baggage with you to other relationships. You experience a lot of unnecessary heartache and confusion. My mind should have been on schoolwork, basketball, and my future, not shagging girls and partying.

All the pornographic images that had been planted in my brain at my dad's house consumed me. My promiscuity was degrading, not to mention dangerous. I graduated high school in 1985 when AIDS was just being talked about. I had never heard about venereal disease.

I had a reputation for being a tomcat, even with the staff. A home economics teacher and a handful of senior girls bought me a plaque when they went on a trip that said, "Way, way oversexed and undersupplied, but always ready."

By the time I was sixteen, I was using alcohol every weekend and smoking marijuana every day. By the time I was a junior, I was using prescription pills like Valium and Xanax that my friends stole from their parents.

Then in my senior year, I got turned on to cocaine. I went over to a dealer's house one day to buy a bag of weed and everybody there was snorting lines of the white powder. I knew cocaine was a deadly drug that was on a whole different level than marijuana.

When they asked me if I wanted to take a bump, I said, "I don't know man, that stuff will hurt you."

They all started laughing, "No way! It ain't going to hurt you. We've been doing it all day. What the hell is wrong with you?"

These kids called me all kinds of names, and I eventually caved and snorted a line. I immediately got a rush and my heart started racing. I liked it a whole lot better than the Valium and other downers I'd been taking. They just made you tired—what was fun about that? But the coke was different. It gave me a burst of energy and made me feel alive.

Cocaine became all-consuming, but I could never do it as often as I wanted because it was so expensive. It took twenty-five dollars to stay high for just a few hours, but I felt so good I wanted more and more, and then twenty-five dollars became fifty. By the time I graduated high school, I was a drug addict and an alcoholic.

One night I got so drunk that I passed out while I was driving. I swerved and smashed into three cold drink machines and destroyed them. I'm lucky; I could have easily killed myself or someone else.

In order to keep from getting into any trouble and having a criminal record, the owner of the store allowed me to pay for the machines instead. They were worth sixteen hundred dollars, which was quite a bit of money for me. I got a job running a chain saw, and every penny I made that summer went to paying my debt. I believe it was a huge mistake to let me off that easily. Perhaps if I had been in more trouble and suffered serious consequences, my eyes might have been opened a little.

I was a total mess. I drank heavily, smoked pot like it was cigarettes, and did coke whenever I had the money. Everyone who knew me assumed I would play college basketball, but I was more interested in cocaine than college. I actually tried out for a couple of college teams but didn't make it. It's tough to play competitive ball when you spend more time putting drugs up your nose than training.

FIVE

Love Hurts

We need to learn to set our course by the stars,
not by the lights of every passing ship.

— Omar Nelson Bradley

IF YOU WOULD HAVE ASKED ME in the eighth grade what I wanted
to do after high school, I would have told you I wanted to get an
education, play professional ball, and then be a high school basketball coach. But within a four-year period, I lost those ambi-
tions; all I wanted to do was stay high, party, and have fun. I was
constantly numbed out; my life was spiraling out of control.

Pomp and Circumstance

I'm burdened with guilt over the things I've done in my life,
particularly the negative influence I had on other kids in high

school. Many of them might have never smoked pot if it hadn't been for me.

In tenth grade I fell in love with a tall, dark-haired beauty named Christy. She was one of the most popular girls in our class. Like me, Christy was an athlete; she was on the basketball team and played a little softball, too. I had dated her cousins and many of her friends, but she didn't want anything to do with me. Every time I asked her out, I ran into a brick wall.

After years of rejection, Christy came up to me unexpectedly at a basketball game during our senior year and said, "Do you still want to go out with me?" *Heck yeah!* I thought. From that night on we were a couple. In the high school yearbook, we were named "Mr. and Mrs. Together."

Christy came from a middle-class, churchgoing family, but her dad was sometimes abusive to both Christy and her mother. One time she came to school with her eyes all swelled up from crying because her daddy had been sitting on her and smacking her in the face.

He wasn't a heavy drinker or drug user, but he was mean and thought he was better than me. I never liked him; I thought he was a hypocrite because he judged me so harshly at the same time he was beating up the women in his family. Still, Christy's home environment was a lot more stable than mine.

Poor Christy had no idea what she had gotten herself into when she agreed to be my girl. She wasn't wild like most of the other girls I knew. In high school she smoked marijuana a few times, but she never got high with me. We drank a couple of times together, that was it. Christy was very good for me in some ways, but she couldn't slow me down—I was a snowball out of control.

Christy and I had an explosive relationship. Only a few months after we started dating we started having terrible arguments. A lot of times it was jealousy on my part; Christy was so beautiful that I didn't think I was good enough for her. I was constantly looking over my shoulder to see if other guys were checking her out. I wanted to have my cake and eat it too, but when she went out with her girlfriends I got really jealous. My selfishness didn't help either. We would schedule a date, but too many times I didn't show up, opting to go out with my friends and party instead. I stood up the most beautiful girl in the school to hang out with my loser buddies. A couple of times she went to my mom's house looking for me and I totally blew her off. The disagreements we had were just shouting matches, but a year later it started getting physical.

After graduation, Christy got a job working at a fast-food restaurant. I didn't know what to do with my life. College was no longer in the cards; I felt like I wasn't smart enough to do anything besides factory work or logging, so I accepted my destiny and sunk into that groove.

Restless, I picked up and moved to Texas with my friend Harold Wayne to seek my fortune. My dad lived in the Dallas/Fort Worth area by this time and set us both up with construction jobs. For a while I worked hard and managed to buy an old Chevrolet pickup truck. Technically speaking, Christy and I were still dating, even though we hadn't seen each other for months. We talked on the phone every week, and she was good about writing letters.

After only about five months I was tired of staying with Dad and was ready to move back to Tennessee and see Christy. When I got back, we picked up where we had left off. I lived with my mom and did odd jobs to make some money and supplemented my income by selling marijuana.

Before we went to Texas, Harold Wayne had been dating a girl from the high school. While we were gone, she broke up with him and started seeing a guy named Mark, who was from one of the wealthiest families in town. Harold Wayne was not happy.

One night after we'd moved back, Harold Wayne and I went barhopping with our buddy Darrel. When we saw Mark's Ford Bronco sitting in the high school lot, I parked my truck and the two of them got out and started tearing it apart. They smashed the windows with a metal pipe and tore off the mirrors, among other things. I stayed behind the wheel of my truck until the very end, and then I got out and took one swing into a window. It was my undoing.

A witness in our little bitty town had seen my truck on the scene and alerted the sheriff. The deputy found me later and asked me if I'd wrecked Mark's car. I denied it, of course. You can call me a lot of things, but I was not a snitch; I never would have told on Harold Wayne and Darrel. They didn't have the same kind of backbone, however. When they were questioned, they squealed on me in the blink of an eye.

I knew there was no way of getting out of it, so I pleaded guilty to vandalism and took my chances. I was sentenced to pay restitution and serve forty-eight hours in jail. The other two guys were never convicted because they made a deal with the prosecutor.

I was nervous as the guard conducted me to my cell. I had no idea what to expect. Although I was no Boy Scout and had done plenty of illegal things, I was still a kid. The worst part of the whole experience was when I woke up the next morning and noticed that a number of my fellow inmates had their heads shaved. I found out later there had been an outbreak of lice in our cell. That really disgusted me.

Unfortunately, Christy's daddy had seen me being escorted from the courthouse across the street to the jail. He went straight home and said to her, "Guess who I saw walking across the street in handcuffs? Your boyfriend!" Not exactly what a father wants for his daughter.

Mom and I constantly fought about my drug use. It was a mystery to me how she did it, but she always found my stash. Sometimes she would hear me pull up, and as soon as I walked in the door and rounded the corner into the living room, she would run to the woodstove and throw my bag of weed into the fire. That inevitably started a huge argument, and I would storm out of the house and leave, gravel flying behind my screeching tires. Mom tried hard to keep me off drugs, but her efforts had little effect.

That living arrangement didn't last long. Mom was no longer willing to put up with my self-destructive behavior and told me I could ruin my life somewhere else. After she kicked me out, I moved into a trailer with two former high school classmates, Jenny and Vicky. Vicky was the same girl who had done my homework all through high school.

Even though Christy and I were dating, I slept with both of my roommates on a regular basis. They both worked at the same lawn-mower factory, but were on alternating shifts. At night I slept with Jenny because she worked days, and when she woke up in the morning and headed to the factory, I crawled into bed with Vicky and had sex with her. To Vicky it seemed to be all about sex, but Jenny wanted more than I could give her—she wanted a husband. I finally moved out of the trailer because I couldn't see eye to eye with Jenny. Surprisingly, my mom let me move back into her house. I'm sure that's hard for some people to understand, but I suspect mothers might relate. Mothers love their children even when they mess us. My mother was no different; she kept giving me chances. After I moved out of the trailer I apologized to her for being so difficult and told her I had no place else to go. Even though I was a grown man, she worried about her baby. She didn't want me living on the streets.

Shotgun Wedding

Every little girl has rose-colored visions of what her dream wedding will be like—fragrant flowers, a handsome groom, smiling guests, beautiful music, and a wedding gown that makes her feel like a princess. Regrettably, my first wedding was a very distant cousin of what you might find on the pages of *Bride's* magazine.

I lived with my mom, but when she went on vacation I had the place to myself. On one of those occasions, Christy spent the night with me. Although she was still living with her parents at the time, she lied and told them she was staying with a girlfriend. That's the night I got her pregnant.

Christy didn't even cry when she called and told me she was carrying my child. Her parents, however, were less than thrilled. They didn't like me for good reason—by the time I was nineteen, I'd already been in jail.

When Christy's parents found out she was pregnant, they pressured us to get married right away. In my heart I think she wanted to be pregnant because she wanted to marry me. But me? I wasn't ready. My idea of a good time was barhopping and sleeping around with different women, not playing house. It's funny in a way, I was excited about marrying Christy and being a family, but the closer we came to tying the knot, the more panicked I became. I knew I wasn't husband or father material and did everything I could to postpone the nuptials.

Then one day Christy came to my house and woke me up. "Get up and get dressed; we're meeting my parents at the courthouse."

Reluctantly, I threw on some clothes and got into her car. When we arrived at the courthouse, her mom and dad were waiting for us outside. I could see their displeasure as soon as I laid eyes on them. A wedding is supposed to be a joyous occasion when the parents of the bride welcome their new son into the family, but Christy's folks were anything but happy. Who can blame them? Their little girl had been knocked up by the person they least wanted her to marry—a known drunk and drug abuser.

Christy and I stood in front of the justice of the peace, held hands, and said our "I dos." After the ceremony there was no reception or celebration. The next day Christy moved in with my mom and me.

I quit the migrant, bumming-around farm work I'd been doing and got a regular job at the lawn-mower factory. Vicky had gotten me a spot on the second shift. She and I continued to fool around after I was married, even though she had a live-in boyfriend. We were attracted to each other like moths to the flame. Neither of us wanted anything out of our relationship other than sex.

After a while, my father-in-law found a little house a mile or so away from them and Christy and I started living like a happy young couple. Despite that idyllic newlywed setting, I got more and more consumed by drugs, especially marijuana. It didn't matter that I was employed; I got high before I went to work and took joints with me and smoked them inside the building with other employees during my shift. At suppertime I went out and got a burger or something and got high after my meal. In other words, I was pretty much stoned my entire shift. There were a lot of potheads in that factory.

Needless to say, the best way for me to pay for my drugs was to supply other people. I bought quarter pounds of marijuana at a time, repackaged the dope into smaller quantities, and resold it for a sizable profit. My coworkers at the factory proved to be a steady, lucrative customer base.

I did my best to convince Christy I was dealing pot so I could make extra money for us. Of course, that never really worked out; instead of spending the money on her or saving it, I went to the bars and blew it on booze.

Things at home were actually pretty calm during the week, but beginning Thursday night and all through the weekend, I was a total playboy. On Thursday nights my factory buddies and I went to a place called the Hut Nut and drank away our pay-checks. It was a popular bar in the black part of town, but on Thursdays they saw an influx of whites looking to cash their checks. A lot of my friends got their money and left, but I usu-ally stayed and partied till the wee hours. Sometimes I was the only white person in the bar, and I sat and drank with the women until 2:00 to 3:00 AM. They liked me because I sold them dope. I liked them because they were fun to party with.

One night I lost my whole check at the Hut Nut after I cashed it. A drunken fool, I had pulled out my wad of cash and dropped it on the floor. Amazingly, not one of the honest, upstanding bar patrons ran after me and said, "Hey! You dropped your money!" When I got home that night, I smelled funky, my mind was gone, and all of my money with it. That money was supposed to buy groceries and pay our rent. Christy was furious! She screamed and hollered, but I was so drunk by the time I got home that I passed out on the couch. She continued to cuss me out while I lay snoring. My wife was mad at me for days, but I cried and apologized and told her I would slow down on the drinking. The same old sob story. I groveled for a week until she got over it—somewhere around the time I got my next paycheck. Then the cycle started all over again.

Sugar and Spice and Everything Nice

The day my daughter was born was one of the happiest days of my life. It was a terrible time for Christy, though. The night before she went into labor I went out and got doped up and drunk. I went to my mom's house instead of home because I knew there would be hell to pay with my wife. Around 4:00 AM I woke up to someone beating on my bedroom window. It was Christy's little brother; her water had broken and she was at the hospital.

I went to the maternity ward, but I was still so drunk I didn't go to the delivery room to be with my wife. Before long, a nurse came into the waiting room and told me and the rest of her family that Sheena had been born.

By the time I saw her, my daughter was already cleaned up and swaddled. Sheena was six pounds, seven ounces and had a full head of black hair and a dark complexion; she looked like she was glowing. My little girl was the most beautiful baby I had ever seen.

It's hard to describe how I felt the first time I held her. It was an incredible moment. I remember thinking that her childhood would be so much better than mine because she would have a dad in her life. I didn't want to be like my old man who had abandoned his kids. I wanted things to be different for Sheena.

After we brought her home from the hospital, I tried to do a little better for a while. I remember going to the bank one day and depositing money after getting paid. It was just me and Sheena. A woman at the bank carried on saying I was the proudest dad she had ever seen.

My role as doting father didn't last long, though. I just couldn't stop getting drunk and doing drugs. I wanted to be a good parent, but I couldn't do it; I didn't know how. When I wasn't working I hung out with my loser buddies instead of being home with my family. They didn't have wives or steady girlfriends to go home to, so all they did was party. They wanted me to go along with them to bars and parties because I was one of the tough guys who could fight.

I hated being married and tied down. It always felt like I was missing something, and I resented the fact that there were things I would never be able to do. I acted like a child; my place should have been at home with my wife and my kid, not boozing it up and getting stoned with a bunch of knuckleheads.

Time and time again I promised Christy I would quit smoking pot. First it was after we got married. When that came and went, I promised her I would stop when the baby came. But I couldn't do it. Things went from bad to worse for us. Not only did I leave the parenting of our demanding infant to my wife, I swallowed and inhaled most of our money.

I worked as hard as I played. During the summer I roofed houses for extra money. The hot, humid Tennessee weather warranted starting very early in the day—if the sun was too high in the sky it was impossible to bear the heat. Christy had a brand-new car, and I used to take it to work. One morning at around

4:00 AM, I was so tired that I fell asleep at the wheel while nego-
tiating a curve. The car ran off the road and flipped upside
down. I totaled her cute little Chrysler.

After that we didn't have a car and I had to catch rides to and
from work. Our lack of transportation also made it impossible for
us to do any shopping. Fortunately, Christy's parents lived just
down the road from us, so we counted on them to help us out.
But they wouldn't; they didn't approve of the way I was living and
refused to "enable" my behavior by going to the store. Most
grandparents would have at least gotten the baby some milk.

In retrospect I don't blame them at all—I was in the frame of
mind where everything that was wrong in my life was somebody
else's fault. My in-laws certainly weren't responsible for taking
care of my family . . . I was, and I fell down on the job. I cast
much of the childrearing off on them so I could do whatever I
wanted. If I would have been a good father, my baby would have
always had milk.

On the other hand, I don't think it's enabling to feed the children of an addict. Some people will disagree with me on that, but
it's not the fault of the children that their parents do drugs or
drink too much, and they shouldn't suffer needlessly because of
it. It would have been enabling to feed me.

Irreconcilable Differences

Christy and I always had a volatile relationship—we started
arguing when we got together in high school and never
stopped. While I had never had a problem pounding another
guy near to death, I'd never been violent toward the women I
dated. But Christy was a hellcat. In school I used to watch her

fight her brother right in the middle of the hallway. Their arguments always broke out into crazy catfights. She clawed him in the face and he slapped her; she punched him and he smacked her right back.

The two of us had brawls too, but ours weren't where everybody could see us. It really was a two-way street. Christy pulled my hair and slapped me. Things got worse after we said our wedding vows. On one occasion we got into a fight when we were sitting in the car in my driveway. We screamed and cussed at each other, and then she slapped me. I returned the gesture, and she leaned back in the passenger seat and kicked me in the face, splitting my lip wide open. I grabbed her by the hair and cuffed her hard in the face. Then all of a sudden it was over. When we fought like that we always cried, not knowing what the hell had just happened.

By the time I was twenty I had become a heavy alcoholic and a very serious drug addict with a violent temper. I dominated my wife and became very physically abusive. Sometimes I picked her up and threw her into the couch or another piece of furniture. I choked her and beat her. The baby used to cry from all the screaming and hollering. Christy tried to fight back, and in many cases, she gave as good as she got, but I was far bigger and stronger. Obviously, it really wasn't a fight—that woman was fighting for her life; I wasn't fighting for mine.

Christy and I could have easily become a crime statistic. I could've gotten her down on the floor and beaten her until she wasn't moving. She could have killed me by hitting me in the head with a pipe or something. I still can't understand why I didn't just leave.

Our relationship came to a screeching halt one blistering

August day. We didn't have air conditioning in our little house, and it was 103 degrees inside. For a couple of days it had been so hot I couldn't sleep at night; I tossed and turned, soaked to the skin while lying in a sweat-drenched bed. I became increasingly short-tempered.

The biggest catalysts for my rage were Christy's parents. I was angry with them because they wouldn't help us with Sheena like I thought they should. When they babysat her at their place, they kept her for entire weekends at a time. I should have been grateful they took her, but I was irrationally angry. To get back at them, I told Christy I didn't want the baby going over to visit them for a while. It was my pathetic attempt to punish them.

I woke up to go to work that hot August morning, all sweaty and cranky, and went to the kitchen to get a bite to eat and see my daughter. When I realized she wasn't there, I flipped out, incensed that Christy had allowed them to take her.

What started out as a vicious verbal argument soon boiled over into a brutal physical fight. Christy had been waiting for that next fight. We'd already split up several times, and she'd gotten to the point that she just wanted to end it for good. She knew I had been running around on her, and she was sick and tired of my all-consuming drug abuse. Substances and other women were obviously more important to me than my family.

After that fight we split up for good. Our marriage had only lasted a year and a half. Christy told people she had stuck with me that long because she knew that deep down, beneath the temper and the addictions, I had a good heart. Christy was a good woman and she didn't deserve the treatment I dished out to her. It breaks my heart to think about it now.

Live and Let Live

On Christmas Day after the divorce, I wanted to drink and forget that I wasn't spending the day with my little girl. It also happened to be my twenty-first birthday, so a friend of mine had a party for me at her place. There were a bunch of people over, including my friend's seventeen-year-old niece who had a serious crush on me. I didn't know her because of the age difference; she was still in high school and I was a grown man with an ex-wife and a child. She certainly knew me though; she'd had a thing for me ever since she'd seen me play high school basketball.

That kid bugged me all night long, trying to get me to go to the back bedroom and fool around with her. I was busy playing cards, doing dope, and drinking with my buddies and wasn't interested in breaking away to be with her.

After the party was over I left the house and headed for home. I didn't get very far down the road before I got to thinking about that girl, and I turned around. I realized that sleeping with her would be a great way to cap off my birthday celebration. When I got back to the house everyone else had left, but that girl was already sacked out for the night in bed beside her aunt (who was my party-throwing friend). I walked into the back bedroom, picked her up, carried her into another bedroom, and had sex with her. We never said a word to each other; I didn't even know her name. In fact, I was so inebriated that I don't think I would have recognized her the next day if she had walked right up to me on the street.

About six weeks later I was rudely awakened by a persistently ringing phone. I stumbled out of bed to get it and immediately felt like throwing up. My head was throbbing, my stomach was lurching, and it felt like I had a whole bale of cotton in my mouth. I'd had a pretty wild night as usual.

"Hello."

"I want to talk to David Parnell," an angry voice said on the other end of the line.

"That's me."

"I'm going to come over and f— kill you!"

That woke me up. At first I thought it was just a prank phone call, but what the man said next stopped me cold.

"You got my daughter pregnant, you lowlife son of a bitch!" It was obviously not one of my buddies.

I invited him to come over and get a piece of me. Of course, I got up immediately and locked my doors. Tough-nut guy or not, you don't mess with "Daddy."

"I don't know what you're talking about," I said, my mind racing. The man calmed down enough to tell me who his daughter was, and things began to come into focus inside my fuzzy brain.

The girl told her daddy I had practically raped her, and she'd been too scared to say anything or fight back. She also let on that she was a virgin when I forced myself on her. We'd definitely had sex—I don't deny it and shouldn't have done it—but I didn't force her to do anything. I don't remember everything in vivid detail, but I can tell you one thing . . . she was definitely *not* a virgin; I'd been with them before. This girl knew what she was doing.

My conversation with her father ended with him informing me that I was expected to pay for half of her abortion. If I did so, he wouldn't prosecute me for rape. I knew there was little chance of him turning me in anyway; one of the conditions of our agreement was that I had to swear to keep the incident a secret. He was more worried about word getting out around town that his precious daughter got pregnant than he was about snuffing out the life of his grandchild.

Actually, it was all a big cover-up. My friend, the girl's aunt, told me that the mother-to-be was dating a nineteen-year-old boy, and when she found out she was pregnant, she decided to pin it on me so her parents wouldn't make her break up with her boyfriend. To this day I still don't know if it was my baby, but more than likely it was her boyfriend's. I guess it doesn't really matter now.

If it hadn't been for my friend clearing things up, I could have been in big trouble. She told the dad that what his daughter was feeding him was a big lie. "She chased him all night long, and he wouldn't go back to the bedroom with her."

With that, I was off the hook. After I gave them some money, I never heard from the girl or her family again. What a relief that was! I was more worried about going to jail, or getting killed by her dad, than I was about the abortion. After the money changed hands, though, it started to bother me that they were killing the baby. Of course, I wouldn't have dared to argue about what they were going to do . . . I knew it was messed up, but I was more concerned about David than any baby. All these years later I think about that girl, and I will for the rest of my life. I wish she hadn't been in that situation, whether it was my baby or not.

This is one of many situations I wish I would have handled differently. Shoot, I wish I would have handled my whole life differently. I squandered my youth and I wasted my twenties, the best years of my life. I don't even remember most of that decade. There are some things in life a person would like to erase. Unfortunately, there are no do-overs.

SIX

The Devil's Playground

Man's power of choice enables him to think like
an angel or a devil, a king or a slave.

— Frederick Bailes

MOST OF MY EARLY ADULT LIFE I MADE one bad choice after another. The worst was choosing drugs and alcohol over my family and my future. I blew a chance to go to college, my wife left me, and I had no money, car, or prospects. Only twenty-one, I was already divorced. I wanted my daughter to grow up with two parents, yet I had walked away from her. To my horror, I had followed in my father's footsteps and had no one to blame but myself. I hit rock bottom—or so I thought. Little did I know there was so much farther to fall.

When Christy left me I was down and out. I had no place to go but back to my mom's house. She watched as I sank further into depression. I was so miserable I quit my job at the lawn-mower factory and did nothing but drugs all day, every day. I had visitation with Sheena every other weekend. Most of the time my mom picked up Sheena at Christy's place while I waited at the house, but on occasion I did it. Oftentimes my sister's daughter, Kimberly, who was a year older, came over so Sheena would have somebody to play with. At first I played with them and colored in their coloring books, but after a couple of hours I got itchy to leave. I had to get high, so I left Sheena with my mom and hung out with my buddies. I was a wretched parent.

Not only was I incapable of nurturing my own daughter, but with no income, I fell apart financially and got behind on my child-support payments. I felt lost and hopeless, and I knew if I didn't make a change in my life, I would go off the deep end. Feeling there was clearly nothing left for me in Tennessee, I headed for Texas.

Chip Off the Old Block

Ironically, as I was going through the aftermath of my divorce, Dad's relationship with Debbie, his wife of ten years, was also ending. Like Christy, she'd had all she could take of his adultery, violence, and drug abuse.

Every time I went over to Christy's to pick up or drop off Sheena, I was an emotional wreck. I begged her to take me back, often weeping uncontrollably. My outbursts just made her laugh: "Don't cry; that's just so silly."

I promised her I would change; I'd get a good job, stop drugging and drinking, and be home more. It was the same old song and dance, and the music had long since ended. I promised Christy I would be the man she always wanted me to be. But it was too late; she had already moved on. I couldn't blame her for wanting to get away from me. I was bad news.

The idea of Christy being with another man made me crazy. Obviously I had always operated on a double standard. The whole time we were married I slept with woman after woman, but once I was free, I stayed away from them. Other than the mistake I had made with that seventeen-year-old girl who'd had the abortion, I was celibate. For years I had slept around with girl after girl, but after Christy and I split, my heart was broken. There was no denying that I had mistreated her and messed up, and that was hard medicine to swallow. I had lost something good, and I kept thinking that if I straightened up my act and prayed hard enough she would take me back. There was no way I should have been doing drugs or drinking; the more I drank and the more I drugged, the easier it was to get lost in my own thoughts and forget what a screw up I had become. But I felt like I could control my sexuality, so I kept women at arm's length. I didn't want to get involved again and risk experiencing that kind of pain.

It was time to put my tail between my legs and run west to Texas. Since Dad and I were in the same boat, I figured it was as good a place as any for me to wallow in my misery. But by the time I got to Texas, Dad had already moved in with another woman; he was like a gigolo to wealthy, unattached ladies. They invited me to stay with them. What a trio we made.

The first thing I did when I got to the Lone Star State was look for a job. I needed a regular paycheck to support my partying. I started working at a wholesale florist making deliveries to flower

shops. It was a great job because making deliveries helped famil-
iarize me with the Dallas–Fort Worth (DFW) Metroplex. Plus,
the owners let me take a van home every night. That meant I had
wheels.

Before long, Dad and his woman started getting at each other's
throats, and I didn't want to live there anymore. I got myself a
cheap apartment in an all-Mexican neighborhood in Arlington,
right across from a car-manufacturing factory. It was a rough
neighborhood. I didn't have much, but I managed to get myself
a phone and cable TV.

When Dad and the woman split up, he moved in with me. Our
father-son relationship was always the opposite of most. He moved
in with *me*. *I* was the one responsible for the rent and the bills. He
paid me rent. Over the course of the next ten years, I often bailed
him out.

Dad had a good job installing air-conditioning units in apartment buildings and made considerably more money than I did.
So I quit my job at the florist and started going to work with him
every day. For a while we did pretty well. We smoked dope all
the time, got drunk, and barhopped all over town, but we were
both steadily employed and got along fine.

Then I was introduced to methamphetamine and began a
gradual descent into true madness. My senses were heightened at
first, I felt alive and empowered, but they eventually became
deadened and I was like a zombie, a heartless corpse walking
around pretending to live. I didn't care about anyone or anything
but getting high. Emotionally, I was a minefield. I could feel
emotions of anger and hatred, jealousy and rage—in fact, they
were far stronger than any positive emotions, such as happiness
or love, which were gone. The closest thing I felt to love was sex,

and even that became negative in the end. I did things I could have never imagined myself doing and am ashamed to admit I did. I didn't see it coming . . . meth robbed me of my soul.

The Workingman's Drug

One night, Dad, his buddies, and I were sitting around our apartment completely stoned, and I noticed something different about the other guys. I'd been a druggie for so long that I could immediately recognize when somebody was high, but this was something I couldn't quite put my finger on . . . these guys were hyped-up! When I asked what they were on, they pulled out some white powder they called crank. I'd never heard of it before.

"It's speed, man. It's like cocaine except a whole lot more potent."

Now they were talking! When I was in Tennessee I had fallen in love with cocaine. It was definitely my drug of choice when I had the money. I would literally lay out lines of cocaine that were six inches long and snort them until I choked and white powder blew out my nose. I'd built up such a tolerance that I had to do tons of it to get high. This white powder was different. Cocaine is unleaded gasoline, but meth is rocket fuel.

Methamphetamine goes by many names: crystal, ice, speed, go fast, glass. Crank, which is what I always called it, is a nickname that came from the habit Hell's Angels had of transporting it in the crankcases of their motorcycles.

Methamphetamine is made from common, easily accessible materials like antifreeze, starting fluids, Freon, drain openers, paint thinner, acetone, and cold medications, and can be manufactured virtually anywhere. Not only is the drug itself harmful, but so is the process of cooking it. The fumes, vapors, and spillage associated with the process are toxic and highly combustible. Meth is poison.

When those dopehead friends of my dad's offered me some meth, they put out a line that was only about half an inch long. "Are you kidding me?" I complained. "You guys are stingy with your dope!"

"This is not like cocaine; you just wait," they laughed.

My first snort was like a line of fire going up my nose. It burned a lot, not like cocaine at all. Immediately, I experienced a sensation so intense it felt like my chest was expanding and my shirt was actually moving. *Oh my God, my heart is going to explode! I am going to have a heart attack!* The powerful rush scared the hell out of me. I had no knowledge of the physiology of taking the drug, but the blood pressure of a person high on meth can exceed 200/150 and the heart rate can run as high as 250 beats per minute. No wonder I felt like my heart was going to jump right out of my chest.

In scientific terms, methamphetamine is a stimulant that affects the central nervous system. In her book, *Crystal Meth: They Call It Ice*, Dr. Mary Holley likens it to the chemical equivalent of a bolt of lightning striking a metal plate in the middle of the brain. The drug stimulates the release of incredible quantities of dopamine, a neurotransmitter in the pleasure center of the brain. Such a surge causes an intensely pleasurable mood as well as emotional and personality changes.

I zoomed for twenty-four hours, rattling on about nothing for half the time. My brain was on overdrive and I couldn't concentrate on anything because my mind kept jumping from one thought to another. One second I was washing the dishes and before I even realized it, I was on to some other project without

finishing the first one. It was like a self-induced attention-deficit/
hyperactivity disorder (ADHD).

A meth high was like nothing I'd ever experienced, particularly because it lasted so long. When I hadn't come down at all
after more than eight hours, it seemed unnatural. I remember
lying in my dark bedroom staring at the ceiling and praying to
God that the high would wear off. "God, if you just slow my
heart down and get this stuff out of my system, I'll never do it
again. I swear." I imagine God was just shaking his head.

When that first hit of meth didn't kill me outright, I knew I
had found my new drug of choice. Crank was cheap, so I could
do it as often as I wanted. Twenty-five dollars kept me high for
three solid days, while a line or two of cocaine lasted only a
couple hours and cost far more.

I believe I became an addict on that very first bump. In her
book, *Crystal Meth,* Dr. Mary Holley estimates that crystal methamphetamine has a 95 to 98 percent addiction rate. In other
words, if one hundred people try the drug, ninety-five of them
will become addicted to it within one year.

Crank scared me half to death, but obviously not enough to
prevent me from trying it again. I started out doing it on the
weekends. Meth made me feel so strong I felt like I could have
walked through a wall. Full of energy, it seemed like I could think
more clearly than I ever had before; my brain was going a mile a
minute. Meth gave me unending endurance, and I loved it.

I sometimes stayed up all weekend smoking weed, doing crank,
and drinking, with absolutely no sleep for two nights. On Sunday
night I finally went to bed and crashed, but sometimes when I
was especially wild, I stayed high through work on Monday and
didn't shut my eyes until that night. Then I would have two fairly

"normal" days where I went to work and just smoked pot, but by Wednesday night I was all cranked up again. It's hard to be on your game and make good decisions when you only sleep a couple of nights a week. Dad was even worse than me. By this time he and his buddies regularly went for two or three days without sleep. It was a weekly ritual and that blew my mind. I tried my best to keep up with them, and before long I was on the same rollercoaster ride.

Some of the older guys doing meth talked about hallucinating and they did some really weird things. I was only twenty-one, strong, and invincible—dope would never control me like it did them. Sadly, it was too late for such bravado; I was already hooked. Back then I would have said I could quit doing crank anytime I wanted to because I only did it on weekends. But by the time I left Texas a year later, I was a full-blown meth addict at a whole new level of addiction.

I had a good job, but I spent all my money on alcohol, pot, and crank. I didn't have an endless supply of dope like I did when I was a dealer back in Tennessee, so I had to buy my own. Every week I blew my whole paycheck; it wasn't unusual for me to go two or three days without eating when the money ran out. If my belly hurt from being empty too long, I guzzled water to trick it into thinking it was full. Then on payday, I'd eat a big meal, like a whole pizza or something.

When the weekend rolled around the whole cycle started all over again. Funny, even if I didn't have a crust of bread in the kitchen, I always managed to have dope. My addiction was my top priority.

There was a war being waged in my soul between evil and good. During the week when I didn't do crank, I'd lay low in my bedroom and read the Bible. The words convicted me, but my cravings were overpowering. The things I'd been doing, like lying, having sex with married women, and stuffing drugs up my nose, were all things I had promised my granddad I would never do. The dark side had taken over and I was hopelessly addicted. I longed for a brief moment of peace. But there was none to be found; my life revolved around seeking pleasure.

Users in the United States account for 70 percent of the illegal drugs used in the entire world. Too many people believe the cultural messages that promote self-indulgence: if it feels good, go for it. Countless vices provide temporary fixes to our problems, but no solutions. I enjoyed being high all the time because it helped me forget the heartbreaks of my childhood and the mistakes I'd made—especially letting my wife, Christy, slip through my fingers.

Dad and I had really become good buddies—two divorced bachelors with no one to tell us what to do. We hung out like roommates would, not like father and son. We hit bars together, chased women together, raised hell together, and got high together. I no longer felt threatened by him, because he was getting older and I was becoming stronger and maturing physically. As far as getting along went, it was a good period of our lives.

I lived my life in a constant state of intoxication. I was on something all day, every day. When I wasn't on meth—or even when I was—I was drunk all the time. Beer was a constant, but I mixed it with whatever was around: whiskey, tequila, whatever. It didn't really matter as long as I was numb.

Although I had always been known as a ladies' man, I wasn't with a woman for nearly eight months after I moved to Texas. Occasionally I got drunk and kissed a woman on the dance floor when my dad's band was playing, but I hadn't been sexually active or even wanted to go on a date.

Dad didn't understand. "What is wrong with you, man? Every night you have three or four ladies approach you at the bar and you dance with them, but you always mess it up. It's like you don't want to have anything to do with them."

He was right. As the night wore on and I got drunk, I would inevitably start thinking about Christy. If I was with a particular woman, I became rude and argumentative to scare her off. It worked every time.

One night my buddy PJ and I went to a cowboy bar on the strip in Fort Worth. We'd always been into cars and hot rods, so when we walked past a beautiful white Porsche right by the front door, we took notice.

After we had a couple drinks, an extremely attractive woman approached me from across the room and asked me to dance. We had a great time drinking and dancing for a few hours, and then she asked PJ and me if we wanted to go out and get something to eat. The three of us walked out of the bar and she looked at me and said, "Why don't you ride with me?" She took my hand and walked me straight to that white Porsche.

I'm sure he felt like a third wheel, so after we had some eggs, PJ took off. The woman took me to her house. She lived in a very nice place in an affluent neighborhood. I was living in a roach motel kind of apartment in a very poor part of town, so to me her place was like a mansion.

Walking in the front door, I got a big surprise. This beautiful woman, who I thought was no more than thirty years old, had two teenage kids. The older girl was driving age, probably sixteen or seventeen; I could have easily been with her instead of her mother. Factoring in her daughter's age, my new lady friend must have been in her late thirties or early forties. To a guy who was twenty-one, forty was old. But, to me, she looked great. Besides, you don't ask somebody you meet in a bar how old they are before you leave with them.

The whole mother-child reunion threw me off guard to say the least. It seemed strange that she would bring a man home when her kids were there, but hey, what did I know? I was just a poor country boy. There were many things about big city life that were brand-new to me.

I felt awkward until we went into the bedroom and she shut the door. At least then I didn't have to look at her kids. We talked for a long time. She told me about all the cosmetic procedures her late husband had paid for and what her life was like before and after he died. I told her about the ex-wife and daughter I had back home and shared how long it had been since I'd slept with a woman. That inspired her—she was like a nurse and I was her pet project.

The next morning we had breakfast and she took me home. When we got to my apartment we kissed good-bye, exchanged phone numbers, and she told me she'd be seeing me. As soon as I stepped out of the Porsche, I thought, *I don't want to see her again.* Even though she was one of the most beautiful women I'd ever seen and had plenty of money and a good personality, I didn't want anything to do with her. My heart was still broken. I never saw her again.

Dad was pretty excited when he saw that lady drop me off in front of our apartment complex. He couldn't understand why I didn't want to pursue her; she was like a gold mine to a guy without any money. Dad was always on the prowl for a rich woman to take care of him. When I first moved to Texas he was living with a rich widow. She drove a Cadillac Eldorado and a Toyota sports car and had lots of money. That woman bought my dad thousands of dollars worth of jewelry and clothes, including seven-hundred-dollar diamondback rattlesnake cowboy boots, a rattlesnake belt, and a band for his cowboy hat. He was like a man-whore, a kept man.

After I slept with that woman from the bar, the proverbial floodgates flew open and I was back in the pickup scene, hooking up with a string of women. I know now that one-night stands do nothing but degrade both people. Somebody always gets hurt, whether they know it right away or not. I got a lot of phone numbers after hooking up with women, but I never called them. I didn't mean to hurt anybody's feelings; it was just that I was so lost that I tried to make myself feel better through casual sex. I didn't want to be attached to a woman and risk experiencing the pain my broken marriage had caused. Sometimes I was the one rejected, so I know how it felt.

Striptease

I started going to strip clubs with my dad and some other guys. Some of them were fancy, high-dollar gentleman's clubs that required customers to wear suit coats, but the one I liked was just a low-rent place in a bad neighborhood. I liked to drink at the Ecstasy Club because I could walk home no matter what condition I was in.

The Ecstasy Club was a dumpy strip club down the street from our apartment. I'd never been in a place like that before; I was still young and green from my upbringing in rural Tennessee. In Dallas there were far more entertainment options.

Most of the girls who worked there had addiction problems. The owners liked to keep them doped up; that way they got back all the wages they paid the strippers. Lisa was addicted to heroin. She and I met one afternoon when I was at the Ecstasy having a few drinks. When she discovered I had a pocketful of crank, she latched on to me right away. She said we couldn't go into the bathroom together to get high because of the club's security, so she begged me to give her my bag and let her go into the ladies' room alone. I didn't buy that for a second; I knew she would steal my dope and that would be the end of it. I gave her a little bit of meth and my phone number and took off, figuring I would never see or hear from her again.

About a week later the phone rang at two o'clock in the morning. When I answered it there was a girl sobbing on the other end. She was crying so hysterically I could hardly understand her. I finally figured out it was Lisa from the strip club. "My boyfriend is going to kill me! He's kicking me out on the street and I have no place to go. Would you please come get me?" This girl had called a total stranger whom she had only met once. Who knows how many guys she called before me? For all she knew I could have been a serial killer.

I woke up my dad and told him what was going on. He didn't approve: "Man, you'd better not do that. It's two in the morning and you don't even know this girl. She's going to bring you nothing but trouble."

"No, I've got to go. She needs some help and I need a woman."

That's really what it boiled down to. I played it off like I was her knight in shining armor, but deep down I just wanted someone to mess around with. I probably would have gone to get her even if there wasn't something in it for me, but those thoughts certainly entered my mind. This girl was very attractive.

Lisa gave me directions and I picked her up at a house a couple miles away. Bawling, she hopped into the van, holding tightly to a tiny plastic bag (the kind you would get at a grocery store) stuffed full of clothes. I figured she was probably hungry, so I drove to the 7-Eleven right by my apartment to get her a chili dog. It was one of the few places open at that time of night.

Pulling into the parking lot, I told Lisa to stay in the car. I didn't want her inside because she was doped up and dressed like a whore. As soon as I walked into the store, I heard the van door shut. I turned and looked and there she was, rounding the front of the van wearing nothing but a see-through halter top, G-string thong panties, and high-heeled shoes. Her bare butt shone in the moonlight. I didn't say anything, just held the door as she click-clacked her way into the convenience store.

The young man behind the counter was appalled. "Man, this is a family store; she can't be in here like that."

"F— you and your family!" she spit out in response. The clerk shut up after that. I just kind of shrugged and shook my head. I was a red-blooded twenty-one-year-old guy. I didn't care if she was naked in a 7-Eleven in the middle of the night. I paid for her food and whatever else she wanted and we left.

By the time we got back to the apartment, it was time for me to get ready for work. My dad was so excited when he saw that half-naked eighteen-year-old running around the apartment that I thought he was going to have a stroke.

He wasn't so overcome, however, that he felt comfortable leaving her in the apartment while we commuted to work. "We don't know this girl; she is going to rob us of everything we've got!"

"But we don't have anything!" I retorted. We really didn't have much. There was a nasty old couch that the landlord had given us when another tenant had moved out, and a TV, but other than that, we didn't have any furniture. We didn't even have a mattress; Dad slept on the smelly couch and I slept directly on the disgusting carpet that had been laid on top of a concrete slab. I ran several miles a day and still played basketball, so I was in good shape, but that hard floor left me feeling sore every morning when I woke up.

"What about my stuff? Who's going to make sure she doesn't steal my stereo and my guitar?"

"Don't worry about it," I reasoned, "I don't think she would do that. She doesn't have anywhere else to go; she just needs a place to stay for a little while."

"I hope you're right about her," Dad said, shrugging his shoulders as we walked out the door. Drug addicts are a motley crew.

To say our apartment was a rattrap is an understatement. There were cockroaches all over the place. At night I could see them skittering around the kitchen. The exterminator sprayed our apartment every month, but it only helped for about a week and the roaches were back in full force.

I knew within the first day Lisa had some serious problems. I was a drug addict, but my abuse was nothing like hers. She was high all the time. I should have listened to my gut; my instinct told me this was going to be a bad deal.

Believe it or not, I didn't have sex with Lisa for several days. I was very gentlemanly with women unless they came on strong to me. The women in my family had instilled in me an ideal of how a guy should treat a girl.

In my mind I was thinking, *Man, I want to sleep with her,* but with Lisa and me, it wasn't a boyfriend/girlfriend relationship. She just needed help and a place to stay. Lisa made a comment that first night about being nervous that I would expect something in return for helping her out, but I assured her I wasn't going to bother her and she would be safe with me.

Then one day she came into the bathroom when I was taking a shower, pulled back the curtain, climbed in, and away we went. When we were finished, we toweled off and went to the bedroom. Dad heard us having sex from the other room and it drove him crazy and ticked him off. I guess he thought that since he was the patriarch, he should be the one having sex and his kid should be in the other room. Our roles had been reversed.

From that moment on, Lisa and I had a little thing going. Dad slept on the couch and we shared a blanket on the bedroom floor. She wasn't exactly the kind of girl you would bring home to Mama for Christmas dinner. I certainly wouldn't have dated a junkie stripper had I not been an addict, but the morals I had learned as a child had stayed on the farm. My relationship with Lisa is a prime illustration of a drug addict's lifestyle. Other than our drug use, we didn't have anything in common. Still, my relationship with Lisa was a turning point. When I was with her I stopped thinking about Christy.

It was just a casual thing for me, but one night after her shift, Lisa told me I could no longer go to the club because we were in a "relationship." I was mad. "What do you mean I can't go back to the club? It's my little hangout dive for drinking beer and doing my drugs!" Because of her I never went back to the club again.

A heroin addict doesn't make a good roommate. Although Lisa made hundreds of dollars a night at the Ecstasy Club, she was always broke. She was supposed to kick in on the rent and utility bills like anybody else, but the most she ever brought home was five dollars. She gave all her money to the drug dealers at work.

For a time we had a buddy of my dad's living with us too. Dick was running from the law and was a total loser. He didn't have a job and contributed absolutely nothing to the rent or other living expenses. We had two deadbeats on our hands.

Lisa was really wigged out. Sometimes Dad and his friends would be at our place doing drugs and watching TV, and Lisa would prance into the living room, turn on the stereo, and start stripping in front of everybody. The music she put on was always satanic, and she did weird stuff like roll her eyes up and growl like she was a demon. She definitely had a dark side.

Many of the guys were in their thirties and forties and were married and had kids of their own, so they thought they had hit the jackpot watching her take off her clothes. I'll never forget the reaction of the guitar player from Dad's band. Nathan was a cool character. He was tall and skinny with beautiful long, dark hair. He loved that hair; if the wind was blowing he would walk backward so the wind would blow it back, like he was a Victoria's Secret underwear model. Nathan really thought he was pretty!

A short time after Lisa's striptease, the guys got up to go home. I stood at the door saying good-bye and Nathan looked at me. "Man, I hate you. I would like to punch you right in the face," he said, pretending he was jealous. Of course, if he lived there he might have felt differently.

Lisa and I fought all the time. She was a smart aleck and had a terrible attitude, especially when she got strung out. If I brought up anything about money, she flipped out. She was really easygoing on the weekends because I got paid and had plenty of dope, but by Wednesday the weed was almost used up and the crank was gone and we started arguing. She was just plain hard to live with. I wanted to kick her out, but I just never had the guts. I liked having a warm body to cuddle up to at night.

Dad's ex-wife, Debbie, lived with their kids, Charlie and Sean, in Dallas. Sometimes I picked them up on a Saturday or Sunday and we hung out with Dad. On those days I didn't go to the bar; I just got doped up and played with the boys. Charlie and Sean really liked Lisa.

One Saturday when I got to their house to pick them up, Debbie laughed and said, "Well, how is your woman working out?"

"It's not working out too good. I think I'm going to have to ask her to leave."

The boys were running around playing and heard every word of our conversation, but I didn't think anything of it. When we got back to our apartment, I told them to hang out with Lisa while I went to the 7-Eleven to get some Dr. Pepper.

Lisa was not a happy camper when I walked in the door. Cussing and screaming, she was throwing clothes in a bag.

"What's the matter with you now?"

"One of the boys asked me why you told their mama you were going to make me move!"

Of course I start backpedaling, "Oh, you don't have to leave. That was just talk."

Lisa had already called somebody from the club to pick her up. "No, I'm leaving and never coming back." The boys had done my job for me. They broke up with Lisa when I was too chicken to do it myself.

More than twenty years later, I still think about Lisa. I hope she got out and got help. If she didn't, then she's dead. She would be close to forty now, and the sad fact is the odds are not in her favor. I suspect her drug abuse killed her.

A couple of weeks after Lisa left everything came to a head for me financially. I was making decent money, but I was spending it all on drugs. We lost the cable first, followed by the phone, and then we received an eviction notice.

I was sick of people mooching off me. I was ticked at Dick because he was so lazy he wouldn't even attempt to look for a job. Dad felt sorry for him and didn't want me to kick him out, but I wasn't as compassionate. I walked up to him and said, "Man, get your stuff and get the f— out of here!" I definitely could have handled it better, but all the frustration that had welled up inside me from Lisa came out in one wave of aggression.

Dick looked at my dad imploringly, and said, "Help me, David."

"I don't got nothing to do with it," he replied. "Everything is Dave's; everything is in his name." Dad knew there was no talking me into anything. Dick called some girl he had met at a bar, and she came and got him.

A few days later I got my final phone bill and it was more than four hundred dollars. While Dad and I had been working during the day, Dick had been making calls to a nine-hundred number. If I had known, I would have at least confiscated his drum set and gotten part of the money back. When you live the lifestyle of an addict, you don't have any real friends. Users value drugs more than honor or friendship. Everybody screws everybody.

Dad and I were forced to pack up our meager belongings and move out. The only place Dad had to go was Tulsa, so we made the five-hour trip to his parents' property. I helped him move in, stayed a couple of weeks, and headed back to my mom's place in Tennessee. I was like a bad penny, always turning up on her doorstep.

Back to Tennessee

I couldn't wait to get back home to my mom's place in Tennessee. It had been a miserable year and a half in Texas. I settled right back into my old routine. I had cravings for meth and told all my friends about how great it was, but since there wasn't any around, I had to substitute other drugs: cocaine, marijuana, alcohol, or whatever I could get my hands on. I snorted up far more cocaine than I used to because I sought the elusive rush I had with meth.

I found a job with a logging company and I grew marijuana everywhere; in Mom's backyard, at neighboring farms, places I knew growing up, places I'd go fishing. Most of it was planted on my uncles' property. They owned seventy-five acres together, but lived in California. I was the overseer of the land, so it didn't look suspicious that I was over there all the time.

I'd always had a violent temper, but when I was drunk I looked for a fight. One of the bars I used to frequent was Maggie Lee's. They were open until 4:00 AM, long after the other ones, so at midnight everyone converged on Maggie Lee's from all over the county. In the wee hours of the morning, it was packed shoulder to shoulder. If you crowd too many rats into a small space, they turn on each other.

One night two guys and I got into it, and we went outside to fight. I suggested we walk around to the side of the building because there was a police car sitting in the parking lot watching us. One of the guys made a move for me and the other one, a guy named Wade, jumped me, right in front of the cop. We hit the ground and Wade landed on me, but I squeezed him and held his hair. When he rose up to punch me, the cop ran over and shouted at us to break it up. I let go of the guy, but he swung at me again and the cop grabbed him, cuffed him, and took him to jail. Nothing happened to me, even though I had started it all, and that seriously pissed off those guys.

The very next weekend I went back to Maggie Lee's. I'd packed in a bottle of vodka. The people who owned the bar had known my dad and let me bring in gallons of booze to drink while I was there. They kept it behind the counter and gave me free orange juice. I didn't have to pay for drinks all night. Free booze is not a good idea for a bloodthirsty alcoholic.

While I was walking through the crowd I ran into Wade. He was stewed about being hauled off to jail the weekend before and was looking for some payback. He acted crazy: "I'm a bear and I'm going to slam you," he said growling furiously.

"It's different this weekend," I threatened. "This time it's not just me and you and your buddies. All these guys are with me." I pointed at a whole wall of big rough-looking hippies with long hair, bushy beards, and bad attitudes. All the redneck guys I ran around with loved to fight, and on this particular night, we were all pumped up on cocaine, especially me. There was so much coke running through my system that sweat was rolling off me, and I had huge circles of perspiration under my arms. It looked like I had just been working out, yet I had just been standing around. One girl thought I was having a heart attack.

The guy kept egging me on. I told him I didn't want any trouble, but he wouldn't stop, and I gave him a mean right hook to the chin. He fell sideways to the ground unconscious and his eyes rolled back in his head. I was so hyped up that I sat on his chest and pummeled him over and over again until he was covered in blood and his face was beaten to a pulp. He couldn't defend himself at all. Every time I hit him, blood splattered all over the people standing around us. It freaked out a lot of people, especially the young women who were just there to have a drink or two. It took three guys to pull me off of him. I would have killed him if they hadn't.

Joe Strauss, the owner of the bar, laughed and said, "Dave, you've got to go. See you next weekend." With that they kicked me out. I got my vodka and moved the party to my house.

I woke up the next morning in the front yard, wet with dew, covered with bug bites, and badly hung over. I had been so drunk that I had walked right through the screen door without opening it. Someone had brought my pillow out to me because I had belligerently refused to go inside.

I was the talk of the town. For weeks people I didn't even know came up to me and bought me drinks or gave me six-packs of beer for beating Wade up because he was such a bully. One girl said, "My boyfriend wanted me to bring you this beer for beating up Wade. Finally, somebody got ahold of him." I didn't even know the guy, so I hadn't heard he hurt girls. I was really no better than that guy, though; they just didn't know me. I was terribly violent in relationships too.

A few years later Wade got into a fight at a house in the town where he lived and didn't want to risk getting his face kicked in. When the guy he was fighting went outside, he walked out of the house with a 12-gauge shotgun and killed the guy.

Wade is in prison. He might have murdered someone anyway, but I can't help thinking my actions might have set things in motion. You never know how things you do in life set off a chain reaction. If I hadn't beaten that kid so severely that night, he might not have been so scared to fight the other guy and he wouldn't have shot him. I hope that man's death wasn't my fault. For years I dealt with feelings of guilt about Wade and so many other things. There are many ways to work through painful memories and emotional issues, but I've relied on prayer, the word of God, and the counsel of pastors and other knowledgeable Christians to overcome my feelings of guilt and shame. In John 8:36 (NKJV) Jesus says, "Therefore if the Son makes you free, you shall be free indeed." I will always feel the shame of letting the Lord down, but I know I've been forgiven.

Drugs are a terrible blight on society but many people condone the use of alcohol. Drinking in excess is just as bad. Alcohol is the number one killer of teens, primarily in alcohol-related motor vehicle accidents. The National Institutes of Health reports that in 2008, more than half of Americans age twelve and older had used alcohol at least once in the previous thirty days. Nearly a quarter of them had binged (five or more drinks within two hours) and an equal number had consumed at least five drinks on five or more occasions during the same period. I certainly met and exceeded that statistic.

I was a terrible drunk, mean and ornery, and I did stupid things. I don't know how many times I passed out in weird places. I woke up once in the ditch lying in my own puke with bugs and flies crawling all over me and my face and arms covered with welts. I'd been there all night. My life continued to spiral downward. I wasn't just allowing it to happen—I was causing the descent.

SEVEN

Both Sides Now

> *Family quarrels are bitter things.*
> *They don't go according to any rules. They're not like*
> *aches or wounds; they're more like splits in the skin that*
> *won't heal because there's not enough material.*
>
> — F. Scott Fitzgerald

MY MOTHER SHOT ME when I was twenty-four. Much of what went on during my twenties is a blur, but I remember that event like it happened yesterday. . . .

Looking for Love in All the Wrong Places

An addict uses every excuse to stay messed up, and mine was that I was either celebrating or mourning something. In those first few years after my divorce, people hated to party with me because every time I got drunk I was a real downer. But we still partied together because we'd all grown up together. By the end of the night we were all drunk. Some of us got sloppy, some of us fought, but we still stuck together. I was actually a pretty fun guy until I went overboard with the booze.

It took me years to get over my first wife. That didn't mean I didn't enjoy other women. I slept with lots of them, even married women. I feel really guilty about that now. Women acted like they loved to sleep with me, but in their view I wasn't husband material. I was the kind of guy to party and enjoy one-night stands with, not marry. Some guys might like that, but deep down it hurt, and I longed to find a woman who would love me unconditionally and settle down.

It wasn't unusual for me to be involved with four or five women at the same time. They didn't seem to mind sharing me. During those years after I lived in Texas, I dated Molly, a girl with whom I'd gone to high school. Molly and I were pretty hot and heavy for a while, but she suddenly disappeared, and I didn't see her for months. Then one day she showed up at my house, handed me abortion papers, and told me I was the father. I didn't know whether or not to believe her, but I had to admit that Parnell men reproduce like rabbits.

The fact that Molly had terminated a pregnancy, one that I supposedly caused, didn't stop me from having unprotected sex with her again. The night she gave me the abortion documents, we smoked pot and she spent the night. Three months later she came by with abortion papers again. We had sex again that night and then I never saw her again.

That was the third time I had supposedly fathered a child that had been aborted. It's something I have to live with, and when I die, I'll have to be accountable for this. In our society many people believe it's a woman's choice, but I've got to tell you, in my heart, I know that abortion is still killing a baby. Sometimes I'll be driving down the road and it hits me and I just start crying over the loss. My lifestyle and bad choices terminated three pregnancies (that I know of) and that is something I will always regret.

I also looked for love and acceptance through my associations with other drug users. Everybody I hung around with got high, and if there were drugs around, I took them, it didn't matter what kind. There was always a variety of mood-altering substances to choose from. I wasn't a discriminating drug addict; all I had to know is what category a drug fit into, whether it was an upper, a downer, or a hallucinogen, and I would take it. I just needed to have an idea what to expect when the drug hit my bloodstream. Drugs made me forget and feel good about myself.

Out in the country, we usually didn't have the hard stuff. I liked crank, but it hadn't hit Tennessee yet. LSD was another favorite. I hallucinated some from blotter acid, but I didn't really get off on seeing things. The reason I enjoyed it so much was that LSD is speed-based and it made me laugh uncontrollably. I didn't even know why I was laughing most of the time, but it felt good.

In order to get drugs like LSD and meth, I had to travel to where they were: the city. Every fall I took the pot I had harvested and dried and made a road trip to Tulsa or Dallas, wherever my dad was at the time, to sell it so I had money to party. Even though we partied pretty hard in the country, I loved the fast-paced city lifestyle. When my drug profits ran out, I went back to logging in Tennessee and started the whole growing process all over again.

Stuck in the Middle

A couple of days after I returned to Tennessee from an extended drug-selling trip to Oklahoma, I went fishing in a local pond with my brother-in-law, Lewis. We got so drunk that we threw our fishing poles down in the boat and spent our time jumping and splashing around in the water instead of fishing.

By the time we got back to my mom's house, it was dark. The two of us stumbled out of the car, totally plowed, laughing about our exploits that afternoon. Lewis and I walked to the front porch and my sisters and my mom suddenly jumped him, cussing and screaming like something you would see on *Jerry Springer*. I walked around them and plopped down on the old wooden church pew we kept on the concrete front porch and happily watched the goings-on.

When the fight turned physical, I sat back and laughed. Lewis wasn't a very big guy, and it was comical to see him fighting and waling on them while the girls beat the snot out of him. They punched him in the head and slapped him; my sister Shantell, who was on crutches at the time, repeatedly bashed him in the head with them. They probably figured it was safe to attack him if I was there to protect them. Drunken Lewis was no match for three enraged women, and they got the better of him. It was a chaotic scene.

My eyes snapped open wide when my sister Shantell said, "You son of a bitch. Don't think I forgot about you kicking Mechell in the stomach and putting her in the hospital!"

What am I hearing? I thought. I assumed they were upset because we were drunk and didn't bring any fish home for dinner, but it wasn't about that at all. Months earlier, when I was in Oklahoma, my mom had called and told me Mechell was in the hospital with a bad case of the flu. The truth was that her husband, Lewis, had beaten her up and kicked her in the stomach when she was pregnant. My mother didn't want to tell me what really happened because she was afraid I would snap and hurt him. She was right. I probably would have killed Lewis if I'd known he had beat up my sister and almost killed their unborn son. I certainly would have never gone fishing with him.

As my sisters took turns smacking Lewis, Mom went into the house, her emotions boiling over. I know she was remembering how my dad used to beat her up. Mom never remarried because of the terrible way she had been tormented by the man she once loved. People who have observed plenty of abused women said they'd never seen anybody banged around like my mother was.

Despite the fact that I was totally intoxicated, when I saw my mother walk into the house that night, I thought, *Oh God, she is going to get her pistol!* Immediately, I came to my senses and ran after her. When she came out of her bedroom there was a gun in her hand.

"Mom! What are you doing?"

"I'm going to kill that son of a bitch."

"No, you're not going out of the house. You're not going to shoot nobody. Put the gun back."

It wasn't about protecting my brother-in-law; he probably deserved to be shot. I didn't want my mom to get into trouble, and I knew if she killed Lewis she would go to prison.

"You'd better move, I'm telling you; you had better move. I'm going to go get him," she said through gritted teeth.

"I'm not moving," I replied calmly. "You are going to put the pistol back up."

Mom and I were in a standoff. By this time Shantell had arrived on the scene and stood next to our mother.

"Get out of the way or I'll shoot you."

With that, I reached out and grabbed Mom's left arm as she was planted in front of me. Boom! I saw the fire come toward me, but I didn't realize I'd been shot. The bullet went through my body so fast I didn't feel it. It wasn't until I touched my hand to my shoulder and saw blood smeared all over it that I understood.

My sister freaked out. She had problems with substance abuse too and overreacted to the situation. Shantell had been introduced to drugs by our father, just like I had been. Dad got high with all seven of his kids.

"Now that you've shot him, you have to kill him!" Shantell shrieked. "Shoot him again! Shoot him again! Shoot him again!"

I know she said that because she was afraid of me, like most people were. I had a ferocious temper and was unpredictable and mean because of my drug addiction. I had harmed people my whole life; some of them had been hurt really bad fighting with me. Once my victim was down, I showed no mercy—I didn't stop hitting until he stopped moving. I was afraid that if I had, I would be the one down on the ground.

I'd become a bully and bad guy because of the abuse I'd suffered at the hands of my Uncle Dale and others. He had wanted to make me tough, but it had backfired. When you beat a dog long enough, it becomes vicious.

When the bullet went through me, I didn't move; I just stood there stone-faced. Most people think it's like the movies when somebody gets shot and they fly backward, propelled by the force of the blast, but it wasn't like that for me. Shantell thought for sure that I was going to attack. After being shot, the furthest thing from my mind was assaulting anybody.

The instant I was shot, my alcohol buzz was gone and my heart started racing. Blood spurted everywhere; the bullet had hit an artery, so every time my heart pumped, blood shot out a foot from the wound. The hole in my shoulder was big—I actually stuck my thumb in it to try and stem the bleeding. I wasn't successful—blood gushed out like Old Faithful. I thought I was dying for sure.

I stumbled out of the room and into the kitchen, eventually collapsing on the floor right by where Granddad and I used to hang out and talk about the Bible. My mom and sisters went out and got Lewis so he could drive me to the hospital, but he was no longer in the yard. As soon as he heard the gun blast he ran, afraid they were coming after him.

My aunt Charlotte found him hiding like a weasel behind a bush in her yard. "Get your butt out, you chicken, and get that boy to the hospital."

On the way to the emergency room, I sat in a puddle of blood in the passenger's seat. I lost all feeling in my arm because the blood flow was cut off. *This must be what it feels like to die,* I remember thinking. *First my arm goes numb, and then my whole body will go numb, and then I'll be gone.* I was completely sobered up and scared to death. I wasn't ready to die. It never entered my mind that I might go to hell, because my thinking was all twisted. Somehow I thought I could do whatever I wanted and there would be no consequences.

Anytime there is a gunshot wound, the police are automatically dispatched to the hospital. I was so shocked by the whole incident that it never occurred to me to that I would have to come up with a story to protect my mother. In my ignorance, I thought an accidental shooting wouldn't be a big deal. When Lewis pulled into the parking lot and we saw the squad cars, I freaked out. I was well known to the local cops.

Nobody from my family was there when we arrived. My sisters

and Charlotte brought my mom a few minutes later, after they had given her Valium to calm her down. My mother had never taken a drug in her life, even though my dad was a drug addict. She was a child of the sixties but had never even smoked a joint. How she ended up with David Parnell Sr. I will never understand.

When the cops asked me what happened, I told them my mom was cleaning the gun and it had accidentally gone off and hit me across the room. Of course, I had a powder burn from being shot at close range, but there was nothing they could do, because the witnesses all corroborated my story.

The bullet had broken my shoulder and gone clean through. When the doctor came in my room, he asked me if I'd been drinking. I had to admit that I had, but I told him I had sobered up. The wound needed to be cleaned, but due to my alcohol intake, they wouldn't give me any painkillers beforehand.

The nurses held me down while the doctor took a long swab that had been soaked in alcohol and ran it through my throbbing wound time and time again to remove traces of gunpowder and other material. After that they poured disinfectant in it; the burning made it feel like my arm was being torn off. I screamed and writhed in agony, cussing at the doctor for not giving me anything to numb the pain.

The ruckus attracted the attention of one of the policemen who was waiting around. Jerry Jones was an old farmer who had become a cop, and I'd known him for years. "What's the matter, Dave? What's going on?"

"Man, this guy won't give me any medicine because he thinks I'm drunk. I'm hurting real bad."

Jerry looked at me, and said, "Well, I can tell by looking at you that you're not drunk; they can just smell the beer. Hang in there for a minute."

A couple minutes later a nurse came in with a syringe and put me out of my misery. Three days later they sent me home with my arm in a sling.

Bad to the Bone

I had no use of my arm for months. I couldn't move it up or down and I wasn't able to hold a chainsaw. There was no way I could work, and sitting around just made me mean and ornery. I was itching for a fight.

Two months after I'd been shot, I saw my sister Shantell at a gas station in town. She was so messed up I didn't recognize her. She had a broken rib and her nose was bloody. Both her eyes were solid black and nearly swollen shut. I had already been drinking, so seeing her like that made me crazy with rage.

She had been at a bar with a big blond-headed guy and he had taken her outside and beaten the crap out of her, kicking her and stomping on her when she was down. It was a cowardly thing to pound on a woman like that. Within an hour after I saw her injuries, I was in front of the guy's house calling him out.

Say what you want about my character, but I stick up for my own. My fighting arm was in a sling and of no use to me, so I fought the guy with my left. When we hit the ground he fell on top of me and my arm popped like a .22 rifle. My arm broke, starting at the point of the bullet entry down to my elbow. I had to go back to the hospital and have a cast put on. Altogether, it took me almost a year to get full use of my arm.

You can still see the scar from where the bullet entered my body. I don't think my mother intended to kill me, but she shot me all the same. I don't blame her for what happened because my actions set all of this in motion. If I hadn't been living the way I was, and treating her and everyone around me so badly, this might not have happened. Because of the pain and stress I caused my mom over the years she snapped when she was pushed too hard. I just happened to be the one who got caught in the cross-fire.

EIGHT

Birds of a Feather

The conscience of children is formed by the
influences that surround them;
their notions of good and evil are the result of
the moral atmosphere they breathe.

— Jean Paul Richter

EVERY COMMUNITY HAS A PLACE like the Andersons' where adults who strive to relive their glory days encourage young people to party at their house. It's like they never truly grow up. In Dukedom, Tennessee, that home belonged to Betsy and Conrad Anderson, a couple who loved to drink. Conrad liked cheap whiskey and his wife preferred Smirnoff vodka. I started going over there after I graduated high school; I always thought it strange that they invited teenagers over when they didn't have any of their own. Betsy had two grown sons from a previous marriage, and together they had a kid in grade school. That's where I first met Amy.

Meet Amy, My Future Wife

When I was over at Andersons' I started hearing about a new girl in town. Amy was just a kid, barely thirteen years old, when I met her. Coincidentally, she grew up in Arlington, Texas, just down the road from the roach motel–apartment where I had lived with my dad. Amy's parents actually lived in the same complex before they rented the house she grew up in. Her childhood paralleled mine in many ways.

Amy's mom was chronically depressed and medicated herself with alcohol. She was usually found lying on the couch passed out or reading. The kids went for days at a time without talking to their mother. Occasionally she'd be on a kick and would make cookies or something with the girls, but generally she was withdrawn and kept to herself. Amy's dad was a drug user with a hot temper. He occasionally spanked Amy and her sister, but he wasn't physically abusive like my dad was. Instead of hitting, he was loud and overbearing and threw things across the room when he got angry.

There was always potential for trouble because Amy's little sister Erin was disobedient and didn't mind causing a fight. Time and time again Amy listened from her bedroom as Erin got worn-out with the belt. Amy, however, kept a low profile around her father. She never talked back, got straight A's in school, and stayed out of the way to keep the household as peaceful as possible. Until she was about twelve, Amy did everything she could to

David and Amy shortly after he'd been released from prison (before he was back on meth).

Hours after David shot himself. (Surgeons temporarily closed up the wounds, but all the bones in his face were broken.)

David after being released from the hospital. (He no longer had a nose and an external fixator bar was in place to hold his face together.)

David after one reconstructive surgery. (Surgeons removed a flap of forehead skin and twisted it to form a nose.

David eating baby food. (Unable to instinctively find his mouth, David had to eat in front of a mirror.)

David after one of his thirty facial reconstruction surgeries.

David after yet another nasal reconstruction surgery.(The green tubes kept David's nasal cavities from collapsing.)

The Parnell family today (from left to right)
Front: Rebekah, Abi, and Gabriel. Back: Josiah,
David, Amy, Sarah, Rachel, and Little David.

avoid rocking the boat. But as her parents' addiction worsened, Amy became more calloused and no longer cared what happened to her. There wasn't one watershed incident that changed her; it was everything compounded. Between the normal teenage rebellion and the stress and anxiety she had been living with, Amy reached a breaking point. She didn't care if she lived or died, much less if she got in trouble for something. Nobody seemed to care about her . . . why should she care about herself?

Both their parents used meth, and their daughters sometimes went for days without seeing them. Though just a kid herself, Amy was responsible for getting herself and her little sister off to school. At the end of the day they were instructed to stay in the house with the doors locked until their parents got home. They weren't even allowed to answer the phone.

Their parents smoked pot with their friends in the living room when they were home. It was a real heavy drug environment. Amy and Erin had to go sit in their bedrooms; it was like being held prisoner. They couldn't have friends over because their folks were always getting high.

Amy, who was just an innocent kid, didn't know what meth was until one of her friends pulled some out of a kitchen cabinet and showed it to her. She'd never even heard of it before.

"This is my mom's ice."

"Well, let's do some!"

"No way, I don't want to touch it. My mom would kill me."

It wasn't until she was older and using meth herself that Amy recognized the signs of her parents' meth abuse: the drama and volatility, their long nights without sleep, the whole atmosphere.

Once, when the girls were ten and six, Amy's parents woke them up before daylight to go on a rescue mission of sorts. They had a completely crazy meth-addict friend named Linda who had two kids of her own. When they got to Linda's house, the kids ran out to the car. Linda walked out of the house backward holding a shotgun pointed toward the doorway. She was covered in blood. Fueled by meth, Linda's live-in boyfriend had freaked out and beaten her up. As soon as he started passing out, she grabbed the gun. Shielding the kids, she held him off until help arrived.

The whole situation excited Amy. She was scared, but the kind of exhilaration one feels upon riding a rollercoaster or going through a haunted house. It's scary, but there is a rush of excitement at the same time. Kids don't sense the danger in real-life situations like adults do. Her mom later told her that there was nothing fun or cool about having a gun held to your head, but it had looked fun to Amy, like watching a movie. In retrospect, this one incident had a profound long-term impact on Amy. It desensitized her and set the stage for finding scenes like this more acceptable later in her life.

In sixth grade, Amy started drinking, experimenting with drugs, and skipping school. It was common for her friends to buy caffeine pills and amphetamines known as "white crosses" and take a whole bunch of them at a time. Of course, Amy's parents' marijuana stash was always accessible.

My dad and I smoked weed together all the time, but Amy only got high with her dad once. He had found out she had been doing it with her friend's parents and said, "I guess I should have been the one to do this with you for the first time." Father and daughter walked around the neighborhood sharing a joint. It was obvious the two were stoned when they got home from their walk, and her mother was really upset about it. That was the one and only time she smoked marijuana with one of her parents. She was twelve.

Like me, Amy gravitated toward the kids who got into trouble. She'd had a couple of friends in elementary school who were considered "good" kids, but when your parents and all their friends are bikers and druggies, parents of the nice kids don't let them near you.

Amy was a frequent runaway. Most of the time she was away from home for just a day or two, but on several occasions she was gone for a couple of weeks. She and another twelve-year-old bounced around from place to place, finding shelter wherever they could. They slept in a friend's garage for a while and then in a tree house. Nobody knew they were there. They found a car that was unlocked and slept there one night and in a culvert another. It was cold.

Young and ignorant, they were targeted by a pedophile who offered to pay them quite a bit of money to stay at his place. He had a warm house, good food, and a hot shower, but they couldn't tell anybody they were going there. Even as screwed up and stupid as she was at the time, Amy knew it was a very bad idea. Sick and perverted people prey on the weak.

Eventually, the two girls were picked up by the police after they were found walking down the street during the middle of a school day. They were charged with truancy and brought to the station. A building full of cops is definitely not where drug addicts want to be, but Amy's parents were forced to go get her. Amy got very sick from eating too little and being cold too long. Her friend contracted pneumonia.

Her parents gave Amy a choice—she could go to reform school or go live with her grandparents. They probably wouldn't really have sent her to reform school; it was a threat they used to get her to leave. Being sent away like that hurt

Amy's feelings, especially since her sister, who was four years younger, stayed in Arlington with their parents. She should have worried about her sister being left in the care of their parents, but she didn't. Amy was going through so many emotional and mental issues of her own at the time that she couldn't think of anyone but herself. In reality, they were probably glad to see her go, so they didn't have to worry about her anymore. Amy told people her parents kicked her out. (Later in her life, Amy's mom and dad apologized for the way they parented her and tried to made amends. While it isn't a perfect bond, they have been successful at rebuilding their relationship.)

Out with the Old, In with the New

Amy was bitter about being shooed off to rural Tennessee. She loved staying with her grandparents in the summer and on school vacations, but living with them full-time was a different story altogether. The town they lived in was in the middle of nowhere with a population that seemed to Amy like it was less than two dozen. Amy was a big-city girl. In Texas, if she wanted to see her friends, she only had to walk down the street. The mall and other hangouts were all within walking distance. She certainly didn't want to leave her party buddies and live in some Podunk town where there was nothing to do.

Newly transplanted, Amy fell in with the bad crowd on her very first day of school. When she got home at the end of the day, she received a telephone call from a girl in her class.

"Hi, I'm Leanne."

"I think I met you today," Amy said, clueless.

"Do you want to come spend the night at my house?"

"Sure," Amy agreed, even though she had no idea who she was talking to. All she knew was that Leanne was in the same grade and liked to party. There is some kind of supernatural, gravitational pull between troubled kids, and Amy and Leanne became inseparable in no time.

Penny and Phil weren't used to having a kid around, and they let her run wild and do anything she wanted. They loved her, but they had no idea what they were doing. Granddad Phil was very passive and quiet, while Grandma Penny was loud and sociable. Penny was a prescription pill addict. There was always a wide variety of downers in her medicine cabinet including Valium, Xanax, Seroquel, and Elavil. Consequently, Penny slept a lot.

Grandma was like a big kid. She enjoyed playing video games with Amy and hanging around with her friends. It didn't bother her at all that her adolescent granddaughter had friends in their twenties and thirties. She bought cigarettes for them so they would sit around and play cards with her. Their home was something of a revolving door—if one of Amy's older adult friends needed a place to live and didn't have a job, Penny let them stay at their place rent free and fed them like they were one of the family. I think she just wanted somebody to talk to.

Amy was free to do whatever she wanted. Her grandparents didn't ask questions and didn't seem to care what was going on in her life. She used to stand and smoke cigarettes while she was waiting for the school bus to pick her up in the morning, thinking she was pretty cool. Shortly after she arrived in town, Amy and her buddies started hanging around at Betsy and Conrad's place with older drunks and druggies like me. That lack of supervision set the stage for Amy's subsequent drug abuse and promiscuity.

That same year, when she was only twelve, Amy was arrested for public intoxication. She had told her grandmother that she, Leanne, and another girl were going to watch basketball practice and would be home by midnight. What girl's high school basketball team has practice at that time of night? Again, there were no questions asked.

Both girls said they were sleeping over at Amy's house. Instead of going to the high school gym, the girls got a ride from a group of boys from Memphis. The group went to the liquor store and paid another customer to pick up some booze for them and bring it back out to the car. Then they parked in an open car-wash stall and took turns passing the bottle. The boys didn't drink much, but the girls got really drunk.

Laughing and having fun, the kids didn't notice a police car had pulled up until two uniformed officers jerked both of the car doors open at the same time. One of the cops slipped on the ice; the other one drew his gun. They ordered Amy and her friends out of the car, shut them in the squad cars, and took them to the police station. After waiting at the jail for what seemed like forever, Amy's grandparents picked her up.

About a week later it was time to go to court. The judge was very upset with Amy's grandparents. How could they allow three twelve-year-old girls to be out that far past curfew, drinking and running around with boys who were in high school? The court should have done more in the way of intervention at that point; the girls just had to do a few hours of community service. There should have been a referral to a social worker or counselor of some kind. There were several times Amy's situation got enough attention that someone could've intervened—a judge, law enforcement, teachers, health department workers, or doctors. People in the community knew her grandparents let her run wild, yet no one ever stepped in.

Despite the fact she had lied, gotten totally drunk, and been arrested, Amy didn't get in any trouble at home. Her grandparents were more upset about what the judge said to them than they were about her behavior. One of the girls, the one who was the basketball player, was grounded, but Leanne and Amy were out partying the next weekend.

She was picked up for drinking again at fifteen when a friend got pulled over. The police poured the alcohol out and took the kids to the sheriff's department to call their guardians, but no charges were filed. The authorities had a talk with her grandmother about how serious the situation was and let Amy go home. Once again, she wasn't in any trouble.

Grown-up Relationships

Within a few weeks of moving to Tennessee, Amy started dating a boy named Tim. He was almost six years older and a senior in high school. When his parents kicked him out of their house, Phil and Penny let Tim move in with them.

Tim was a psychopath and sexually, physically, and emotionally abusive. He didn't get Amy down and beat the crap out of her; it was the little things with him. He listened in on her phone calls, dictated who she could see, and even picked out her clothes. He threw lighter fluid on her, threatening to light a match. He'd grab her hair and slam her into the wall, choke her, twist her arm, or hit her in the leg where most of the time people couldn't see the bruises. The first time he left visible marks on Amy, Tim freaked out; he was worried her grandparents would be really mad.

"Look at this, we were just wrestling. I didn't mean to do this," he said apologetically.

Penny just smiled and said, "Well, Amy just bruises easily." That was it.

The couple frequently had sex right under the noses of her grandparents. They did it in the bathroom or in Amy's bedroom after her grandmother fell asleep. She definitely knew what was going on because Penny took her granddaughter to the doctor to get birth control pills. It was ridiculous how her grandparents just let it all go on. In any state, a sexual relationship between an eighteen-year-old and a seventh grader would be considered statutory rape.

Amy and Tim went out from the time she was twelve until she was fourteen. When they finally broke up for good, he stalked her. He called and called, filling up the answering machine tape with threatening messages. It got so frightening that Amy's family left the phone off the hook most of the time. But Tim would convince the operator to break into the line, claiming there was an emergency at the Goodyear plant where Amy's grandfather worked. So if Amy or her grandparents put the phone back on the hook to make a call, the operator would say they needed to clear the line. Then the "emergency" call would come in and it was always Tim. He must have waited for hours for someone to actually be on the phone. He also went to the house and knocked on the windows and doors. The police suggested Amy's grandparents file a restraining order, but they never did.

Then one night the stalking came to a head. An older friend of Tim's went to Amy's house and told her that Tim was threatening to kill himself if she didn't at least talk to him. Amy took the bait. When she got to his parked truck, Tim had a gun. She didn't want to go anywhere with him, but he promised to take the gun home and put it away if she rode with him so they could talk. He didn't act like she should be afraid.

Tim drove over to his house, and when he and Amy went into his dad's bedroom, he flipped and started ranting and raving. "You're getting back together with me," he warned, putting the gun to her head. "If you don't, I'll kill us both."

The friend came into the bedroom when he heard the yelling to try to talk to Tim. As soon as Tim let go of her, Amy bolted out the door, jumped over the porch railing, and ran down the driveway in the dark. Unfortunately, he heard her and took off after her, quickly catching up. He smashed her head into the truck a couple of times and choked her. Then he pulled the gun back out, "You're not leaving me," and tossed her back into the truck.

Tim later forced Amy to have sex with him. When they were finished, she was dismissed. "Okay, you can get out of the truck now," he said, and left her standing by the side of the road. She walked home alone in the dark. Despite the obvious danger of this particular situation, Amy was relatively unfazed by it because others like it had occurred throughout her relationship with Tim. It wasn't until years later that she realized it was wrong for a grown man to have a relationship with an adolescent girl like he had done.

A Perfect Couple

Amy was well on her way to being an alcoholic and a drug addict. By fourteen, she was stealing her grandmother's pills and taking anything else she could get her hands on. People didn't even have to tell her what they were; they would simply hand

Amy some pills and she'd take them—green, purple, red, white, or yellow—it didn't matter what color they were. She also drank every day. She kept bottles of vodka or Southern Comfort under her mattress.

For some reason, Amy was attracted to older bad boys; the more horrible, the better. She had a few nice boyfriends along the way, the kind that were mild-mannered and would do anything for her, but they just didn't have the right chemistry for her. I think it was because subconsciously she was looking for someone like her dad. Maybe she was just bent on self-destruction.

I certainly fit that profile. I had a terrible reputation and was trouble with a capital T. That's what drew Amy to me. She liked troubled boys, and I was the worst of the worst. I was dangerous and crazy; when I walked into a room, it was like a tornado hit. I was loud and obnoxious, the life of the party. The first time Amy saw me, I walked into a crowded room, grabbed a beer, popped the top and shotgunned it, drinking the whole thing at once. She had never seen that before.

Guys were afraid of me because I was so violent and aggressive. People used to say when I showed up that there was going to be a fight or somebody was going to jail. Yet for some reason, I was attractive to this little fourteen-year-old girl. Even though I was raising hell, I was always really nice to Amy, and she never felt threatened by me. She thought I was a diamond in the rough, her knight in shining armor and protector. If she was with me, nobody would ever mess with her again. She also figured if she was with me, it would raise her status and she would be more popular. In her eyes, I was perfect.

She couldn't have been more wrong. It breaks my heart to think about how she thought I was her savior. Later, when everything went to hell, I turned into a monster and Amy needed protection from me.

I'd seen Amy around at parties, but I didn't really know her. One night I was at home and she and her friend Leanne called me. They wanted me to come over because they thought there was somebody fooling around the house. I didn't want to go, but they bribed me with pills. As soon as I walked in the door, I knew there wasn't a prowler. It was all a ruse to get me over there. I hung out with them for a while, popping pills. A couple of weeks later when I was out drinking, I ran into Amy again. We ended up having sex that night. She was fourteen and I was twenty-three.

When I sobered up, I was terrified that I would be charged with statutory rape. I actually called Amy after it was over and apologized. We slept together a number of times after that and every time I sobered up, I freaked out and promised myself I wouldn't have anything to do with her. I couldn't believe I slept with a girl who wasn't yet in ninth grade. There I was—a grown man! I'd been married, had a kid, and I was involved with women who had grown children of their own. There I was having sex with a kid! Amy couldn't even go the places I went because she was too young. I only saw her at house parties.

Sometimes I didn't answer my phone and avoided her at parties because I was so plagued with guilt. I looked at her as a kid and thought, *What am I doing?* People kidded me about robbing the cradle. I know a lot of the guys were jealous that she was with me instead of them. Truthfully, the least of my worries was having relations with an underage girl; I was an alcoholic, addict, and drug dealer. Yet I was so attracted to her I couldn't help myself. When I was drunk, I just didn't think about the consequences. Everything revolved around David Parnell's self-gratification.

Just to be clear, it wasn't like I was a pervert in a chat room looking for teenage girls to prey upon. Amy hung around my group just like a lot of other kids. Nearly all of the people she socialized with were my age or older, and she slept with a lot of older guys. Amy's grandparents certainly didn't care if she was with me. If my fourteen-year-old was going out with a man who was in his twenties, I'd go ballistic. It just wasn't that way with them. Still, I should have never had a relationship with such a young girl. It was totally inappropriate. The lifestyle I was living had completely dulled my conscience. I would do almost anything if it made me feel good.

At the time, Amy was also going out with a twenty-two-year-old guy named Brian. She was crazy about him, but I didn't like the guy at all. But what could I say—it's not like Amy and I were in an exclusive relationship. I slept with a lot of women.

If you play with fire long enough, you are going to get burned. When I was with Amy I didn't use condoms and she got pregnant. I knew I was the father because I could pinpoint the night it happened, but Amy told everybody it was Brian. When Amy's belly started swelling up, I decided to take my marijuana harvest and head to Oklahoma. I was actually in love with her, but I remembered the things other women used to tell me about not making a good husband, and I wasn't eager to prove them right.

Brian was really mean to Amy. He hit her for no reason at all; she'd walk by and he would just frog her hard in the side of the leg. I couldn't stand to watch it, especially knowing she was pregnant with my child.

I ended up punching Brian at a party once before I went to Oklahoma. Amy wasn't there and I knew it was my opportunity to get back at him. We were by a lake in a really rough area of

Tennessee called Samburg where a lot of bikers hung out. Brian was being very aggressive with a girl, and even though she kept telling him to stop, nobody intervened. I finally got up and told him to leave the girl alone. He was ticked off that I had interfered, and we got to shoving and cussing.

The argument finally turned to Amy. I reminded Brian that she had been my woman before his and that I was in love with her. Besides that, the baby was mine. Of course, that didn't go over very well. He swore at me and grabbed me between the legs, squeezing my balls so hard they turned black. The pain was so excruciating I saw flashes before my eyes and nearly passed out. As soon as my head cleared, I punched him until he was bloody and black and blue. I beat the crap out of him, and it felt good.

All Amy ever wanted was to get married, but I wouldn't do it. Brian acted a thousand times more interested in her than I ever did and agreed to become her husband. Brian didn't care that he wasn't the father; he really just needed a place to live. His mother had kicked him out of her house for stealing, and so had his aunt, his cousin, and his sister. Playing house with Amy seemed like a pretty good deal. Amy's parents and grandparents didn't care if she got married at sixteen and willingly signed the papers. That way she was no longer their responsibility. Amy was excited about the baby, and she quit drinking and doing drugs during the duration of her pregnancy.

Brian's Song

It definitely wasn't wedded bliss. Brian had three strikes against him—he was a cheater, a nasty alcoholic, and a thief. Brian actually slept with Amy's little sister Erin when she was only twelve years old. Evidently, he wasn't too worried about statutory rape. Their granddad's stuff came up missing all the time, things like tools and other expensive equipment. He was also very cruel, sometimes slapping Amy for no reason. Brian never hit Amy in front of her grandparents, but they knew what was going on.

One night after baby Sarah was born, the couple and their infant daughter went out with Brian's brother, Jeff, his girlfriend, Carla, and their baby. Brian was so drunk that within a quarter of a mile he nearly drove off the road three times. Jeff had to grab the steering wheel and right the vehicle's course so they wouldn't land in the ditch. Amy finally told Brian to pull over, pretending she needed to adjust the car seat. She knew if she said something about him being drunk that he would refuse to pull over and terrify them even more. It didn't bother him that there were infants in the car.

Of all places, Brian pulled over in my mom's driveway. My sister Shantell was leaving for work when they pulled up, but turned around because she had forgotten something. Brian stepped out of the car to speak with Shantell, and Amy took the opportunity to get out, too.

"Get back in the car," Brian hissed

"No—you're drunk, and you're not driving."

"You are going to get back in that car." Amy jumped into the driver's seat, but he forcibly pulled her back out and slapped her. "No, I'm driving. Get in the backseat."

When Amy wouldn't comply, Brian grabbed his loaded deer rifle and pointed it at her. She grabbed the barrel and tried to push it away from her head. Brian hauled back and punched her in the face and knocked the gun out of her grip.

Shantell came up around the car behind Brian, grabbed the

rifle, and jerked it back over his head. "What are you doing hitting her like that?"

Eventually, she emptied the bullets out of the gun and handed it back to Brian on the condition that he let somebody else drive. Jeff cussed out Amy, saying, "You should have just let him drive." Can you believe that? Like the whole episode was Amy's fault.

After they dropped Jeff and Carla off at their place, Brian and Amy went to a party. As soon as he went into the house, Amy put the car in gear and drove back to her grandparents' house. When she walked in the door, she was carrying the rifle and Sarah, her face swollen to the point that she could barely talk. If one of my daughters came home today and told me her husband or boyfriend had hit her and tried to shoot her, I would immediately call the police and do whatever I could to protect her. But when Brian showed up, Amy's grandparents merely told him to leave. It amazes me how blind Phil and Penny were when it came to Brian. Another night he got a DUI and Phil bailed him out of jail, taking money out of his savings account to do it.

At twelve, Amy's sister Erin was in the same boat as Amy had been at that age, running wild and getting into trouble. Her parents no longer wanted to deal with her and shipped her off to Tennessee. Brian and Amy lived with her grandparents until Erin moved in, and then they moved into a small trailer with baby Sarah. The marriage only lasted a few more months.

NINE

A Menace to Society

We are all serving a life sentence in
the dungeon of the self.

— Cyril Connolly

I DIDN'T SEE MY DAUGHTER SARAH when she was born. Not because I didn't want to, but because I was in prison.

After I found out Amy was pregnant, I ditched. Frankly, drugs were more important than she was. Even though I hadn't had any in four years, I still thought about crank all the time. I craved it. I wanted it. I would do almost anything to get it.

Unfortunately for me, methamphetamine still hadn't hit Tennessee. One of the best places to buy it was in Oklahoma where my dad was living. To chase that high, I left everything behind—the woman I loved and our unborn baby—to go where the action was.

I headed north to Tulsa with twenty-five pounds of marijuana in my trunk; the harvest had been good. I told people I was going to go out and make some fast, easy money, but the truth is there is no such thing when it comes to selling drugs. I don't know any millionaire drug dealers, but I know a lot of people in prison from selling drugs and an equal number who are dead from using them. I definitely don't know anybody getting rich.

By this time my dad was on wife number five, a woman named Tracey, who was only two or three years older than me. There were four little boys in the house: Dad and Tracey had a son together, she had a boy from a previous marriage, and Dad had Charlie and Sean from his relationship with Debbie.

Tracey and my dad had been using crank for years and were full-fledged addicts. The household rocked with violent explosions of anger, and the couple had become sexually deviant. While Dad played music, Tracey picked up women and then they all went home together. It was a vile place for four little boys to be raised. You know if I call a situation deviant that it must have been bad. I was no altar boy.

Caught Red-handed

I had been in Tulsa just three weeks when the FBI, the DEA, and the state police kicked in our door. They'd received a tip that I had come across state lines with dope. I'm guessing one of my dad's friends got a nice little reward for turning me in.

By that time I only had thirteen pounds of marijuana left; the rest had been sold or smoked. The authorities kept asking me where the other stuff was because their informant told them we had crank and LSD on the premises. I know they were disappointed that all I had was weed. To a hillbilly like me, thirteen pounds is a lot of dope, but in a place like Tulsa, it is just a drop in the bucket. The police were used to busting people for hundreds of pounds.

To keep Dad and Tracey out of trouble, I signed the necessary papers and pled guilty. The judge wasn't available on that Friday to pass sentence, so I had to spend the weekend in the Tulsa County Jail. I'd been in jails before for minor offenses, but rural county jails were like resorts compared to this big-city version.

Before I went in, Dad told me to stand my ground right away or it would be a bad experience for me. He had learned that in his own stint in prison. Jail bullies like to mess around with weak victims; they don't want to go after a guy who will fight back when they try to rape him. Young guys are usually the targets; vulnerable eighteen-year-olds who are still a little wet behind the ears and don't know when to keep their mouths shut.

Incarceration is all about humiliation. When I was first brought to jail, I was stripped down, paraded around naked in chains, and then finally given a uniform. Yet there were no catcalls like you might see in the movies because everyone had been demeaned in the same way. Once or twice a week the guards made the inmates strip to change into clean uniforms. In our case, there were eighty-four nude men standing in line.

The inmates were also stripped down when they were being sent to different locations, like to and from court or to different areas of the facility. During those times each man took his turn bending over and coughing so the guards could search his body cavities.

A man loses his dignity in jail. There are no private moments; you eat, sleep, shower, and relieve yourself in front of others. Open showers were positioned in a row on one wall and toilets on the other in a cell that housed eighty prisoners. It took me days to be able to go to the bathroom in front of them. A roomful of guys could really stink up an enclosed space. Sitting on the toilet in front of fellow inmates was one thing, but female guards could also see.

County was a tough environment. Most of the time the jail was in twenty-four-hour lockdown, and inmates were never allowed outside for a breath of fresh air or exercise. The layout was like an army barracks, with bunk beds on each side. My first three days, there were only ten beds for forty-three inmates. There were bodies everywhere—we were so tightly packed a guy couldn't even stretch out his legs. Tulsa County Jail was later closed down by the Feds due to overcrowding.

When I was put in my cell there was a group of guys sitting in a circle doing a Bible study. I walked over and asked if I could join them. We read and prayed and discussed the Bible. I think that decision had a critical impact on the rest of my time at County.

During my stint in jail, the chaplain gave me a New Testament that was small enough to fit in my back pocket. I used to pack that Bible with me when I did dope deals, like it was some kind of lucky rabbit's foot. I figured if anything went down at the drop and I was killed, I would go to heaven, that the Bible would protect me. Other druggies made fun of me for carrying it.

I went into jail a drug addict and alcoholic. Contrary to Hollywood movies and urban legends, not everybody who goes through drug withdrawal flops around on the floor like a fish or curls up in a ball in the corner begging to die. There is a wide range of reactions. Some guys in prison had it so bad that they actually ate the scabs of other meth addicts because they thought the meth that has been secreted in the scabs would help them through their withdrawals.

I was one of the lucky ones and my symptoms were much milder. I had terrible headaches and body cramps when I first arrived because of the abuse I had put my body through, but I slept for at least fourteen hours a day that first week because I was so wiped out. I think that healing sleep saved me from other withdrawal symptoms.

Believe it or not, out of all the drugs I did, I craved tobacco the most. In Oklahoma, the jails were smoke-free and I wanted cigarettes more than anything. I'd been a smoker since I was a kid and it proved to be an especially tough habit to break.

After I sobered up and started exercising, I felt much better physically, but emotionally I was still an addict. I thought to myself, *I don't ever want to see that stuff again. I hate it, look where it got me.* But the next day I would be craving it all over again. It was an emotional roller coaster. I struggled with depression, understanding that I had ruined my life.

I was scared to death to be in jail, but I tried to stay positive and psych myself up every day, telling myself I could live without the drugs: *You can do this, you can do this. You can survive without the drugs. You can make it through.* And thank God, I did.

Later I was transferred to a different cell that had sixty-four beds for eighty-four men. I slept on the floor for three weeks; no bunk was available until it was almost time for me to leave. There were times, lying on that cold jail floor, that I bit my lip so hard to keep myself from crying that it bled and my whole body shook from holding back. I just rolled back so nobody could see me and sobbed quietly, the tears rolling down my face. I didn't want anybody to see me cry because it would make me look weak.

Like the army, jail has a certain pecking order. The inmate in charge of our cell was a freaky-looking green-eyed black guy. He called his pack of brothers the "Dog Pound" and they ran the place. You didn't want to mess with the Pound. The cell was segregated by choice, the blacks on one side and the whites on the other. I slept on the black side next to a Native American.

On my third night a big blond brute of a guy challenged me to a fight. I didn't want to do it, but in jail you don't have much choice; you do what you have to do to survive. I was just a skinny country boy with long hair and a beard, and by this time I was such a heavy drug user that I had lost a great deal of weight. Normally I tipped the scale at about 215 pounds, but I had dropped down to 165. I guess I looked like an easy mark.

Fighting isn't about brawn, it is about technique, and I knew how to take care of myself no matter what. Apparently that mouthy blond guy didn't have the moves, because I whupped him. I was scared, but I fought that guy with everything I had. On my first lick I broke his nose and blood spurted everywhere. He didn't stand a chance after that. I hit that towheaded kid like the one I thrashed in the bar many years earlier, the one who couldn't move when I was done with him.

My dad had told me that if I got into a fight, I'd better be prepared to finish it strong or I would wake up with my opponent in my face. That advice ran through my mind as I landed blow after blow. Nobody tried to pull me off, and his buddies never stepped in to help. By the time I was done with that kid, he wasn't moving much, and I was soaked in so much of his blood that I had to take a shower. I broke my hand pounding on that kid, and my knuckles have never been the same. The blacks said it was the best fight they had ever seen and started calling me "Rocky."

Twenty minutes after the fight, the guy's buddies packed him to the front of the room and called the guards to come get him. When the guards asked who had beaten him up, I confessed and was handcuffed. In unison, the ten blacks protested, chattering and hollering at the guards, taking up for me. They said the other guy had started it and I had just defended myself. Since the blacks were standing up for a white, the guards believed them. My hands were freed and I was left in the cell.

The guy I beat was sent to the infirmary and then moved to a cell on the other side of the unit. I saw him when we lined up for meals. His "friends" flipped the guy off and called him names when they saw him. They turned on him like snakes.

It was like a school yard—after my victory I was propelled from the bottom to the top of the white pecking order and started running things on our side of the invisible line. It wasn't my choice; I didn't want to be the enforcer at all. I just wanted to be left alone. But I guess being the boss is better than being picked on. One time there was a great big corn-fed guy who wore bib overalls who refused to take a shower. He reeked; I could smell him four bunks down, which is not a good thing in close quarters. I had to convince him to take a shower or they would force him to do it, and that would be bad for him.

That weekend in jail was rough. When Monday finally came and I was back in court, the judge sentenced me to two, two-year terms in state prison: one for attempt to distribute marijuana and the other for failing to obtain a drug tax stamp—in other words, neglecting to pay taxes on my dope profits. What a crazy law.

The Process of Repentance

I was sent back to Tulsa County Jail and spent the next twenty-four days waiting for the chains. That's what they call it when you go to prison, because they chain your hands and feet together. Now, you don't go from county jail directly to prison—first you spend time in a processing center where they determine where you will serve out the rest of your sentence. I was processed at Lexington Assessment and Reception Center. With a name like that, it sounds like you are going to a wedding party instead of jail.

The first person I met at Lexington was a young man who couldn't have been more than nineteen. He cried as he told me his story. He and some friends had broken into a house and robbed a drug dealer, not knowing his girlfriend was home. They ended up beating her to death and throwing her body off a bridge in Tulsa. She missed the water and landed on a sandbar, but she lived long enough to identify her killers to the police.

The young man was sentenced to life plus ninety-nine years. I remember looking at him when he told me that and everything went into slow motion. This guy was never getting out of prison. He was never going to have a woman, never going to drink a beer, never going to walk the street again. The thought blew me away completely. I'd been pretty sad up to that moment, feeling sorry for myself, but his reality actually lifted my spirits. I knew I could do my few years standing on my head. Somebody always had it worse.

After I had my new uniform, I was brought to a barber shop where my head was shaved and my face buzzed. The shaver didn't do a very thorough job, so I was given a cheap disposable razor to clean up the remnants of my beard. Fifty guys had probably used that blade before I did; it felt like I was pulling each whisker out individually. Then I was fumigated for lice and had my picture taken.

The processing center was a whole different environment from the county jail; still tough, just different. I was in solitary confinement for thirteen days; I showered once a week and my meals were brought to me. They did all kinds of medical tests and then checked my IQ and aptitude. I felt like I was at a stockyard where cattle are checked to see if they are sick before being butchered.

I sat in my cell and thought about the path I'd taken to get there. For hours I stared out the window. It's funny how watching a bird can bring freedom to mind. There I was, a grown man, and I was locked in a room like I had been when I was a little child. It's weird to think we lock people in cages like vicious dogs. It's sad that people can't behave and remain part of society, but I know I needed to be locked up for my own good and for everybody else's. I understood that my own stupid choices had landed me there, and I hoped that by being incarcerated for a while I would be able to get off the meth and stay off it when I was back on the outside.

Shortly after I went to jail I found out my thirty-two-year-old cousin Frankie had been killed in a logging accident. Although he had bullied me when I was a little boy, the two of us had become party buddies and logged together before I went to Oklahoma that last time.

Frankie had married a girl who was a drug addict and who had slept with nearly every man in town. But Frankie loved her. Needing the extra money, he took a more dangerous job cutting down trees, which paid better. On December 2, a tree fell on Frankie and killed him. Right away his mom and his sisters suspected foul play.

Our boss was a drunk and a womanizer. Recently divorced, he had constantly cheated on his wife. Frankie had agreed to testify against him in court so his ex-wife could get full custody of their son. I warned Frankie against it: "Man, you don't want to be doing that—you work for the guy. Just quit!"

Frankie refused. "They ain't running me off!" Frankie was always stubborn and domineering.

It's easy to kill somebody in the woods and make it look like an accident. All you have to do is hit a guy in the back of the head and then throw a tree on top of him. Nobody would know the difference.

Ultimately, my aunt Charlotte and my cousins blamed me for his death—if I hadn't run off to Oklahoma to sell my dope and subsequently been caught, I would have been working with Frankie and could have maybe done something to prevent his death. Better yet, maybe it would have been me who was dead instead of him. That's how Charlotte felt. Frankie was dead, I went to prison, and it was all my fault.

That was also the last time I talked to Grandma Williams. She called crying because Frankie was dead and I was going to prison. I'd only seen her cry one time before and I feel terribly guilty that I put her through that. The hurt in her voice is something I will never forget. Frankie died because of drugs, and I was in prison because of drugs. She was terribly disappointed in me.

Shortly after I was locked up Grandma Oma had a stroke. I thought for a long time that it was my fault, but I found out later that she had taken the wrong medication and it had shocked her system. Deep down, I still think I had a part in what happened to her. Grandma lived for several more years, but was never able to speak again. She lived long enough to see me transformed and healthy, speaking to kids about the dangers of drugs. I could see by the look on her face and her beaming smile that she was proud of me and knew I had made it.

A convicted felon's stint in the processing center was intentionally unpredictable. It could be a month or it could be three or four days; you just never knew when they would come for you. The element of surprise was designed to minimize the likelihood of escaping—if an inmate's friends knew when he was going to be transported, there was potential for a hijacking. I remember lying on my cot listening to the cold metal doors being locked and unlocked and wondering when it was going to be my turn to be processed out.

My time came on my thirteenth night at Lexington. Several guards came for me at about 2:00 AM when everybody was asleep. "Parnell. Get up. Get ready." I climbed out of bed robotically, put on my jumpsuit, and stood by the door, putting my hands through the bars to be cuffed.

When I arrived at the loading dock my hands were shackled to a belt that encircled my waist and chains were put on my feet. When you are chained like that, you can't even scratch your nose—it made me feel terribly claustrophobic. There were a number of other inmates waiting to be transported to one prison or another. We all took baby steps in single file toward the open bus door. It reminded me of the movie *Cool Hand Luke* when Paul Newman was on a chain gang.

I was petrified. I had no idea where I was going or what to expect when I got there. I'd gotten used to the facilities I'd been in, but prison was like diving back into the abyss. My mind raced as I sat on that vinyl bus seat. How in the world had I gotten to the point in my life where I was going to prison? How had I followed so directly in my father's footsteps? I came to the realization that my own bad choices had put me there. I believe God gives us the freedom to choose right from wrong and I chose the wrong way. That was my downfall.

Doing Time

When I was in a high school, the administration brought in a group of convicts from a local prison for an assembly. As the students watched from the bleachers, three guys in orange jumpsuits inched their way to the podium in shackles. They talked about how selling dope had ruined their lives. Because of what they'd done, they had lost their families and their freedom. I'd already been selling drugs for years.

The principal made me go listen to the drug program, and I was mad, so I got high before going. Sitting next to Christy I was a real jerk, talking loudly and heckling the speakers. One of the inmates knew I was stoned and watched me. He said something like, "You young guys with the cocky attitudes had better be careful. This could be you someday." He was obviously talking to me.

While the guy was speaking I looked up at Christy and said, "What the f— do I have to come in here and listen to this for? I'll never end up like these losers!"

Almost exactly ten years later I was sitting in a big old rolling cage as it lumbered down the road in the dark toward the penitentiary. What that inmate had said to me during that school assembly suddenly hit me like a ton of bricks. I wish I had listened to him. My heart weighs heavy thinking there are kids out there who also believe it will never happen to them.

Everybody in Oklahoma knew of Big Mac, a state penitentiary located in McAlester, Oklahoma. A big riot had taken place there on July 27, 1973, the most costly in the history of the nation. Big Mac was a foreboding structure with its twenty-foot block wall and old-fashioned guard towers. In front of the maximum-security facility, there was an old electric chair on display. When I saw it I thought, *Oh God, this is the one I've heard about! I was just selling pot; I didn't have a gun or anything when they raided the house.* McAlester prison was my worst possible scenario.

The guard on the bus called out a bunch of names, and the doomed inmates shuffled off to their new home. Some of them were in the "shock program," a military-style boot camp for non-violent, first-time offenders. When the driver shut the doors and gassed the bus, I let out a big sigh of relief. *Where in the world was I going?*

At the bottom of the hill sat an old hospital that had been converted to a minimum security prison named Jackie Brannon Correctional Center (JBCC) that didn't even have a fence around it. That's where I got off. Maybe prison wouldn't be so bad after all.

Orientation took place the next day for the hundred or so new inmates. Our jumpsuits were traded for prison uniforms—blue jeans and blue button-down work shirts with "CORRECTIONS" stamped prominently on them.

The clothes were sewn by inmates in the in-house factory who weren't exactly gifted tailors. I was issued a few pair of blue jeans, mismatched garments that were so poorly made they wouldn't even be considered "irregulars" in the garment industry. Most of the time one leg was tight and the other loose, and one was always shorter than the other.

My fellow inmates laughed at me when I complained that all of my pants had a hole in one pocket. They informed me that that was where an inmate put his shank, or homemade knife. I was pretty green when it came to prison life.

We were also issued a pair of uncomfortable black work boots. The shoes didn't come as a pair, we just had to reach into a big box and grab a left and right shoe in our size. One of my boots was far more broken in than the other, which made for awkward walking.

JBCC had three stories. The bottom level housed the infirmary where the AIDS patients were kept, along with anyone else who was sick. I stayed on the second story in a room that was fondly nicknamed the "Drunk Tank." The Tank was much better than county jail. We actually had our own bathroom with a shower. It was the first time I had been able to go to the bathroom and shut the door in months.

I was a lot older than many of my cellmates; they were in their upper teens and I was twenty-seven. Some of them probably looked upon me as an older brother. We were a racially diverse group; one of my buddies, a fat black kid named Gump, slept above me. We talked for hours at night after the lights went out. He cried over a girl he had gotten hooked on crack cocaine. She had been a nice, churchgoing girl and had turned into the biggest whore in town because of drugs. Gump loved that girl.

Prison food was pretty good. There was a salad bar every night, but you needed to be one of the first guys in line to get things like peppers and tomatoes. I usually just had plain lettuce.

There was a medium-security facility next door that was situated behind a barbed-wire fence that was actually a working farm. The inmates raised cattle and we got all our milk and beef from there—we actually had steak once a week. That's far better than I ate at home.

As soon as you went upstairs you could smell pot. Everybody knows there are drugs in prison. Inmates could get any kind of drug they wanted in prison—pills, meth, cocaine, whatever. Guys were shooting up all over the place to pass the time. It wasn't hard to smuggle drugs into prison either. When inmates are allowed to have physical contact with visitors, something is bound to sneak through the cracks. Beyond the obvious hand-to-hand exchanges, visitors use a variety of means to get their loved ones high. Heroin was sometimes inserted between the layers of a paper greeting card. Women who came to see their partners would put balloons filled with drugs in their mouths and transfer them during a passionate kiss. The inmate would then stick the balloon into his rectum until he reached the safety of his cell. After most visits, the guards patted down the inmates, but they normally didn't check body cavities.

Of course, there were always a few corrupt guards who looked the other way and profited from the drug trafficking, but in most cases, the guards did their best to eradicate drugs in the prison. Unfortunately, they just couldn't catch it all because they were outnumbered ten to one, or even worse. The guard station was located on the bottom floor and they only checked us every two hours. It didn't take very long to take a few puffs of a joint without the guards knowing. The inmates knew how to work the system.

I didn't do any meth while I was incarcerated. I thought I would go crazy locked up when I was on speed. My thing was marijuana. My dad never visited me in the county jail, but he came to see me once at JBCC. He slipped me a little bag of marijuana while we sat at a picnic table in the visitor's area.

I smoked in the bathroom because there was a window. I wondered why there weren't bars on the windows; if someone wanted to commit suicide they could easily jump out. One time I sat out on the roof ledge and smoked a joint with a couple of cellmates. It was pretty easy to find places to get high, but I only did it four or five times when I was locked up. I had lost everything because of drugs, yet I still wanted to get high; that shows you how severe my addiction was. I don't want to give the impression that prison was like a frat party. I got high on occasion, but I was still locked up. I was in fear for my life every day. I missed my freedom.

Prison isn't about rehabilitation, it is about punishment. Criminals are put in prison because we need a place to house them and remove them from society. Putting an addict in jail with other addicts and criminals doesn't improve their character, particularly if they don't receive drug treatment or education that will help them once they are back on the outside. I wasn't rehabilitated at all.

On Wednesday nights a van picked me up so I could go to a Pentecostal church. My motivation wasn't to worship God; it was just to get out of prison and be around normal people for a while. I'll never forget my first night at the church. Everybody was friendly and wanted to shake my hand, but I just wanted to blend in and be anonymous—like I could do that wearing a blue work shirt with "CORRECTIONS" stamped on it in big black letters.

One man had such a firm handshake he about broke my hand. As soon as I looked at him, I knew he was some kind of law enforcement. He had the buzz cut and that redneck look about him: "I'm a guard at the prison. We're watching you." It's hard to feel the Holy Ghost when you are shaking in your shoes and looking over your shoulder. I went to that church every week until I got caught smoking dope and lost my privileges. After that I never left the prison building again except to go to work.

Early every morning a big orange county truck picked me for my job, which was to fill potholes. The other prisoners said there was no way they would let the system work them like that, but for me, it was a little taste of freedom, and I loved being outdoors. The driver was a little guy named Broom. He was quite a character. The workers nicknamed him "Clean Sweep" because he made prisoners fill potholes the size of quarters. Broom had been shuttling prisoners for years.

For my midday meal, the cafeteria staff packed a sack lunch with a peanut butter sandwich smeared with some kind of syrup and an apple. They never sent a drink. I always thought the prison staff did that on purpose; they probably smirked knowing my tongue would stick to the roof of my mouth while I was working in the hot sun. At least there was some water on the truck. Filling potholes is hard work, and that measly little lunch didn't do much to satisfy a grown man, but complaining wouldn't have done any good.

Broom often stopped at a convenience store on our way back to the prison and let me buy a little cup of vanilla ice cream. I made about fifty cents a week doing that backbreaking work, and between that and the few dollars my mom sent me, I had just enough to treat myself. You don't realize how important little things like ice cream are until you lose them. That frozen treat was like heaven.

Prison wasn't wrought with widespread violence like I had expected. I only saw one fight the whole time I was there. It had been a common occurrence at the county jail. Being a minimum security facility, the majority of the inmates were nonviolent offenders there on drug charges. It was also the last stop in the McAlester chain. Guys who got long sentences for crimes like rape and murder started out at Big Mac, and with good behavior they worked their way down to medium security and then to our place until they were released.

Everyone wanted to be on his best behavior so he wouldn't be sent back up the hill. We all just wanted to do our time and get out. Sometimes I heard men screaming at night and knew something was going on, but I never asked any questions. Out of the nearly one thousand inmates, there was only one guy I would have called a friend. Other than that I kept to myself.

The prison was so crowded that the corrections department offered to release me on house arrest after I'd served only four months. Of course, I took the deal. As I walked out the door of the prison for the last time, I had mixed emotions. The sense of freedom I felt defies explanation. I was glad they were letting me out, but I was also upset I wasn't able to go home to Tennessee. I hated the idea of going back to my dad's place. I had to stay in the state until I was up for parole.

Dad and his wife, Tracey, picked me up. By the time we pulled out of the parking lot, I was already getting high. I hadn't had any meth for four months and fell right back in the groove. I was totally cranked up when we got to their place in Tulsa. On one hand it felt great to be out and high again, but deep down I was disappointed with myself. There I was right back in the same old rut . . . nothing had changed.

Wicked, Wicked Ways

I was on house arrest for about seven months in a dope house —not a good place for rehabilitation, that's for sure. I would have been much better off staying in prison. Still, house arrest was a piece of cake compared to being in prison. This was back in the early '90s and I didn't wear an ankle bracelet like they do now. Upon my release, technicians came to my dad's house and set up a computerized monitoring system. Several times a day the computer called and said the name of a state. I had to repeat it, and it was recorded. They claimed they would be able to tell if I had been drinking or taking drugs, but I doubted that was possible. How could they tell if I had been smoking pot by the way my voice sounded on a recording? I fooled that computer the entire time I was on house arrest. I was also warned that I would be subject to random urine tests, but I never had one. If I'd had to pee in a cup, I would have been sunk. All I did was party.

I was allowed to be out and about until 8:00 PM, but I still didn't have my freedom, and I wanted that more than anything. I had the freedom to go out, take a shower whenever I wanted to, and use the bathroom in private when I wanted to, but that wasn't what I really wanted. From the moment I walked out of prison, I longed to go back to Tennessee and I begged my parole officer to let me leave. I wanted out of Oklahoma. I didn't want to live with my dad because it was such a sick environment. Many times I wished I hadn't taken early release because I had to go back to his place. If I had just stayed in prison I could have gone home to Tennessee and things might have turned out differently.

My dad dropped a bombshell shortly after I moved back in with them. He told me he had become impotent as a result of back surgery and his meth use and he could no longer please his wife.

"If you really love me, you'll take care of her. If you don't sleep with her, she is going to go somewhere else and find a boyfriend. You would be saving my marriage."

Several of my friends had told me that Tracey was attracted to me, but I certainly hadn't done anything about it. She was pretty enough, but I didn't like her at all. In fact, I thought she was kind of a bitch.

"No way, man; that is just weird. You're freaking me out—I can't do that!" But I hadn't been with a woman in a long time, and the more he tried to convince me to have sex with his wife, the more I bought in to the whole idea.

"Just think about it," he said. "I'm taking the boys to a babysitter and then going out for a while. When we get back, if you've had a shower then I'll know you'll do it. If you haven't, then I won't say nothin' else about it."

As I considered his proposal, I came to the conclusion that I really would be doing him a favor if I slept with his wife. Plus, at the same time I would be gratifying myself. Deep in my spirit I knew not to do it, that sleeping with my stepmother wasn't right. I knew it was way over the line, but I had never been very good with boundaries. I understand now that they are very important in our lives. Boundaries keep us in line, keep our society functioning, and keep us from totally anarchy. I had to cross a lot of lines to learn that, but boundaries keep us healthy and safe.

When Dad got home I was doped up and had taken a shower. In other words, I would do it. He was pleased. Later that night Tracey, Dad, and I were sitting around doing more dope. After about an hour or so, Tracey looked at me and said, "Are you ready?'

The two of us walked into their bedroom and my stomach

started churning. What in the world was I doing? As I started to shut the door, Dad walked in.

"What in the f— are you doing here?"

"Well, I'm coming in, too."

"What do you mean? I thought you wanted me to shag this woman."

"You didn't think I was just going to sit out there, did you? That's not how it is going to work. I want to see it."

I was horrified. I knew my dad was kinky, particularly since he'd been turned on to meth, but I never dreamed he would want to watch another man make love to his wife—especially his own son.

Tracey and I got on the bed, and Dad settled into a chair. We put pornography on the TV and started in. Meth affects women in a strange, sexual way, and she was wild. When she climaxed, my dad flipped and stormed out of the room. Tracey ran after him, and I heard him hollering, "I can't believe you let him on you!" I went to my room and let them argue.

Later, when he had calmed down, Dad came in and apologized. He asked me to screw her again, but I said, "Man, that crap is over. Don't ever bring it up again." I'd had sex with Dad's former wife Terry after they divorced, but sleeping with his current one was too creepy, even by my warped standards.

A month or two later, Dad and Tracey went to the bar and I stayed home and babysat the boys. When they showed up in the wee hours of the morning, Dad woke me up. "Get up, get up. Let's get high. We brought a woman home with us!"

Dad acted like he had brought that strange woman home for me, but I knew better. He wanted us all to have sex together. I staggered out of bed and got high with them for a while, and we had some laughs, and then Dad started rubbing around on the woman to try and get something started.

I pulled a fast one on them that night and rearranged the party in a way they weren't expecting. The woman had been flirting with me all night, so I invited her to my room and we shut the door. My dad and stepmother were left staring at each other. Their well-orchestrated plan had failed. They never bothered me about that kind of thing after that.

I only lived with Dad and Tracey for a couple more months. As soon as I was off house arrest I moved in with my cousin Lavonne and her husband until I badgered my parole office often enough for him to let me return to Tennessee and finish my parole there.

Sleeping with my dad's wife was one of the worst things I ever did—I wasn't kin to that woman, but it was still like incest. My choice that day profoundly affected my life and my psyche. I didn't realize until I was older just how much it traumatized me. I was a terrible man, a menace to society.

I was mad at my dad for the rest of his life for the way I was brought up and the things he exposed me to from a young age. Twenty years later, I'll randomly start crying because I feel like I was cursed from the day I was born. I pray about those feelings often and take comfort in Scripture. My dad made a lot of mistakes in his life, but I've learned that God loved him, too.

TEN

The Road to Hell

The safest road to hell is the gradual one—
the gentle slope, soft underfoot, without sudden turnings,
without milestones, without signposts.

— C. S. Lewis

FROM THE FIRST TIME we were together, I was in love with Amy.
I didn't recognize it at first because she was just a child, but deep
down in my heart I knew I would spend the rest of my life with
her. I'd made a mess of every relationship I'd ever been in, but
something in my spirit drew me to her.

A Match Made in Heaven

After Amy and Brian split up, she took the baby and moved
forty miles away to Murray, Kentucky. She got her own apartment

and a decent job at the Fisher-Price factory making toys, and things were going well. But when Amy heard I was back in town, she immediately drove back to Dukedom to look for me. She found me on the first night when we both happened to pull into a parking lot at the same time. I could tell she was excited to see me, and it was obvious I was happy, too. We found out we had both been looking for each other. We had a brief conversation and then before going our separate ways, we exchanged phone numbers and made a date to get together a couple days later.

Over dinner we talked about my time in prison and I told her that I had been thinking about her the whole time I was in Oklahoma. She had been dreaming about me too. That night, we told each other that we loved each other. It felt so right.

Within two weeks, Amy quit her job and she and Sarah moved in with me. At least she was of legal age by this point. Amy was eighteen and I was twenty-eight. Living with her was a big change for me; at the time I was sleeping with four different women. Suddenly I was a family man.

Stepping into a ready-made family wasn't easy, especially with my alcohol and drug addictions. I didn't know the first thing about being a daddy. Sarah stayed with her grandparents quite a bit the first month or two because having me around was such a difficult adjustment for her. She had just turned two and wouldn't acknowledge that I was her daddy. It broke my heart; I wanted her to automatically love me like I loved her, but I was a stranger. A father/daughter bond was a long time coming. It wasn't until her little brother was born that my daughter started calling me "Daddy."

Not long after I got home from Oklahoma, I received a notice informing me that a registered letter was waiting for me at the post office. While I had been incarcerated, my ex-wife's new husband had adopted my daughter Sheena. They said they had tried to contact me for a year, but didn't know where I was. I don't believe that for a second.

Before I left for Oklahoma, Christy had asked me to relinquish my parental rights, saying Sheena wanted to have the same last name as her stepfather. I steadfastly refused; at six years of age, Sheena wasn't mature enough to make that kind of a decision. If she still wanted to change her name when she was twelve, I would sign the adoption papers without further argument.

Christy knew how I felt, so when I was in prison she put the wheels into motion behind my back and finalized the adoption. I found out years later that Sheena hadn't wanted to change her name at all; it was all her mother's doing. When our little girl asked what happened to her daddy, Christy told her I had just left them. That was one of my greatest fears; I never wanted a child of mine to feel abandoned like I had when I was a little boy. It was painful wondering why my dad didn't love me. It would have been far better if Sheena had been told the truth— that I was a terrible husband, messed up on drugs, and in prison —than to make her feel like I didn't care. Finding out about the adoption put me into a tailspin. It was just another excuse to drink heavily—like I needed one.

Second Chance

Amy and I had been living together for about six months when we discovered she was pregnant. On July 3, 1995, three months before she gave birth to our son, David, we went to the courthouse in Murray, Kentucky, and got married. Amy's grandparents, our daughter Sarah, and my stepbrother Jessie were our only guests. It wasn't a fancy wedding: I wore jeans and a T-shirt and Amy wore maternity shorts, but we were incredibly happy. Amy told me we could have gotten married on the street for all she cared. The two of us became a couple in every way, including our drug abuse. Soon, we would face the dragon together.

I had been an everyday pot smoker for more than ten years. Amy never liked marijuana much; it made her paranoid and nervous, and she was afraid to be around other people when she was high. Still, I relentlessly hounded her to smoke with me so I wouldn't have to do it alone. She finally agreed, but on two conditions: I had to lock the doors, and if anybody knocked, we had to pretend we weren't home.

Amy became a brand-new person on weed once she knew we could do it in private. It mellowed me out, but it made her giggly and silly, and we laughed for hours; I laughed at her and she laughed at everything.

I was usually in a foul mood when I woke up, but Amy knew if I smoked a joint I would be my regular jovial self, so she did it with me. The two of us were high on marijuana from morning until night nearly every day. We certainly weren't very nurturing parents, but we provided basic care. It wasn't fair to our children and I deeply regret it.

One thing Amy wouldn't tolerate was drinking. She had been around alcoholics her entire life and had been adversely affected by their behavior. I'd been an alcoholic since I was in high school, and had become meaner and more volatile with every passing year. When I drank alcohol, I was out of control and crazy. Oftentimes I blacked out and didn't remember anything, even if I had run my car off the road.

I remember one night in particular when I walked in the door of our house drunk and ornery. One minute I told Amy I was going to kick her butt, and the next I was laughing hysterically. She was both angry and scared. As soon as I passed out, Amy grabbed our daughter and drove to my sister Mechell's place.

When I woke up later and found a note saying where she'd gone, I snapped, smashing dishes and pulling doors off their hinges. It looked like a tornado had gone through our house when I was finished. Then I rushed over to my sister's and raised some more Cain, screaming and swearing at both women. Amy finally agreed to come home with me to spare Mechell my wrath.

Amy panicked when she got a look at the havoc I had wreaked at home, but I never threatened or laid a hand on her. In the morning, I begged her to forgive me and stay, and Amy gave me a warning: if I didn't stop drinking, she would leave me for good. I promised never to drink again, and I actually didn't for several years.

In 1995, methamphetamine hit Tennessee and Kentucky with a vengeance. Our region of the country has always been famous for growing marijuana. The climate is just right: green and tropical. I used to cure the weed I'd grown by hanging it in the upstairs rooms of our house. At times I would have those three rooms so full we could hardly walk through the upstairs. The freezer was usually full too.

Suprisingly, it was actually easier to get crank than pot. Entrepreneurial-minded druggies started cooking it all over the place. Meth is especially popular with truck drivers because it gives them energy and endurance on long hauls. That's how I got sucked back into using it—I got my commercial driver's license and started driving a semi for a logging company. Getting zipped up on crank helped me bring the goods in on long hauls.

I liked to eat my meth. I rolled a chunk of it in toilet paper or paper towels and swallowed it like a pill. In my view, smoking it was a waste—too much of the drug was lost in the vapor. Guys who smoked it seemed like they always wanted more in only fifteen or twenty minutes. Eating it was safer and produced a longer-lasting high that was more intense. The one drawback was that when I swallowed the ball it took about twenty minutes for the high to hit.

At first I only used crank while I was working. When I arrived home and made love to my wife, she noticed that I was more aggressive than usual and she asked me what was going on. Amy didn't know what to look for when somebody was on speed; that my pupils would be dilated or that I might talk rapidly. I didn't want to tell her I was using meth again, so I said I was just hyped up from driving sixteen hours.

In only a month or two I went from using crank a couple of days a week to staying awake four or five days in a row. Running that long without sleep is called "tweaking." I know people who tweaked for more than twenty days at a time. Going that long is dangerous; addicts become explosive, violent, and unpredictable. All you have to do is say the wrong word and they freak out and pull a knife, or gun, or beat you half to death.

Crank Bugs

Methamphetamine releases a surge of dopamine, which causes an intense rush of pleasure. With repeated use, the drug affects the brain's chemistry, making it impossible to feel pleasure at all. Meth is highly addictive, and a user quickly develops a tolerance, needing progressively larger amounts to get high.

Chronic use can cause a variety of devastating physiological changes. You've perhaps seen pictures of the transformation of meth addicts. Within a very short period of time men and women age drastically and appear significantly older than their years. They become haggard looking, their skin lacks luster and elasticity, and their hair becomes dull and lifeless. Because meth speeds up the heart so dramatically, there is also an increased risk of heart attack and stroke.

A powerful appetite suppressant, speed causes users to lose massive amounts of weight until they are gaunt and frail. They are just not hungry. In many cases, weight loss is what draws women to the drug.

Meth inhibits the production of saliva, allowing acids in the mouth to eat away at tooth enamel. That dry mouth, coupled with bad nutrition, poor dental hygiene, and repeated tooth grinding, results in severe dental decay, also known as "meth mouth." Teeth break, turn black, and rot, eventually falling out completely. I think the reason my teeth didn't rot right out of my head was that I became compulsive about brushing them. My mouth was so dry that I brushed my teeth five, six, seven times a day on a regular basis.

The psychological implications are even more frightening. Users are both anxious and depressed, and become increasingly violent. Long-term, habitual use can result in full-blown psychosis, and addicts become highly paranoid and experience disturbing hallucinations. The fight-or-flight response is enhanced and addicts constantly struggle for survival. The sensation of bugs crawling beneath the skin is a common delusion, and users develop sores that won't heal because of obsessive scratching.

I didn't suffer many of the physical side effects of meth addiction, but my psychological breakdown was just as bad, if not worse, than rotting teeth or sores that wouldn't heal. Crank got ahold of me fast that second time around. I didn't want to ever come down; the craving I had was much stronger than when I had used it in Texas. I knew I was in trouble from the minute I took that first bump, but I didn't care—it just made me feel too good.

Meth had a profound impact on my family. Once, after an especially long shift behind the wheel, I walked into the house and plopped down on the couch of our living room. Like many couples do when they see each other, I asked Amy if anything had happened that day.

When she told me someone had called but she didn't know who, I flipped out. "You didn't get the phone number?"

"Well, I didn't think it was a big deal; it was probably a bill collector or something."

I snarled at her. "You don't think it's a big deal when somebody is calling your house?" I completely freaked out.

Amy jumped up and started crying.

"Wait, wait, wait, I'm sorry. Give me a minute. I'm sorry, it's not a big deal, you're right."

I knew there was no way to hide what I was doing, so I finally broke down and told Amy I was using meth. She was shocked at first, but then my strange behavior finally made sense. I didn't tell her that I had started seeing things.

Cold as Ice

Time and time again I promised Amy I would quit. But in no time I broke down and was back to using again. She nagged at me constantly. I figured if I could get her to try crank, she would leave me alone and I could use as much as I wanted. I also knew

I would be able to control her. Most men know if we get our women hooked on cocaine or meth or any kind of stimulant drug that we can use them and abuse them.

It sounds cold-blooded because it is cold-blooded. Meth robs people of the ability to love and feel compassion for other human beings, whether it's your children, your wife, your mother, or your father. I had no problem hating and wanting to hurt people when I was on it, but I could not love myself or anybody else.

I told my wife, "Try it—it will make you feel good. Plus, this stuff will help you lose weight." She had been struggling with a few extra pounds since David had been born. She saw me go for days without eating, so she knew that would give her the boost she needed. But you don't want to be on that diet, because it will actually starve you to death.

If you push something on somebody long enough, they will eventually cave in and try it. She was curious—what was it about this drug that made me keep going back to it, even though it made my life a living hell? She'd done pills and speed for years. Could meth really be that different? She had one other motive: she wanted to prove to me once and for all that quitting could be done, so I could no longer use a sorry defense for falling off the wagon. Ironically, she would later make every excuse in the book to keep using crank.

The first time Amy and I did meth together, we got somebody to watch the kids. First I showed her how to snort it properly. If you don't do it right, snorting meth feels like burning battery acid. If you tilt your head back and put water down your nose immediately after inhaling, it won't burn so bad. When Amy tried it, she thought she was going to puke, so we started eating it instead.

When the rush hit her, Amy felt better than she ever had in her life. "I've been wrong; this stuff isn't bad at all. This is great! I can't believe I've been giving you such a hard time about it."

I won't deny it: meth feels great in the beginning. But you can't imagine how awful you will feel after six months of abuse. I'd been warned, but I didn't want to believe it. A meth high doesn't make you feel woozy like you do when you are drunk. You feel like you are thinking more clearly and are more in control. The world is better, the air is cleaner, everything is just better.

All of a sudden Amy was up and cleaning the house with energy to burn. She was naturally a very shy person, but meth made my wife feel more outgoing and confident. As soon as she took that first hit, Amy had a perfect, clear thought that she would be chasing that high for the rest of her life. And she was right; my sweet baby was already hooked.

After we got high together the first time, I was heartbroken. I couldn't believe I'd given my wife this stuff. "I'm so sorry, I'm so sorry. We'll never do it again."

In no time at all we did it again. "If you ever feel like this is getting to you like you can't control it, then we'll quit."

Amy would say, "Yeah, I promise. Hand over the dope."

As time progressed, Amy became very competitive with regards to our drug use. She wanted to use as much—if not more—than I did. If I was splitting the crank up into portions, she was right there next to me making sure my portion wasn't larger than hers. It didn't make sense—she was half my size—but she didn't care about that; in her view, fair was fair.

Out of Sight, Out of Mind

There are a lot of empty refrigerators in the homes of meth addicts. Parents and caregivers who are dependent on the drug lose the ability to nurture their children, and instead focus solely on feeding their growing addiction. Parents will stay up for two to three weeks at a time without sleeping, and when they do pass out, they're out for a couple of days. During that time children are left to fend for themselves, even at the mercy of drug-addicted friends who frequent the house. As their parents get high and then crash, older siblings assume the role of caretaker.

There's certainly no time for grocery shopping or food preparation, and when the parents aren't hungry, they're probably not going to make food a priority for the kids either. Even if they are hungry, their stomachs get so sick that they just won't eat.

The vicious cycle of intoxication and withdrawal makes it difficult to hold down a job, so money is tight. Instead of using limited funds to put food on the table, provide routine medical and dental care, or pay utility bills, addicts use the money to buy drugs. Their children are sick, dirty, hungry, and cold.

Drug-endangered children often struggle in school. Neglected kids mimic the sleep-wake cycle of their parents and alternate between hyperactivity and crashing. Secondhand exposure can result in symptoms of attention deficit/hyperactivity disorder (ADHD) and make it nearly impossible for students to sit still and focus in the classroom. They also can't stay awake in class; school is a neutral zone—when it's not safe to sleep at home, they'll do it in school. They may get into trouble by doing it, but at least nobody is going to hurt them.

Our children started suffering when Amy started using meth with me. Before that, they'd always had their mother to take care of them when I was getting high. I would have told you back then that I was a good parent. I justified my drug use by saying I didn't do it in front of the kids. But the truth is that they were very neglected. Many times they came and knocked on that bedroom door and I screamed at them, "Get out of here! Leave me alone! Don't be bothering me, I'm not coming out." I was never there for them.

Amy's cravings became intense. In the beginning, she still remembered the importance of paying the electric bill and putting food on the table, but before long all she could think about was getting more crank. Tweaking became our new lifestyle, and normal family routines went by the wayside.

Despite the fact that the two of us were hard-core methamphetamine addicts by this point, Amy quit doing it every time she got pregnant. Meth made us both crave sex, and since we didn't use any form of birth control, we had a lot of babies. It was a cycle: Amy binged five or ten times, got pregnant, quit the drugs, had the baby, breastfed, and then started the whole thing all over again. She smoked marijuana to manage her cravings, but stayed away from crank. Marijuana isn't good on a baby, but I think it saved our kids, because it was better than speed.

Miraculously, all of our children are healthy. They are either very athletic or top-of-the-line, straight-A students. Our daughter Rachel just earned the Presidential Physical Fitness Award, which was bestowed upon only five students out of nearly 500 in her school. Our son, David, is ranked in the top 5 percent nationally for his intellectual ability. All of our kids regularly receive the "Citizen of the Month" award, and the school principal often tells us we have the most well behaved kids in the school.

I walk around scratching my head about their success nearly

every day. It is far beyond my understanding how this happened, but I don't question it, I'm just grateful that God has made them happy and healthy. I certainly can't take credit for any of it. Some of the credit needs to go to their grandparents on both sides who faithfully took them to church and Sunday school so they might turn out better than I did.

Amy was so addicted when she got pregnant with our last daughter that she couldn't wait to give birth just so she could get high again. With our first daughter, Sarah, Amy couldn't wait to see what she was going to look like. But she didn't even breast-feed Abby like she had done with the other babies. She was in a hurry to get it all over with so she could start cranking again.

My wife didn't handle being a drug addict and a parent very well. Because of the bingeing, she would be awake for a week and then sick for a week, and then have a few good days when she got caught up on the laundry and other household duties before it all started again. Amy's grandparents were down at our place all the time, and for a while, my mom lived with us in a different part of the house. Between the three of them, there was always milk for the kids.

We were both terribly neglectful. Baby Abby basically lived her entire life in her crib and was completely accustomed to entertaining herself. Amy was fairly attentive during the day, but after I came home from work, our lives revolved around getting high. Amy and I spent most of our time in the dope room; if there was a crisis, or the baby needed feeding, Amy ran out to handle it and then ran right back to me. I stayed behind, focusing on my drugs rather than my family.

We have one videotape that is especially painful to watch. It was Christmas morning. While the other kids were on the floor opening presents, one-year-old Abby stood in her crib perfectly still, just watching the festivities. She didn't even cry. A child raised in a normal environment would want to get out and be in that paper and all the toys and everything. On the shelf in the background, you can see piles of foil we used for smoking meth. Amy and I are joking around about her having a black eye, like that's funny. It makes us sick to watch that tape.

The last couple of years, Amy and I locked ourselves in our room for days at a time instead of playing with and nurturing our six kids. They had to fend for themselves; we forgot to feed them because we weren't hungry. Sometimes it would be nine at night and we'd suddenly remember, *Oh my God, we haven't made supper!* The older ones ate whatever they could find and fixed bottles for the smaller ones.

Even though Sarah was just a little kid, she became a surrogate mother. If somebody wanted something, Amy said, "Go ask Sarah," or, "Sarah, go outside and keep an eye on them." At the time it didn't seem like a big deal to Amy, like maybe she was asking Sarah to fill in just every so often, but it wasn't every once in a while, it was all the time.

While we were on a binge, the laundry didn't get done, the house was filthy, and the kids didn't get bathed, but we weren't living in a garbage house either. I've been in houses where my feet didn't hit the floor until I got to the kitchen. In homes where meth is manufactured, there usually aren't cockroaches. It's not because they can't handle the chemicals in the air—a roach can live through a nuclear bomb—it's because there's no food to eat in the house. On the other side, I've been in houses where I'd hear a thump and see roaches literally falling off the ceiling onto the kitchen counter. We didn't care, though; we were all busy smoking crank. It's disturbing to think that innocent children live in those houses.

Our kids missed a lot of school, but Amy managed to get them on the school bus most of the time. She wanted them out of the house so she could use her drugs in peace. Amy became a shut-in; she never left the house, not even for school functions. As a trucker I was gone for days at a time, and when I wasn't working, I'd be out looking for dope. Amy didn't have any friends or look forward to anything except getting high.

Amy was a hopeless addict. Even in the hot Tennessee summer, she sequestered herself in that stifling back bedroom. She didn't turn on the air conditioner or the fan because she needed to be able to hear the baby cry. She sat back there in the dark all alone for hours so she could see headlights pull up in the driveway or hear footsteps. My mother still lived with us, and Amy was paranoid she would catch her with the dope. Of course, Mom already knew what was going on, but we did our best to keep our drug use hidden. It was a terrible existence. I'm grateful that our kids were so young during this time period and don't remember.

Happy Birthday

Children's birthday parties are usually joyous occasions filled with laughter, balloons, and birthday presents. They are some of the most memorable moments in a person's life. My daughter Sarah's sixth birthday is one such memory; except it left an indelibly negative stamp on her psyche. I don't know if she will ever forgive me for what I did.

Every time I woke up, whether in the morning or after a nap, I was angry. My family never knew what to expect, other than that I would likely start a fight for no reason. It got to a point where I was ticked off about something all the time.

For Sarah's sixth birthday we bought her a decorated chocolate cake to celebrate. Before the birthday party I went into the back of the house to lie down, with specific instructions to be roused when it was time to cut the cake. When Amy came in and woke me, I went into the living room with her to sing "Happy Birthday" and watch Sarah open her present from us, a sleeping bag. I ate a couple bites of cake, but it made me sick to my stomach because I hadn't eaten anything in a few days. Chocolate cake on an empty stomach that has been worn down by meth is very unpleasant.

After the party, Amy's grandparents took the younger kids so we could have a special time just with Sarah. After they left, I flipped out at Amy, chasing her around the room with a big hunting knife: "You knew this was going to make me sick! You're glad I'm sick! You want me to be sick! You should have fixed me something else to eat before giving me that cake!"

I threw her down on a chair and threatened to cut her throat. It was the first time I had ever pulled a knife on her. Then I got a gun, shot at the dresser a couple of times, and shot holes in Sarah's new sleeping bag while she and her mother stood in the doorway crying. Sarah finally calmed down when I gave Amy the gun, and she promised our daughter there would be no more fighting. Amy did her best to play with Sarah and pretend like nothing was wrong. I was mad the entire day, but I didn't scream in front of Sarah.

Time and time again I told Amy I would quit, but I just couldn't do it. I just substituted one addiction for another. I remember saying a bunch of times, "I'm not going to do any more meth; I'm just going to stick with smoking marijuana." It only works for a little while, because you have to be around drug addicts to get that pot. One night you are going to be around them and be stoned like I was so many times and use poor judgment, thinking, *One time isn't going to hurt me* . . . Then you are right back to the drawing board. If you really want to get away from crank, you have to quit *everything* and get rid of *everything* you are subject to relapse to, including alcohol and pills. You have to be completely clean.

Children living in homes with meth users often witness domestic violence against one or both of their parents. It didn't take long before my threats and violent attitude morphed into physical abuse. I didn't do much to help with the kids or the house— I just waited for Amy to serve me.

Oddly enough, I didn't want our kids to attend public school because of what they would be exposed to there. One day when we were getting ready to leave to visit a local Christian school, I languished angrily on the couch, copping an attitude as I waited for everybody to get their act together so we could leave.

"Are you ever going to get ready?"

"It might be better if you'd get up off the couch and help me."

I came unglued, grabbing my tiny wife and choking her, screaming about being disobedient and sassy. Then I slammed her into the washing machine, badly bruising her back.

"Look what you're doing to Rachel and Sarah and David! Look what you're doing in front of these kids!" Amy pleaded. Our three kids sat openmouthed on the couch, completely freaked out.

"Well, good! I hope they learn not to talk back to me."

If you throw a frog in a hot pan it will jump out, but if you put a frog in cool water and slowly warm it up, the frog will stay in the water until it is cooked to death. That's what it was like for Amy living with me. I went from being her savior and protector to the person who bullied and abused her. She needed protection from me.

It seemed to me like Amy nagged me all the time, and one day I snapped. I smashed the alarm clock and threw Amy down on the bed. I reached under the bed and grabbed the 12-gauge shotgun and threatened to kill her. What I did next is unthinkable; I put the barrel up to her head and pulled the trigger.

Fortunately, there were no bullets in the chamber. We always kept it unloaded because of the kids, but I was still taking a chance. How did I know Amy or one of the kids hadn't loaded it? I wasn't thinking clearly in those days, and I didn't stop and ask, "Hey, did anybody load the gun?" I could have blown off Amy's head and I could have gone to state prison for life, or it could have been a murder-suicide and I could have killed the whole family. The idea is horrifying. Our family would have been destroyed.

As soon as I fell asleep, Amy grabbed all the kids except little David and drove to the sheriff's department. He was curled up in bed beside me and there was no way she could get him out of bed without waking me up too. David was just four or five years old and often slept with me. I rocked him to sleep even when I was doped up and there was turmoil in the house. Somehow I made him feel more secure—go figure.

Although I was obviously a horrible father, I didn't want my kids to grow up the same way I did. With my dad, anything went, but I was a strict parent in many ways. I didn't let them watch movies that contained violence or nudity, even when I was messed up. I didn't talk to my son about women or say filthy things in front of him like my dad did. I wanted to be friends with all my kids, but I wanted them to see me primarily as a father rather than a buddy. Today, David and I do everything together, and I am close with all my kids. Instead of going to a smoky honky-tonk like I did growing up, they travel with me and go to my drug-awareness programs.

When I woke up, nobody was home except for David and me. I figured Amy and the kids had gone to the grocery store to buy some milk, but after an hour passed, I knew something was up. I wasn't certain though, so I didn't get rid of my dope; a guy doesn't want to do that unless it is absolutely necessary.

I was outside burning the door I had busted chasing Amy when three squad cars pulled into our driveway with lights flashing. I had a reputation with the cops, and when they came to my house, they came loaded for bear. Of course, I was terribly remorseful and promised to never touch her again, but the cops loaded me up in one car and put little David in another. Then they searched the house and found a small amount of marijuana. I didn't have very much by that time because Amy had taken my big stash and thrown it in the woodstove.

In Tennessee, the police are only required to keep people who are charged with domestic violence for six hours. Amy wanted them to hold me for twelve or twenty-four to give me a chance to cool down. They kept me for the full twenty-four; I was well known to the authorities and not popular.

When I was released, I stayed with my sister for a couple days because I'd been slapped with a pretrial restraining order. In the meantime, Amy wrote a letter to the judge asking to have the assault charges dropped. I'm sure they thought she was an idiot, but they dropped the felony assault and only charged me with misdemeanor marijuana possession. I was sentenced to two days in jail, a pretty lame sentence, if you ask me. I should have been charged with domestic assault or wonton endangerment, and as a convicted felon, I never should have had guns in the house. They could have easily sent me back to prison for six years or more. For some inexplicable reason, I got off virtually scot-free.

Episodes like that didn't happen every day, but 99 percent of the time I lost my cool because I hadn't smoked a joint to mellow out. People—usually stoners—say marijuana isn't addictive and that there are no symptoms of withdrawal, but I know from personal experience that when I didn't have THC (tetrahydrocannabinol, the active chemical in marijuana) in my bloodstream, my body reacted negatively. My nerves were on edge, and I couldn't control my temper. Everything bothered me. Everything made me mad. Those are signs of withdrawal.

That was certainly true many times in my former life. I hate when people say marijuana is not an addictive drug. I smoked it for twenty-three years, and when I quit, I had strong cravings for it. They weren't as bad as the ones I had with cocaine or methamphetamine, but I know I was addicted to marijuana.

One day my wife asked me to go to the grocery store to buy a gallon of milk for the kids because they didn't have anything to eat. I told her I wouldn't buy it; all I had in my pocket was thirty dollars and I needed that to buy a bag of weed. If she wanted milk, she could ask the children's grandparents to buy it. I'm ashamed to admit I chose getting high over feeding my own kids. If it's not addiction to do a thing like that, there's no such thing as addiction.

It's hard to understand why Amy stayed with me through the abuse. I know now that it was because she had been slowly and methodically brainwashed. It wasn't like one day she was confident and independent and the next she was isolated and taking all kinds of abuse. Her own upbringing in a volatile drug home may have also played a role; for Amy, our dysfunctional family seemed "normal."

Domestic violence is a process, and it cycles through generations, usually going from bad to worse down the line. My dad was abused by his dad, my dad abused his kids and beat his wives, and now I was the bad guy, beating on my own wife. Drugs and alcohol played a role in all of these situations. The cycle needs to be broken.

ELEVEN

Shadow People

Those who play with the devil's toys will be
brought by degrees to wield his sword.

— R. Buckminster Fuller

I CROSSED THE LINE FROM BEING an addict who occasionally hallucinated into a full-blown psychotic. I started believing that everything I saw and imagined was real. Conspiracy theories formed in my mind. Every time the phone rang and it was an unknown caller, I was convinced it was someone calling for Amy trying to lure her away from me. Invisible people whispered all around me in an unknown language. In the quiet of the night, I heard their footsteps around the house and knew they were listening to me.

Seeing Is Believing

Derangement is a slow process; one rarely loses touch with reality overnight. Research conducted by the Wyoming Methamphetamine Treatment Initiative has shown that the psychosis an addict experiences as a result of meth abuse is scientifically indistinguishable from classic paranoid schizophrenia. In many cases, the symptoms last for years after withdrawal from the drug.

My dad's buddies told me they saw things back when I first started doing meth in Texas. I never believed them, though; I thought they were just trying to scare me. When I started having hallucinations of my own years later, I knew those guys had been telling the truth.

I never saw anything that was pleasant to look at when I was on meth. There were no talking bunny rabbits or smiley faces. I would have killed to have seen a pink elephant like the ones in the Disney animated classic *Dumbo*. All of my hallucinations were dark and scary. I saw shadow people.

It started early one morning when I was driving a large load of logs through a hilly area of Kentucky that was dense with trees. As I was getting close to crossing a big river on a two-lane road, I slammed on the brakes. Somebody was standing on the edge of the bridge looking like they were poised to commit suicide. There was no way to survive a huge drop like that. When I got to the bridge there was nobody there—I had imagined the whole thing.

A couple hours later I came to a rise and freaked out when I saw a car stopped at the bottom of the hill. Once again I locked up the semi, tires squealing and smoking as my heavy load shifted around on the trailer. Breathing heavily, my heart nearly jumped out of my chest. When I got over the hill there was no car. *Oh my God. What in the heck is the matter with me?*

My hallucinations shifted from imagining shadowy figments to seeing sudden movement out the corner of my eye. When I turned to look, there was nothing there. Paranoia will destroy you.

I started packing a .38 revolver like an old police pistol. It was the same gun my mom accidentally shot me with years earlier. Then I got a 12-gauge shotgun and a .22 automatic rifle. One of those guns was with me everywhere I went. When I started seeing things in the bushes, thinking they were other drug dealers trying to rip me off, I carelessly shot them up without thinking. It could have been one of my kids playing! Thankfully, it never was.

My aggression toward Amy and people in town intensified, and I became violent like I had been when I was drunk. I got into it once while I was waiting in line at the local McDonald's drive-through. It looked to me like the carful of black women ahead of me were staring at me in their rearview mirror. *What the hell were they looking at me for? They were after me!* I snapped, screaming curse words and threatening them. It was just a fast-food drive-through!

My schizophrenia really kicked in after that, and I no longer just saw shadows in my peripheral vision. One evening I saw a shadow walk across the room, swinging its arms like a person. Instantly, I knew it was a demon. The first time it happened, I jumped back, scared to death. Meth addicts around the world see the same shadow people. I believe in my heart they are evil spirits.

Amy's hallucinations were particularly awful. The first time she saw a mangled cat crawling toward her. The worst thing she ever saw was an image of our two-year-old son lying decapitated in his crib. He was talking to her. It's common for meth users to see bugs on the floor; I talked to one woman who described seeing worms all over the carpet, and she wouldn't put her feet down for hours. Another one said she was convinced the gateway to hell was in the trunk of a junk car parked by her house because she'd seen zombies and demons entering and exiting it. I never heard anybody tell me they hallucinated about something nice.

My hallucinations became dangerous to those around me. One hot and humid summer night—it must have been at least ninety-five degrees—Amy and I were driving down a country road on our way home. Amy asked me why I was driving so slow; the speedometer showed me hovering at only fifteen mph. In my mind it was snowing so hard I couldn't go any faster—a blizzard in the dead of summer. White lines of frozen precipitation angled down on the windshield as I crept along the country roads away from prying eyes. I could have easily driven into the ditch and killed us both.

Meth addicts are especially prone to abusing their children. Violent reactions to otherwise innocent stimuli are common. While tweaking or crashing, for instance, a hungry baby's cry is ten times louder, and minor misbehavior can be overwhelming. Tweakers often experience delusions and hallucinations; the last thing they want to hear is a kid, particularly if that kid doesn't look like their kid, but instead like a shadow person or something. A common reaction is to literally kick their children away and then stomp them, resulting in broken bones and other permanent injuries. Many children are kicked to death. Perhaps my one redeeming quality was that I never physically injured my kids.

Green-eyed Monster

When I started hallucinating, I started changing. I'd always been a violent man, but meth made me about a thousand times worse. As time marched on and my dependence on methamphetamine became more debilitating, I took my anger out on my wife, the person I loved the most. In many cases, my violent outbursts were sparked by jealousy. I became paranoid that Amy was running around on me.

I beat the crap out of her when I was tweaking. She tried to fight back, but she didn't stand a chance. When I became enraged, the adrenaline coursed through my veins with such power that nobody could stop me, especially a woman who was only five feet four and weakened by her own drug abuse.

My brain was twisted. Not only did I think Amy betrayed me with other men, I thought she was my enemy; a disloyal foe who might turn on me at any moment. I got so mad at her that I saw blood-red flashes and lashed out. When I came down from the high and saw the physical damage I'd inflicted, I was always horrified. Finger bruises covered her arms from where I had grabbed and shaken her. My own wife was deathly afraid of me.

After the fact, I went for days with my head hung low. "I'm sorry, I'm sorry, I'm sorry. I'll never do that again." I tried to control myself, but when I got high, I always thought she was looking at somebody, and I'd lose it again. Then I went back to questioning her, back to accusing her. I punched the walls and then transitioned from pounding the Sheetrock to slapping Amy. She threw things at me and tried to hit me back, but that just made me crazier. I pulled her hair and threw her around, choked her and held her down, screaming in her face. My violence became worse and worse as the months passed.

According to a report in the *Journal of the American Medical Association* (JAMA), 92 percent of domestic abusers reported using alcohol or other drugs on the day of the assault. Drug use is known to impair judgment, reduce inhibition, and increase aggression. Methamphetamine damages the limbic system of the brain, and addicts lose the ability to control their tempers. They fly off the handle over the smallest things and become obsessed over perceived offenses. Eventually they blow. Drug-related homicide is the most frequent cause of death in methamphetamine addicts.

One night as I was lying in bed, it hit me—I had turned out just like my father, if not worse. I remember being so angry with him that I vowed to kill him—and look at what I was doing. Why was it so natural for me to slap my wife around when I got mad like he had done? No man should ever put his hands on a woman in anger. I felt remorse like most abusers do, but not enough to get help.

Dirty and Depraved

I don't care how tough you think you are, if you use meth long enough it is going to make you sick. Meth abusers become compulsive about whatever it is they are doing, whether it is cleaning the house or having sex. Meth addicts are hypersexual, meaning they become excessively active. They often become unable to control their sexual behavior; rape always happens more frequently when the drug hits an area hard, as do child abuse and molestation. Sexually transmitted diseases like AIDS also rise because sexually charged addicts forego safety precautions, such as condoms.

My mind was completely consumed with thoughts of sex; I craved it all the time. Fortunately, my wife was an addict too and had the same tendencies. We had a ritual: I got home from work, we put the kids to bed, turned on some pornography, and did drugs and had sex all night long. Sometimes we stayed naked for twenty-four hours going back and forth between getting high and having sex. We only took a break to use the bathroom or get the kids off to school. Run-of-the-mill sex was no longer enough; the pornography we watched became more hard-core and we got into S&M. The sex was so aggressive at times that I rubbed myself raw.

Making love to my wife had always been a beautiful thing to me, but meth made it ugly and weird. I did things that were disgusting, and the farther my addiction progressed, the kinkier I became. When I sobered up, I was ashamed and felt dirty and cheap.

To some guys this might sound like a dream come true. But in the end, my sexual marathons were replaced by frustrating dysfunction. Meth causes delayed ejaculation in men and renders them impotent. Side effects are generally reversible after drug use ceases.

Hanging in the Balance

My meth use was like peaks and valleys. I would tweak for days at a time and then have periods of recovery before bingeing again. One of my worst experiences happened after a meth binge. Amy had taken the kids to her grandparents because she knew what I would be like after the meth was out of my system. It was a preemptive action on her part.

After I walked through the empty house, I sat out on the porch crying, swallowing a random combination of downers like Valium and Xanax to help me come down from the crank. I thought for sure I was going to have a nervous breakdown.

I'd made a terrible mess of my life, jeopardized the welfare of my family, and put them through hell. And there was no end in sight. I knew what meth was doing to me, but I couldn't quit; its hold on me was far too powerful.

Suddenly, I heard a harsh, deep voice. It sounded like a man was standing right next to me, but there was nobody in sight. There was something in that voice that frightened me—instinctively I knew I was talking to the devil.

"You know, your wife and kids would be better off if you were dead. The world would be a better place without a guy like you."

"I don't want to hear it—leave me alone!"

What the voice said next broke me. "Do you really think God is going to forgive you for the things you have done and the people you have hurt?"

"No, I don't think He will," I answered, sobbing. I'd done so many terrible things and hurt a lot of people, both physically and emotionally. There was no forgiveness for a guy like me.

With that, I got up out of my chair and walked straight to the barn. I was no longer crying, I was determined; it was like a switch had flipped and I knew what I had to do. All I could find to do the job was a heavy nylon fishing line, the kind you would string fish on, but it was strong enough to hold me. I tied a slipknot on the end so it would tighten when pressure was put on it. I didn't know how to tie a hangman's noose.

Focused, I pulled my riding lawnmower beneath the dangling rope and stepped on. Then I stood on my tiptoes, grabbed the rope, slipped the noose around my neck, and stepped off the mower.

Instantly, I gasped and choked, my tongue suddenly becoming too large for my mouth. My head felt like it was swelling up, and my face turned red, like when you were a kid and you held your breath too long. The pressure was intense; it felt like my eyes were going to pop out of my head. The nylon noose brought all the blood to the surface and cut my throat from ear to ear.

When I felt the pain and pressure I panicked and changed my mind. I didn't want to kill myself after all! But my thrashing legs couldn't find the mower and my fingertips barely grazed the rafter. I knew I was going to die.

I woke up on my back looking straight into the face of my sister Mechell, who was shaking me and crying. The rope had shredded and broken in two. Evidently when my body convulsed it had snapped the line. Suddenly, I was back to my senses and no longer felt crazy. I couldn't believe I was alive!

Everything looked more beautiful. The sun seemed like it was shining brighter, the sky was bluer, and the flowers looked prettier. I couldn't speak, but I sat up and cried, so grateful to be alive.

Mechell called my cousin Debbie and the two of them brought me to see a preacher named Billy Patterson. Billy and I went into a room at his church and talked; I cried uncontrollably as I told him my story. He shared how he had been an alcoholic when he was young and had thoughts of suicide. He had been so bad that he had been locked in an insane asylum. Billy understood what I was going through.

I stayed off illegal drugs for five months, thanks to Billy. It was the first time I had been sober since I was thirteen. I'd forgotten what it felt like—it felt great! Amy and I got baptized and went to church regularly. We were both sober for the first time in years, because of God. We slipped back into the parent mode, helping with homework, playing games, watching TV, and having supper together. We were there for the children for five or six months. We even had a birthday party for Jesus on Christmas Day. Everybody was happy.

I'll never forget the day Billy Patterson brought me in front of his congregation, saying, "Satan just about killed David, and if he gets back on drugs, it's going to be far worse than it was this time." It was a foreshadowing of things to come.

A couple of days after the hanging I went back to work. I told my manager that I hadn't been to work for a few days because I was depressed and suicidal. They sent me to the factory nurse who suggested they immediately send me to a psychiatrist. At my first appointment, the psychiatrist asked me about the marks on my neck. I still had burn marks and scabs from the nylon rope I had used as a noose. When I told him I had hung myself, he suggested I not tell the company; to this day I'm not sure why.

I stayed out of work for about four months. The psychiatrist treated me for a sleeping disorder as well as depression and anxiety. I had a medicine cabinet full of prescriptions, Paxil, Lithium, Buspar, I couldn't stay sober, so there was no way to prescribe the right medication. He finally found a medication called Neurontin—a drug normally used to control seizures—that leveled me out. He just kept increasing the dose until I was swallowing a staggering amount.

I saw the psychiatrist off and on for more than a year. As soon as I started feeling better, I'd run back to the drugs. Then when I felt suicidal again, I'd make an appointment and he'd adjust my meds. Eventually he threw up his hands and told me he couldn't help me any longer. I wish he would have had me hospitalized.

Working the System

It's probably hard to believe, but throughout all my years of drug abuse, I always held down a job. I wasn't a model employee, mind you, but I was gainfully employed. For years I worked as a truck driver, but my family had grown so large that I needed to earn better wages. When I found out the local tire factory was hiring I applied there. For five years I worked at the General Tire factory in Mayfield, Kentucky, in the chemical room where we mixed compounds to add to the rubber before tires were manufactured. My job was easy, so it was no problem being high on the job.

When I went back to work after my doctor-ordered leave of absence, I had to go back to the same old environment and the same guys I'd been selling dope to. They were good guys; they were just addicted to drugs like I had been. I didn't think it would bother me if they smoked marijuana because I had it kicked. I actually thought I could turn them around and get them to go to church with me.

I didn't know anybody who didn't use drugs. I'd smoked pot for twenty-three years, and as soon as I got back around those guys who were all doped up, I was right there with them. It is impossible to hang around your old buddies and not use. You might tell a probation officer that, but you can't fool me—I tried and failed miserably. If you really want to live a life of sobriety, you have to surround yourself with sober people.

At the time I was tied up with one of the biggest drug outfits in west Kentucky. Our night-shift plant superintendent and another guy bought huge amounts of meth from California and had it shipped into the factory through the mail. When the police honed in on their operation, the buddy made a deal and sold out his partner. The superintendent paid him back by beating him to death with a claw hammer. He is now in Kentucky State Prison for murder. Those were the kind of people I was hanging around.

As soon as I smoked that first joint with my friends, I quit going to church. I didn't want to sit in a pew like a hypocrite after I'd told all those people I was clean. It was a terrible mistake—I should have run *to* the church, not away from it.

As my drug use escalated, so did my altercations with fellow employees. At one point, my supervisor ordered me to take a drug test because I was getting so out of hand. One of the biggest advantages to belonging to a labor union is how difficult it is for management to terminate an employee. When I failed my drug test they still couldn't fire me, so they had to put me on a year-long probation period during which I would be subject to random drug tests. Every day for the next eleven months, I carried a pill bottle full of someone else's pee to work. It might have been from one of my kids, or a nephew, or just some random kid at a doper's house. I paid five dollars for someone to urinate into a cup for me.

They called me in three times for a random urine test. I had ten minutes to get down to the nurse, so I went and got a cup of coffee, heated the pee in the microwave, and stuck it down my pants. I passed every one of my tests operating that way. That's how I kept my job.

Back to the Future

When I got back on crank, I did it with gusto. I started staying up for eight or nine days in a row and would only eat a couple of cheeseburgers the whole time. When you don't eat for a week or more, it's like you forget how to swallow. The back of my throat was so raw that it took me a couple of days just to be able to start eating again. When I did, it had to be something simple and soft like pinto beans. During that period of time I lost more than forty pounds and became emaciated and sickly. After four or five days down, I tweaked again. The cycle continued for three years.

Thoughts of suicide came roaring back. When I came down off a meth high and looked at my family, my heart broke. My kids were afraid to be in the same room with me, and Amy's face was often bruised and battered. I was a monster.

My paranoia also grew worse. The people I was dealing with were ruthless drug addicts. They didn't have jobs; they just cooked meth and broke into other people's houses. I had thousands of dollars worth of marijuana drying on the second floor of my house, and I was convinced those guys were going to steal it and sell it out from under me.

I talked Amy into buying me a couple of guns in her name—the ones I'd owned previously had been confiscated by the police when Amy had me arrested years earlier. This time I picked out an SKA assault rifle and a .22 automatic. I couldn't sign for them myself because I was a convicted felon. I sealed the deal when I told her those dopeheads were going to break in the house and kill her and the kids. I knew that would scare her enough to buy me some guns. Many times Amy wished she hadn't done it, because I ended up turning those guns on her. Our house has more than two hundred bullet holes in it from me freaking out.

TWELVE

Assault with a Deadly Weapon

There is hardly a man clever enough to recognize
the full extent of the evil he does.

— François de La Rochefoucauld

I DIDN'T WAKE UP THAT MORNING THINKING, *Today I am going to blow my face off.* It just kind of happened.

Hitting the Wall

When I first started using meth, a typical dose was about the size of a pea. In the end, the wad I swallowed resembled a big grape, a massive amount to use at one time. I frequently tweaked for nine or ten days straight. Near the end, my motor skills were shot and I could hardly talk. It was impossible for me to put words together in a sentence, let alone carry on a conversation.

202

I was like a zombie. For up to eighteen hours I'd sit on a chair and stare at the floor or the walls, my gun propped up next to me for quick access. The only time I moved was to put more dope in my mouth.

When my body could no longer take it, I ate enough downers to pass out and then stayed in bed for days. Sometimes I stopped breathing in my sleep, rising up in bed gasping for breath. Amy had to shake me to get me breathing again.

When a run like that was over, my energy was completely zapped and body aches made me feel like I had the flu. My body was empty and dehydrated because I hadn't put anything in it besides dope, and when I tried to eat, I got severe cramps and diarrhea. I was literally starving myself to death. There was another reason I didn't want to eat, though: I thought my wife was trying to poison me. I got so sick every time I ate that in my paranoid mind I thought she must have been doing something to my food. A drug addict always blames their problems on some-thing, or somebody, else, never on the drugs. I didn't want to accept that it was the meth making me sick.

People hardly recognized me. My eyes were sunk into my head, and my skin was so jaundiced my feet looked as yellow as Bart Simpson's. It was obvious to everybody that I was sick, but they didn't know what to do. There was no rehab in our area, and even if there had been, I couldn't have gone. We didn't have the money for treatment; I had totally bankrupted my family. If my mom hadn't let us stay in my childhood home, we would have been out on the street.

I didn't want to quit; it was easier to keep the meth flowing through my veins than risk suffering painful withdrawal. Every time I started sobering up, I went into convulsions—meth addiction can cause symptoms that mimic those of Parkinson's disease—and my whole body, my arms and my legs especially, twitched uncontrollably.

Over the course of the last year of my addiction, I was obsessed with dying. I used to go on binges and think, *This is going to be the time.* I wasn't courageous enough to kill myself; I hoped the meth would do the job for me. I expected that I would eventually overdose or my organs would shut down and kill me. I almost welcomed it. One time I consumed about a gram and a half of meth, and Amy found me in the middle of the driveway having a seizure, gagging on my tongue.

Your Cheating Heart

At the end of those long meth runs, I exhibited a physical symptom that was humiliating to me: I became impotent. Amy and I had always been enthusiastic sex partners, but I became too sick and weak to perform. I tried Viagra to get an erection and it worked for a few days, but even a prescription medication couldn't compete with the ravages of methamphetamine.

I accused Amy of adultery, assuming she was getting elsewhere what I couldn't give her at home. My imagination went crazy. I got it into my head that Amy had slept with my friend Eric. Several years earlier, Amy ran into him at school when she was registering our daughter. He told Amy that his wife wanted to meet her. She was on leave from work and suggested Amy stop over sometime for a cup of coffee. She didn't think anything of it at the time.

Later, when Amy told me what Eric had said that morning, I became very agitated. She should have known Eric was coming on to her! Not long after that, when Amy was at the grocery store, Eric stopped by our house when I was supposed to be at work. He made up a lame excuse about wanting to see if I was home, but I knew better. I never believed him and stewed about it for years.

When my paranoia and delusions reached a crescendo, I became convinced that Amy and Eric had a thing going. The idea was completely irrational; there was absolutely no reason to believe Amy had been unfaithful to me. But once my mind latched on to it, the idea spun around until I could think of little else.

One day, after we'd been arguing about it, I finally snapped. I dragged Amy to the van, shut her in the back, and drove off. When we reached an isolated spot, I climbed into the back with her and started questioning her.

"You had sex with Eric, didn't you?"

"No, you're wrong," she said calmly. "I think he was hitting on me, but I haven't done anything."

I physically tortured Amy until she broke. I choked her until she almost passed out and slapped her until she was red in the face.

"Yes! I did it!" she screamed finally, saying anything to get me to stop hurting her.

I grabbed my gun and jumped back into the driver's seat. I distinctly remember having the thought that I was going to murder that snake, his wife, and their two kids—all of them. Then I would turn the gun on myself.

Screeching to a stop in Eric's driveway, I bolted up the steps and pounded on the door. When his wife answered, I shouted, "Your husband has been screwing my wife. Where is he?"

That woman knew me and understood how dangerous I was. "He would never do that to me!" she argued.

"Well, he told me he slept with another girl when he went for training to be an ambulance driver."

"Let me talk to your wife," she demanded.

"No, you're not talking to her. She's already been through enough over this guy. . . . Did you ever ask him to invite my Amy over for coffee?"

"No."

"That's what Eric told me the day I found him sitting in his car in my driveway. He said you wanted him to ask Amy to come over because you wanted to meet her."

"No, I never told him that."

She refused to tell me where Eric was. The fact that he wasn't there that day saved everybody from getting hurt. I know in my heart if he had been home, I would have killed him before I even opened my mouth. I probably would have gotten out of the car, knocked on the door, and blown him away right there on the front porch.

On the way home, Amy denied she had done anything wrong. "I didn't do anything with that guy; you made me say that. You're insane; you need some help!" When she changed her story and said she had never been unfaithful to me, it didn't appease me, it enraged me even more. Amy and I fought for the rest of the night. I screamed and hollered, and said hateful things that I am so ashamed of.

Eric called crying the next day and insisted he had never had sex with Amy. I didn't believe him for a second; he was the kind of guy who went to church every Sunday and tomcatted around the rest of the week. The whole thing about him going to church infuriated me. Christians were supposed to be better than that. What a hypocrite. Everybody who loved me, my mother, my in-laws, my sisters, and my cousin Debbie and her husband, Jim, tried to convince me to get off drugs and get right with God. I was sick to death of hearing about how God could change me and what He could do for me. I wanted to blame God for everything that happened. In a powerful act of defiance, I threw my Bible in the woodstove and watched it burn.

I threatened Eric and hung up. He called my cousin, Mark, and asked him to talk to me because he was so scared. He had good reason to be. Fortunately, I passed out and nothing more ever came of it. That happened sometimes with me. I would be agitated over one thing or another when I was on a meth run, but when I came down I became indifferent and forgot why I was so mad in the first place. My brain just bounced to the next delusion.

Of all the terrible things I've done in my life, torturing my wife is the one of which I am most ashamed. That was the pinnacle of my insanity.

My unwarranted jealousy also had a profound impact on our children. Amy once found Sarah's journal. In her ten-year-old words, she wrote about how I beat up her mother because she had a boyfriend. Sarah had heard me threaten to cut off Amy's head and threaten to burn her with cigarettes to get her to confess to her adultery. Amy ripped the pages out of that diary—it's too bad I can't erase those things from her memory as easily.

Another time, shortly before the holidays, Amy and I slept under the glow of the Christmas tree lights. It was supposed to be a special time, but it just turned into another nightmare. I was obsessed with the notion that she had cheated on me. I hit her repeatedly that night, telling her everything would be okay if she just confessed and asked for forgiveness. So of course, she did it to get me to back off, but things were far from okay. I pounded her.

Sarah came in the room crying, trying to get me off her mom. "Your mother has been sleeping with other men. She is destroying our family. Look what she is making me do to her and to you kids!"

I went on for days at a time screaming at Amy, calling her a whore and ranting about the kinds of sexual acts she had probably been doing with all these men—all in front of, or within earshot of, the kids.

On one occasion I hit her for so long that Amy couldn't take it anymore. She went into the kitchen, grabbed a knife, and slit her left wrist several times, leaving nasty gashes that should have had stitches. Amy wouldn't go to the hospital because she was afraid they would lock her up. I followed her into the room and wrestled the knife away. There was blood everywhere.

My mom, who was living with us at the time, heard the commotion and ran in. "Stop it, David! Not in front of Josiah!"

"I don't care; I can't help it if his mother is a whore."

Mom took Amy to her bedroom and taped the wounds together with supplies she had in a first-aid kit. I was never concerned that she had sliced herself up—I saw red as she was bleeding all over the kitchen floor. Little Josiah saw everything from start to finish. He was only four.

Holidays were always especially turbulent at our house. One Thanksgiving Day, as the whole family sat around the table, someone said something about how much Sarah looked like Amy. Rachel, who was only five at the time said, "Yes, Sarah looks just like Mama. When she grows up, she'll have bruises all over her face, too."

Things got so bad that Amy actually left me and the kids. She waited until I was asleep and left a good-bye note on the table. Amy didn't have enough money to buy the amount of meth she wanted, so she took along a bottle of my prescription painkillers to trade.

While she was waiting to meet a girl who was going to help her find some drugs, Amy took too many of the pills and passed out in the parking lot of a Cracker Barrel restaurant. Knowing there was no going home after that, she had decided she would kill herself. It was my fault that she felt so hopeless and alone.

When I woke up and found Amy's note, I packed little David into the car to go look for her. I found her sitting in the car, so I pushed her over to the passenger seat and drove back home. Amy doesn't remember much about that night, but she does remember our little boy crying, "Daddy, please, please, take Mama to the hospital." I wouldn't do it.

It probably sounds crazy, but ours is truly a love story, even though it's a twisted one. I know that if Amy hadn't stayed with me, I would be dead now. She prevented me from totally spiralling out of control. She tried her best to keep me grounded, but I still went off the deep end. Had she not been with me, it would have happened much sooner. I'm the happiest man in the world today because of her, and because of my amazing relationship with our kids. Ten years ago I could have never imagined that.

Say Uncle

In November of that same year I attacked one of my heroes, my uncle Larry. Amy and I had gotten into another fight, and she'd gone over to my mother's house to escape my anger. I went after her, doped to the hilt as usual. I tried to get her to accompany me home, but Larry stood in front of me, blocking the way. I tried to push past him, and when he grabbed hold of my arms I shoved him backward—hard. My aunt and my mom both thought I was going to hit him, so they called the police. Not wanting me to get into any trouble, Amy left with me.

We didn't go home right away; instead we drove around talking. When we got home, the yard was full of police cars and officers standing with guns drawn. The house was surrounded. I quickly turned around and drove to a little town about a mile from our house. I stopped at the store to get a drink, and when I walked out again, there were cops taking Amy out of our car. I ran back into the store, out the back door, and into the woods. After running for about a mile and a half, I was back at my mother's house. By the time I got there, I was coughing up blood. I found out later I had congestive heart failure from the methamphetamine. It felt like I was suffocating.

Within a few minutes thirteen squad cars arrived, some from Tennessee and others from Kentucky. They surrounded the house and arrested me. I didn't have a gun with me at the time, but I had a knife in my pocket that wasn't in a sheath, so I was arrested for carrying a concealed weapon and spent the next ten days in jail. If they had sent me back to prison, things would have turned out very differently.

Sold Out

My life was unraveling. I was addicted and sick, my marriage was a disaster, and my kids were scared of me. I remember seeing the fear in their eyes and thinking how much better off they would be if I were dead.

Several weeks after I got out of jail, I drove to Oklahoma to get some dope from my dad. By then my stepbrother Charlie was in prison. He was a meth cook and had been convicted of forgery and possession of a controlled substance. Dad asked me if I would go with him to visit Charlie one Saturday after I had just gotten to town.

At this point in the conversation my sister chimed in. "I guess Dad told you they've got a warrant for your arrest."

"No, he didn't mention that. He wants me to go down to the jail and visit Charlie." I wasn't aware there was a warrant on me for an unpaid fine. "Dad, why didn't you tell me they had a warrant?"

Dad's face turned red. "Well, they would have never checked your ID down there at the jail."

"What—are you completely insane?" I replied, incredulous. "They check everybody's ID when they go to visit somebody in jail. They just don't let you go in there!"

My relationship with my dad was already strained by that time. The only time we ever talked to each other was over a drug deal. He called me every so often to borrow money, but that was about it. We didn't even exchange birthday cards.

This deal with Charlie was the last straw as far as I was concerned. I truly believe my dad was trying to have me arrested so he could make some kind of deal and get Charlie out. Without his son, it was harder for Dad to get his dope; Charlie was the cook. Plus, I think he thought if he got me put in jail he could sleep with my wife. I'm sure that sounds unbelievable, but my dad was strange when it came to women; he didn't hold anything back. Over the years, he'd made completely inappropriate comments about how hot Amy was. The drugs had warped his mind and twisted him so far out of the norm that he would sleep with anybody who would have him; it didn't matter if it was his brother's wife or his son's wife. He didn't have boundaries—after all, he had asked me to sleep with his wife.

That's how it ended with me and my dad. I never saw him again.

Acting on Impulse

One particularly cold day in February, I started out in the early afternoon shooting pool at my friend Donny's house. Donny was a Vietnam veteran and really liked to smoke marijuana. It was a daily thing for me too, and I smoked even more after I'd been doing meth for a few days straight. I'd already been on a meth run for three days without a wink of sleep, so I was in rare form. I'd also started drinking again, even though I'd been on the wagon for ten years.

After several hours of partying, I started eating Klonopin, a potent anticonvulsant and muscle relaxant that is used to treat seizures and panic disorders. My psychiatrist had prescribed it several months earlier because I was fighting anxiety and depression from the meth.

I didn't want Amy to know I'd been using crank, and for some reason I thought taking the pills would help me come down. That's how crazy I was thinking—I hadn't been home all night, and she knew I'd been on meth for days, but in my psychotic state I thought if I took some pills, she wouldn't be mad at me. I'd totally lost touch with reality.

I don't know how many pills I took that night, but Donny later told me I was just pouring them into my palm and taking handfuls at a time. Normally I could take just one or two pills and sleep for hours, but this time they didn't cut through the powerful stimulant I was on.

At about midnight I left to give my dealer a ride home. Anne was a meth cook and supplied a lot of the drugs in the county. I generally had a very good memory when I took methamphetamine, but the combination of drugs had made me such a mess that I barely remember Anne getting out of my truck. I'm sure I spent some time doing more meth at her house. When I left her place just before daylight, I went back to Donny's to party for a couple more hours. Eventually I ran into my buddy Randy.

One of the worst side effects of methamphetamine is paranoia. I felt like people were out to get me all the time, so I started packing an SKS rifle everywhere I went. The SKS is a gas-powered, semiautomatic rifle that uses the same ammunition as the AK-47s that are being used to kill our soldiers in Iraq. They are so powerful that they can penetrate soft body armor. I'd lost more than fifty pounds and was too sick and weak to fight, so I kept the gun in my truck to protect myself. I'd actually shot at a person or two, including Anne's boyfriend.

The gun was important, but it wasn't nearly as crucial as the next high. Unfortunately, I'd run out of both money and drugs, and when my friend Randy started eying the rifle, I asked him if he wanted to buy it. The gun was actually registered in Amy's name, so about 9:00 AM he followed me home so she could sign a bill of sale.

Going home turned out to be a very bad idea. Amy knew I was blitzed out of my mind and she was clearly upset. When I asked her to sign the paper, she said there was no way she would sell her gun to a known drug user. If something happened it could come back to haunt her. I went out and told Randy the deal was off, and when I got back inside, I was ready to fight.

For the next couple of hours it was a nonstop confrontation.

Four of our six kids were home that day—ten-year-old Sarah was sick—she'd had a temperature of 104 degrees the day before—as were seven-year-old David, five-year-old Josiah, and our little Abigail, who was just a toddler.

Our out-of-control screaming and hollering really scared them. Over the years they had seen me hurt their mother many times; I'd put knives to her throat and shot bullets beside her head, threatening to kill her and myself. This time it didn't turn physical; I was too sick and weak to push Amy around. Crying, they pleaded with us to stop fighting and asked their mama to take them away.

Amy had quit using meth a few months earlier. The guilt over what our drug use was doing to the kids had built up over time and every time she got sober she felt horrible. They had seen and heard the most horrific things you can imagine. Sarah used to beg us to stop fighting just so she could go to sleep before it was time for school. Rebekah shook and had terrible stomachaches. Josiah barely spoke at all.

One day it just got to be too much for her and Amy drew a line in the sand and vowed to quit using meth and pot. She could no longer take the insanity of our lifestyle, the violence and the crazy highs and lows. To stay sober, she started going to church regularly and focused on her relationship with God and taking care of the children instead of doing drugs with me. Amy had tremendous support from the kids, her grandparents, and the other people in the church and she was able to stay clean. She quit cold turkey, and it was especially hard for her to kick the habit with me in the back room using all the time and hounding her to get high with me. I'm amazed she was so strong.

That morning I told my wife I hadn't been using meth, it was just pills and booze, but she didn't buy it. Instead, she dropped a bombshell. She'd had enough of my temper and the meth and was leaving—and taking the kids with her. Amy was determined to leave because she knew that every time I got high, I physically and verbally assaulted her for days at a time. She understood that was the price she had to pay to get high, but she was no longer willing to live with the pain and fear she saw in the eyes of our children.

I begged, bargained, and badgered, and somehow I convinced Amy to head to the back bedroom to get away from the kids and talk. I had to—I was so sick I couldn't stand up any longer.

The back bedroom was my "dope" room, the place in the house where I used and sold drugs. That was perhaps my only redeeming quality; I never did drugs in front of my kids. I had become so physically sick I put a mattress in there, got high, and slept alone much of the time. By the end I didn't get out of bed unless I needed to leave to get more meth—I rotted on the mattress for two or three days at a time, mesmerized by the music of counterculture bands from the '60s and early '70s.

When Amy and I headed to the back bedroom that morning, I brought the rifle along—I never went anywhere without it. I propped it up in the corner next to Amy's side of the bed where I could reach it, and asked her if she would lie down next to me and talk. She figured the tranquilizers I'd taken would eventually kick in and I'd fall asleep, which would allow her to sneak out of the house without an altercation. She had a good reason to be afraid—more than once I'd threatened to kill her if she ever left me.

But I didn't fall asleep, and rather than using common sense and lying like she should have done, Amy settled down next to me and told me that no matter what, she and the kids were out of there. When I heard that, something in me snapped. I realized with absolute clarity that meth had robbed me of everything: my health, my family, and my future. It was all over. I didn't even think about—in a split second I made the snap decision to blow my head off.

Remembering that I always kept a bullet in the chamber, I grabbed the SKS rifle, laid it on my stomach, kicked off the safety, and positioned the barrel under my chin. Amy screamed and reached for it, but before she could grab it, I pulled the trigger.

The initial blast felt like opening the screen door during a violent thunderstorm—the wind just sucked the breath right out of me. The bullet rocketed through the roof of my mouth, up my nose, and finally exited between my eyes. Deafened by the blast, I felt the whole front of my face blow apart.

As the impact catapulted me onto the carpet, I grabbed my face on both sides, trying to hold it together. The damage was extensive: every bone in my face was broken except for my left eye socket; the tip of my tongue was blown off and the rest was split in two; the roof of my mouth was completely disintegrated; and twenty of my teeth were missing. My whole body went into shock; my feet even throbbed because of the wound in my head.

When I pulled the trigger, I assumed there would be a big flash and my life would be over. I certainly never expected to wake up again. Believe it or not, methamphetamine is such a powerful stimulant that I never even lost consciousness. Vivid memories of my failed suicide attempt are still crystal clear.

After I hit the floor, Amy tried desperately to pull my hands away from my face to assess the damage. The next thing I heard was a sound I will never forget as long as I live—the horrified pitch of my children screaming. I'd never heard anything like it before—and I hope I never do again. They were primal, almost inhuman, howls from four innocent kids who were in a living nightmare.

Little David jumped up and down in a circle waving his hands and shouting, "Daddy's dead! Daddy's dead!"

I begged Amy not to let the children see me, but I was too late. The image of me lying on the bedroom floor in a puddle of blood is forever burned on their brains. Thank God, they didn't see my face. Blood was splattered everywhere—on the bed, the floor, the walls, and the ceiling, and Amy was dripping wet. Her hair was matted with my blood and tissue, and her right arm had tooth and bone fragments embedded in it that she had to dig out later. In shock, she didn't think I was hurt that bad. I knew I was dying.

The next thing I heard was my mother's voice. Mom lived about half a mile up the road from us, and the kids had called her earlier that morning, wanting her to come calm everything down like she had done so many times before. But it was too late—she arrived right after I pulled the trigger.

Standing over me in the pool of blood on the bedroom floor, she yelled, "Why did you do this?"

I told her the same thing I had told Amy, "I'm sorry, I don't know." I really didn't know why I'd done it. Amy was leaving with the kids, but all of a sudden that didn't seem like reason enough to kill myself.

It probably seems implausible that I could form words after sustaining such a devastating injury, but I actually spoke more clearly lying in a heap on the bedroom floor than I do now after more than thirty surgeries. The only way I can explain it is that I believe God gave me the ability to speak that day so I could tell the two women I love the most that I was sorry and to try and ease their shock and panic.

The last thing I remember saying was, "It hurts; it hurts so bad." There's just no way I can put into words the kind of agony I was experiencing. It was a red-hot, searing pain from the top of my head to the tips of my toes.

Amy raced to the phone and called 911, but she was too hysterical to speak coherently. My mother grabbed the phone and told them to send an ambulance. We lived on the state line between Tennessee and Kentucky, and authorities responded from both states. Surprisingly, rather than getting me ready for immediate transport to the hospital, the police busied themselves taking crime scene photos of me in different positions. The minute they saw me, they wrote me off for dead, thinking there was no way I could survive with such serious injuries. I couldn't understand why they seemed to be standing around waiting for me to die.

At least one of them tried to save my life. A paramedic named Richard Arnold got an oxygen tube down my throat when it swelled up so badly I couldn't breathe. It was impossible to tell where my airway was since everything was so messed up, but somehow he found a way and saved my life.

A call was then put in to have me airlifted to a trauma center in Nashville, but the weather was bad and the skies were overcast. The only helicopter pilot who could fly by instruments alone was already transferring someone else. The decision was made to take me to Parkway Regional Hospital, ten miles down the road in tiny Fulton, Kentucky, population 2,700.

The emergency room doctors at the little bitty rural facility took one look at me and knew they weren't equipped to handle injuries so severe. If I was to have any chance at survival, they had to get me to Vanderbilt University Medical Center in Nashville where they had more experience with gunshot wounds.

When doctors told Amy they were going to transport me by ambulance two and a half hours to the city, Amy said, "What do you mean?" She had no idea I was hurt so badly. "But he was just talking to me."

The doctors were stunned by her statement; they assumed it was a medical impossibility for me talk without any semblance of a mouth and told both Amy and the police so. How could a guy talk without his tongue and the roof of his mouth intact? Yet the police and my family said I talked plainer that day lying on that floor than I do right now. It took me more than two months to learn how to talk again so people could understand me.

Amy never saw my gaping face. At the first hospital they bandaged me with six-inch-thick gauze, so all she could see was the tube sticking out of the middle that allowed air in and out. She didn't actually see the damage until my face was all sewn up in Nashville.

It's a miracle I was coherent the entire time—from the shooting itself right through my time at that first little hospital. For example, when Amy told me they were going to send me to Nashville, I raised my arm indicating that I understood. Fortunately, I don't recall any of what happened there. I was in so much pain that my brain must have dealt with the trauma by shutting down certain functions. I'm glad I don't remember all of it, but I'm also glad that I didn't black out entirely. Otherwise, I wouldn't be able to share the most miraculous story of all.

I began this book with the story of my incredible near-death experience, because that is the day my life, and my eternity, changed forever.

When I flatlined in the ambulance on the way to the hospital, I knew instantly that I was dead. The events that transpired next proved to me that both God and His enemy are real. Hell is a real place, not some twilight zone conjured up by the church to scare people into believing in God. I am totally convinced that God allowed me to visit hell so I would know what my eternity would be if I didn't change my ways. And believe me, I will do whatever I can to keep myself, and everybody else I come in contact with, from winding up there. It's that bad. Not even my worst enemies deserved to be there.

I can't explain the anguish I felt when I realized I was in hell . . . it is truly beyond description. How do you describe an oppressive black void that instantly sucks the joy right out of your soul? How do you explain the fear that comes from knowing you will spend forever with demons in a place filled with despair? How do you explain a place that is far worse than your worst nightmare? The terror was palpable and unforgiving.

Even though there were people with me in the darkness, I felt utterly alone. In that moment I realized I had made a mistake that was irreversible and for the rest of time I would be separated from God and the people I loved. I couldn't bear the thought of being without my wife, Amy. So when I woke up in the hospital three days later, I was overwhelmed with gratitude for getting a chance to be a better man.

THIRTEEN

Over the Rainbow

The soul would have no rainbow
had the eyes no tears.

— John Vance Cheney

THEY CALL ME THE MIRACLE MAN at Vanderbilt University Medical Center. From a purely medical standpoint, there's no way I should have survived a gunshot to the head with an assault rifle. The first surgeon who cared for me in the trauma unit told a local television station I was the luckiest man he had ever seen. It wasn't a fluke that I was unsuccessful at my suicide attempt; I know I was saved for a reason. There was a message to be told.

221

Waking Up on the Other Side

The ambulance ride from Fulton, Kentucky, to Nashville was touch and go. When hospital personnel met us at the emergency room entrance, the paramedic was ventilating me to keep me breathing. It took more than an hour for the doctor and his team to stabilize me; every time my vitals plummeted, the angels at Vanderbilt did something heroic to keep me alive.

As soon as I was out of immediate danger, I was wheeled into the operating room for a lengthy surgery to debride (remove dead and damaged tissue) and close my face to prevent me from bleeding to death. At the same time, they did a tracheotomy so I could breathe, and inserted a catheter called a "subclavian line" into a large vein in my neck to administer medications and fluids. After I had been in the recovery room for an hour, they roused me to make sure I came out of the anesthesia. I couldn't talk, so they gave me a black marker and a notebook in case I needed anything.

I don't remember any of that. In fact, my first three days in the hospital are a complete blank. When I finally came to my senses, I was terribly disoriented. I was struck hard by what I had done. Why did I shoot myself? I had a beautiful wife, six wonderful kids, and a good job. I recalled in vivid detail the horror I had experienced in hell and lay in terror.

The trauma unit at Vanderbilt was a big room filled with severely injured people, many of whom were on their deathbeds. Each of the eight "treatment booths" in the big circle were separated by curtains. There were no family members present—all I could see were the injured and the machines keeping them alive. As I lay alone in agony, I knew Amy and the kids were gone. My last memory was of her saying she was leaving me.

My right eye was so swollen and full of blood that I couldn't see past the foot of my bed. It wasn't until she was bending right over me that I recognized my wife. My God! She hadn't left me! Amy smiled, told me she loved me, and said I was going to live. She didn't tell me then, but the doctors had said I had come very close to dying.

What she said next was music to my ears. Amy had purchased a test in the hospital pharmacy and had just found out she was pregnant with our seventh child. I couldn't smile, but she knew I was thrilled with the news. I believed with all my heart that our baby was going to have a better start than had the rest of our kids. My doping days were over.

My ability to speak was eliminated due to my injuries. Flustered, I tried to tell Amy about my near-death experience, but couldn't.

That's when Amy pulled out the notebook I had written on when I first came out of surgery. Doctors had advised her against showing it to me because they were worried I would be upset. But Amy knew me, and she knew that the words on the pages of that blue-lined tablet wouldn't upset me, but be inspirational.

When I paged through it, I got a chill down my spine. On the first page I had scrawled, "JESUS LOVES YOU ALL" in big, black letters. On another page I wrote that I had died and gone to hell and that the devil was trying to get me. One page contained the names of Peter and Paul, two of Jesus's apostles, and an upside-down cross.

For a guy who was raised in the church that might not seem out of the ordinary, but to me it was striking. I'd been carried into that ambulance in absolute rebellion against God. Several months earlier I had drawn a line in the sand when I threw my Bible, the one I'd been given after my baptism, into a roaring fire. To me,

God was dead. I had convinced myself that there was no after-life. When you were dead, you were just dead. No heaven, no hell, just nothing. I steadfastly refused to believe what I had been taught my whole life; it was all just a bunch of brainwashing. I didn't want anything to do with God. My visits to heaven and hell changed all that.

There were some other fascinating things scribbled in that notebook. I didn't understand all of it, but the page that said, "E. V. Hill" was the most mysterious. I assumed it was somebody's name, but I didn't know anybody named E. V. Hill. Amy reminded me that I did, in fact, know who he was.

Dr. E. V. Hill was the pastor of Mount Zion Baptist Church, in Los Angeles, California. One morning years earlier, while Amy was watching him preach on television, I walked into the room and cussed at him. "He's a fake! Why do you listen to this garbage?" I didn't think there was room for a con artist like that on national television.

A couple of weeks after the shooting, I learned that E. V. Hill had died three days after I'd shot myself, the same day I came back to my senses. Why had I written down his name? Why had I jotted down "Peter" and "Paul"? Had I met them all in heaven? The whole thing boggled my mind.

I had so many unanswered questions, but I knew one thing for certain: in a matter of thirteen hours I had been completely transformed. Instead of being consumed by anger toward God and blaming Him for everything bad that had happened to me, my heart was actually filled with joy. Without a doubt, I knew that as soon as a man's heart stops, he goes to one of two places—one is evil and the other is full of peace and love. I never wanted to go back to the demonic abyss I'd seen; it was utterly terrifying.

Nightmares and Delusions

The best word I can use to describe my first week in the hospital is disorienting. It's like being in another world. A different language is spoken, and the sounds, smells, and tastes are different. The first time the nurse came into my room to give me a bath, I didn't know who she was or what she was doing to me. It freaked me out.

I suffered from what is called "intensive-care unit psychosis." It is a form of delirium post-op patients often experience, particularly those who are under general anesthesia for extended periods. Anxiety, paranoia, and hallucinations agitate patients, often causing them to become violent. Being in the ICU is disorienting; lying in bed hooked up to countless machines, I had no concept of day or night. The lights were always on, there were no windows, and there was the constant hum of life-support machines in the background.

On the third day of my hospitalization, I decided it was time to escape my confines. I noticed a window in the corner of the room and thought if I could just bust it open I could go home. Of course, I didn't realize I was on the tenth floor and that there were no windows. I could have sworn I saw one.

I was in a morphine fog. Every time the pain got to be too much to bear, I pushed a button and a pump delivered a small dose to my IV. It left me numb, and the worst of the pain abated. The morphine drip continued for four days before they decided to cut me off. I flipped, tearing out my catheter and thrashing about until several male nurses were able to restrain me. In the process, one of them bent my thumb back so hard his colleague got on him about being too rough. In the back of my mind I heard him say something like, "I know how these people are; he is one of those whackos who get off on pain."

They ended up giving me a shot of Haldol to subdue me and then tied me to my bed. Hours later when Amy came in, I was sitting in a rocking chair unfettered, once again calm and happy. I was doped up on the tranquilizer.

The medical staff thought I was insane because I wrote the same things over and over in my notebook. Sometimes they would come into my room just to flip through the pages; occasionally they asked me about what was there, but most of them thought I had simply lost my mind. I heard more than one tell Amy I might not ever be right again.

I had horrifying nightmares about the devil that I found both disturbing and curious. It was like the devil was chasing and tormenting me. In one of the most memorable dreams, my head was completely bandaged up. When the nurses took them off, there was absolutely nothing wrong with me—it was like my face was healed and I was perfectly normal again.

A dark-headed young girl kept running up to me, smiling and laughing as she said, "He's almost ready! He's almost ready! It's almost time!" Then she ran off for a minute and came back again, always saying the same thing. The scene repeated several times until I looked up and saw a body suspended in midair, wrapped in a white burial cloth from head to toe, almost like it was mummified or in a cocoon. I got the feeling it was a man. His hands and feet were spread wide, tied to what, I'm not sure, but the positioning made it look like he was tied to a cross.

Suddenly, it dawned on me who that little girl was talking about—Satan was the one being suspended. He was preparing to be born. She was saying that he's almost ready, it's almost time for Satan to be unveiled and set loose, his power revealed. Helpless, I couldn't do anything but watch.

My paranoia was out of control. I felt like the doctors and nurses were Satan's messengers and were out to get me. They wanted to kill Amy too; the male nurses wanted to take her away and murder her. Once when she came to visit me I wrote down in the notebook that I wanted her to go home and leave me alone. She started crying; she didn't understand that I was just trying to protect her. She even skipped one of the visits so I wouldn't get upset.

I also told Amy to "turn me off." She thought that meant I wanted her to remove me from all life support, but that wasn't it at all. I'd been hallucinating that I was on a TV show called *The Gunslinging Bambinos*. I wanted Amy to go home and turn off the TV—I felt like I was trapped inside.

There was a lot of commotion in ICU, but in my muddled brain, I couldn't always understand what was happening. There was a gunshot victim in the bed next to mine. I found out later he had been shot in the stomach and part of his intestines had been removed. One day he was having a bath, but I thought there was a party going on. I heard splashing and what I thought was the whoosh of beer cans opening. I couldn't believe they were getting drunk next to me in the hospital!

Being in the hospital was surreal—I really have no idea how long my dementia lasted, but my wife says it was three or four days. When I came back to my senses, I felt a tremendous sense of peace because I knew God had saved me.

Mirror Image

I remember the first time I saw my face really well. About a week after the shooting, I started coming back to my senses. By that time I had been moved out of the triage unit to a room of my own in a rehabilitation center a block away. I kept hearing everybody talk over me about how I looked, and I wanted to see the damage for myself. Still unable to speak, I wrote a note asking for a mirror. Nobody would bring one, not even Amy, because they thought I wasn't ready to handle what I would see.

I had finally gotten strong enough to sit up. One night, as I sat up on the edge of my bed, I turned to the right and noticed there was a window directly behind me. What I saw in its reflection was unimaginable. It was like looking at a monster.

I'll never forget that horrifying sight for as long as I live. I had no nose, almost no mouth, and hundreds of stitches from my forehead all the way down to underneath my chin. I had needles and different things attached to me from the tips of my toes to the top of my head. There was a tracheotomy tube inserted into my throat so I could breathe, and the doctors had sewn two thick green tubes into the spots where my nostrils should have been to keep my nasal cavities open—I could see them sticking out of my face. It would be a year before I could breathe through my nose or experience the sensation of taste. I had blown off 70 percent of my lips, so there was no mouth to touch. I was heartbroken. I sat alone in my hospital bed and sobbed.

In fact, I cried much of the time I was in the hospital, my emotions raw. My doctors thought I was depressed and upset that I had been unsuccessful at killing myself, but it was just the opposite—most of the time I cried because I was happy to be alive and knew I had been given a second chance.

The first time I was helped out of bed so I could stretch my legs, Amy was on one side of me and the nurse on the other. As we walked in a circle, I bawled uncontrollably, tears rolling down my face in streams. All of my emotions came flooding out, both positive and negative. My eyes had been opened to what I'd done to my wife and kids, but from the moment I woke up in that hospital, I was grateful I hadn't died. Most people who attempt suicide don't really want to die; they are just eaten up by despair and want it to end. I had made it out of the pit and was thrilled to be alive. That's why I was crying; I wasn't suicidal at all.

Growing Pains

Don't get me wrong, there were many, many bleak times. My recovery was excruciating, especially when I was taken off the morphine. The only way I was able to make it through the day was by reminding myself that I had been given a second chance. Any pain, any hardship was better than going back to that dark place.

At times it was hard to keep up my spirits. Time creeps by when you are bedridden; I felt too horrible to watch television and reading was out of the question. The only break in the day was when the nurses came to attend me, and they were usually not welcome breaks. I couldn't even look forward to meals.

I remember the first time I had a bath. When they poured water on my head I started shivering and shaking, causing me to hurt all over. If I lay still, I didn't hurt, but every time I moved or they started fooling around with me, the pain came on like a tidal wave. Having my mouth cleaned was the worst. The nurse used a stick with a green sponge on the end that had been soaked in peroxide. She swished it around my mouth—or what used to be my mouth. The right side was particularly painful because the few teeth I had left were sore and loose. The girl who did it was very rough, almost like she was trying to punish me, and I hated seeing her come through the door.

Still, nothing came close to the pain I experienced lying on my bedroom floor the day I blew my face off. It was indescribable. I have no idea how I lived through it. I never want to forget that pain, because it is part of my recovery. I did it to myself—I made the decision to put poison into my body for decades.

Other than my family, I didn't have many visitors. You don't really have friends when you're in the world of methamphetamine; you have drug associates. I knew literally hundreds of people—I sold drugs to them and got high with them—but not one visited me the whole time I was in the hospital. Not one person called and said, "How ya doing?" or "We're glad you lived." Not even my own father. Dad knew I'd shot myself, yet he never bothered to pick up the phone. That hurt me; I can't imagine my son getting hurt like that and then not even calling him. Later, after I did a lot of self examination, I came to understand that my dad's addiction was a severe illness. I saw tremendous potential in him, but it never came to pass because he was high or drunk all of my life. If he had been sober, he would have probably been a very different person and we would have probably had a very different relationship.

Building a New Face

The blast totally obliterated my face. Other than my left eye socket, every bone was broken. My nose was gone and most of my mouth was completely pulverized. All of my front teeth had been blown out; to this day I only have twelve teeth, which makes chewing very difficult.

Once the doctors knew I was going to live, it was time to start the rebuilding process. When I first arrived at the hospital, surgeons closed up my face, but didn't fix anything. Everything in my face was shattered and scattered; bone fragments floating under the skin.

The first major surgery took place six days after my injury. The maxillofacial surgical team opened my face back up and fashioned a network of pins and plates to put my sinuses and other bones back together. Altogether, I have more than thirty titanium plates and screws holding my sinuses in and my face together.

An external fixator, a piece of equipment designed to hold fractured bone in place during the healing process, was placed on my face using pins through my skin and attached to my jawbone; it looked like a torture device. The procedure was difficult because my bones were so shattered that there were no "landmarks" to go by. Bone and bullet fragments, teeth, and dental work were also removed from the soft tissue inside my face. Finally, the surgeon replaced the stomach tube that had been inserted earlier with a more permanent one. This complex surgery took nearly thirteen hours.

The second large-scale operation didn't take place for six months. In it, the first of several bone grafts were done. I've had five bone grafts, a surgical procedure that replaces missing bone from other material in the body. Bone grafting is usually done to make repairs that are very complex. Cartilage was taken out of my rib and my ear, and two bone grafts came from each hip. During those grueling procedures, a bone doctor and a plastic surgeon worked in shifts.

A new top palate was formed in my mouth and bone was put into my chin where it was missing. They also built a nose for me from scratch and re-formed my lips.

Although it has been difficult to come up with an accurate count, it is safe to say I have had at least thirty surgeries since I blew my face apart. In a split-second, impulsive decision, I had done horrendous damage. Most of the medical expenses incurred during the first year were covered by my company-provided health insurance. After that, I was on my own. We'll be paying off that debt for the rest of our lives.

Home Again

After a week in the trauma center and three weeks on a rehabilitation ward, it was time for a change of scenery. Doctors tried to get me into a lockdown psychiatric ward because of the suicide attempt, but they couldn't find one that would take me with such severe injuries. Instead, they sent me home and ordered me to go to an outpatient treatment facility for six weeks.

I was eager to see my kids. We'd kept them out of the hospital intentionally because we didn't want them to see me all messed up. The first thing Amy and I did when we left the hospital parking lot was to go to my sister's house where the kids had been staying. They were grocery shopping, and rather than waiting for them to return, we headed to the store to look for them.

We found them sitting in the car in the Walmart parking lot with their cousins. Not thinking, I got out of the car, walked up to their window, and knocked. My niece freaked out and screamed; the rest of them had blank looks on their faces, staring at the spectacle before them. They showed no emotion—no smiling, no frowning—just shock. Nobody recognized me until I spoke.

It broke my heart to realize I was a total stranger to my own kids. Who could blame them for not knowing me at first? I looked completely different from the father they had seen a month earlier with his bloody face hanging on the floor. I had stitches all over, tubes stuck in my nose, and a tracheotomy.

It took a long time for us to get to know each other. I was a completely different man, and they weren't sure how to react at first. On the inside, I had been transformed from a drug addict to the man I had been before I ever discovered methamphetamine. For the first time in years I felt like myself again. But the kids remembered their daddy as a mean drug addict. Rebuilding trust and making them feel safe again was a long, gradual process.

I remember my two oldest, Sarah and David, sitting on the couch watching TV one day about six months after the shooting. They were acting weird—I couldn't put my finger on it exactly, but I could sense something was wrong.

"What's going on with you guys?"

"Nothing."

"You think I'm going to use drugs again, don't you?"

In perfect synchronization they replied, "Yeah."

"I don't blame you for not believing me. I've lied to you a thousand times and said I wasn't going to do it anymore. The only thing I can do now is show you. After a while you'll realize I'm serious about staying sober."

It was about a year before I could ask that same question and they would say, "No, Daddy is never going to use drugs again." I am so grateful I now have a great relationship with all of my kids and they trust me completely. We are a healed family, and I truly believe God is responsible for that.

Believe me, it wasn't always easy staying clean. The outpatient treatment facility I was referred to when I was discharged from the hospital wasn't equipped for the likes of me. Bless their hearts, there were good people working there, but most of their patients suffered from depression and/or had been sexually molested; I was the one meth addict in the place, and they didn't know what to do with me. At lunchtime the other patients took their sack lunches to the cafeteria. I stayed in the classroom with the teacher and injected a can of Ensure into my stomach tube. I just didn't blend in with the other students.

They really had no idea what was going on in my mind because I could hardly talk. How can you counsel a guy if he can't share his heart? I was supposed to go there every day for six weeks, but after just three, they said they didn't think there was anything wrong with me and signed my release papers. I was a hard-core meth head, and I never had a minute of drug treatment. I really should have been locked up for a while for mental evaluation.

From the jaded viewpoint of an addict, I hit the medicinal jackpot after the shooting. I took Lexapro and Depakote for depression. Lortab, Darvocet, and Percocet were for pain. Risperdal was to keep me from having "drug dreams"; a lot of addicts are plagued with dreams about using when they try to quit. Zantac, which is often used to treat ulcers caused by excess stomach acid, was prescribed because I spent so much time lying down. I also took arthritis medication because of all the bone surgeries.

My cravings for meth were virtually gone, but I had a terrible time with pain medication. After each of my major surgeries, doctors gave me liquid Lortab in a stomach tube to manage the terrible pain. Due to my addictive nature, they all knew it would be no picnic weaning me off. Sure enough, when they pulled me off of it, I thought I was dying. I was put on Suboxone to manage my withdrawal and get me over the hump. Even today when I have surgery, doctors give me just enough painkillers to get me through—not one pill more. Sometimes I'll go through days of agony without taking one because I am afraid of relapse.

Daily Life

The business of living completely changed when I got home from the hospital. At first I required constant care and assistance with everything from eating to bathing. As time went on, of course, I learned how to do more things for myself, but in the beginning, poor Amy ran ragged.

I slept in a hospital bed in our bedroom for the first six months because we were worried one of the kids would hurt me in the regular bed; I couldn't handle jostling of any kind. An adjustable bed was also more convenient for feedings. I needed to be propped up in order for the liquid nutrition to be pumped into the feeding tube in my stomach. We hung the bag from the hook on the hospital bed.

I had to be extremely careful around water. Once I was strong enough to stand up, I was able to shower, but it was critical that water didn't run into my tracheotomy. If it did, I would literally drown. Doctors gave me a little cap to place over the opening, but when I used it, I couldn't breathe very well. Instead, I tried to remember to put my finger over the hole.

One of the biggest adjustments to being home was learning how to eat again. I'd blown off nearly 70 percent of my lips, so the surgeons had to create a new smaller opening to serve as a mouth. For a couple of months I used a product like Ensure that was injected directly into my stomach tube. Then I started lique-fying real food in a blender and injecting that. It was nearly six months before I was able to supplement my liquid diet with spoon-fed baby food.

My hand-eye coordination was so bad I usually hit the side of my face with the spoon. I was forced to prop a mirror against a soda bottle on the kitchen table and feed myself while looking into it. Otherwise, there was no way I could find the hole. It seems crazy, because eating is such a natural thing. You don't even think about the process of feeding yourself; the spoon just goes directly to your mouth without you even thinking about it. I had to really concentrate.

Learning to Love Again

An old English idiom reads, "Absence makes the heart grow fonder." Given my own experience, I'm not sure I always believe that. Sometimes being away from the one you love just makes the two of you uncomfortable with each other.

During the end of my meth use, Amy would have loved to have seen me knocked down a few notches. I had been so cruel and demeaning to her that she wanted to have the upper hand for a change and give me hell. But after I was hurt, she softened and focused on helping me.

She mixed my medication several times a day, cleaned my wounds, and coordinated feedings. That by itself was time-consuming, but when you add in caring for six children between the ages of one and ten and managing the side effects of early pregnancy, you can only imagine her stress level. My poor wife was absolutely exhausted.

As mentioned earlier, the day I regained my senses in the hospital after the shooting, Amy came to me with wonderful news. She was pregnant with our seventh child. To me, that was a powerful sign of hope. When we found out it was a boy, I told Amy I wanted to name him Gabriel after the messenger angel, because he was definitely a message from heaven for me.

It was a difficult pregnancy. Gabriel was in distress several times and doctors fully expected Amy to miscarry. At thirty-two weeks she was put on full bed rest, a very tough order for Amy. She was busy caring for me and our six kids, so in her mind there was no time for lounging around. Still, she did her best to comply and get much-needed rest. Our families were wonderful, it seemed like somebody was always there to cook meals or help with the kids. Gabriel was born completely healthy three weeks early by C-section. He is our miracle baby.

I cried when all of our kids were born, but Gabriel's birth was special because I was sober on his birthday. It was the first time I wasn't high on something, which makes me feel terribly guilty about my other kids' births. All of our kids deserved a good father from the very beginning, and they didn't get one.

My post-shooting relationship with Amy went back and forth. One day—or hour—we would be getting along fine, happy to be together, and the next we would be fighting. At one point Amy told me she would only stay with me until I got better, and then she was leaving for good. Neither of us thought there was much long-term hope for our relationship; there was just too much water under the bridge. After all, we were both recovering meth addicts and had been through a great deal of trauma—Amy from all the violence and me from the shooting. It's a huge adjustment for anyone to get off drugs and learn to live sober, even without a huge family and a life-threatening injury with which to contend.

Our kids got to see us at our worst: a mother who was neglect-ful and depressed and a father who was a junkie and did mon-strous things, but they also got to see us recover and learn to love each other again. We learned to love each other by following the examples we read in the Bible about unconditional love. After years of abuse and horror, she came to see me as more than a drug addict. I was a new creation. I came to see her as a saint because she had stuck with me despite my destructive behavior. We are living proof that joy can come after the pain

Therefore, if anyone is in Christ, he is a new creation;
old things have passed away; behold,
all things have become new.

(2 Corinthians 5:17, NKJV)

FOURTEEN

The Man in the Mirror

We need to learn to set our course by the stars,
not by the lights of every passing ship.

— Omar Nelson Bradley

REGRET IS A TERRIBLE THING—left untended it festers and robs you of your joy. Believe me, I've relived some of my bad choices a thousand times, and probably will continue to do so until the day I die. I wish with all my heart that I could erase the hurt and pain I have caused other people—family, friends, and even strangers—but I can't, because there is no going back. The best I can do is live my life going forward as a reflection of the man I have become. The old one is dead and buried. No matter what you've done or how bad things are now, you can always start fresh. I am living proof of that. You have the ability to change your future to a brighter one, but it takes commitment and self-discipline.

A Sad Ending

Harriet Beecher Stowe, the author of *Uncle Tom's Cabin*, once wrote, "The bitterest tears shed over graves are for words left unsaid and deeds left undone." That's how I feel about my dad. David Parnell Sr. was a troubled man and a drug addict. He introduced all of his children to the world of drugs. A number of us have become addicts, and more than one has gone to prison—not the kind of legacy most fathers would want to pass down.

My dad died on May 30, 2009. He never quit using drugs, and it killed him. He had cirrhosis of the liver from meth and hepatitis C from sharing needles with other junkies. My family encouraged him to go to treatment many times, but he wouldn't—or more likely couldn't—stop. He was really screwed up because of meth.

Dad died alone in a filthy, beat-up old camper, like the prodigal son who went to live in a pigpen. Unfortunately, my father never realized the error of his ways like the prodigal son did. He died a slow, agonizing death. At the time of his passing, I hadn't talked to my dad in more than five years, since before I'd shot myself. I feel guilty about that now. I intentionally cut off contact with him so I could stay clean; I knew if I spent any time with him that I would most likely go back to using. It had always been that way between him and me; we were little more than party buddies. Sadly, even though he was married five times, he had no wife with him when he passed away.

After my transformation I wished I had tried harder to turn him around, but at the time I was angry and bitter. He was never much of a father to me; in fact, he was just the opposite. He set me on a very dangerous path, a life filled with violence and addiction, although I realize I am ultimately responsible for staying on that path. One of my biggest regrets is that it took me so long to forgive my father for what he did to me, and it ate me up inside for a long time. The two of us missed out on a lot. We could have had a relationship like I now have with my children. A relationship like that, however, is a two-way street. In the end, my dad chose drugs over me.

It hit me hard when Dad died, which surprised a lot of people. Although I had hard feelings toward him for the things he'd done (and hadn't done) over the years, we were buddies for a long time, and I loved my dad. After my own experience in hell, I didn't want him to go there. I remember weeping and praying hard, begging God not to send him to that dark, terrible place. I didn't want him to be one of the screaming voices I had heard that day. I don't care how bad he was; I was actually far worse. Grandma Parnell told me at the funeral that Dad had made his peace with God. That was a comforting thought.

Paying the Price

My story is miraculous in so many ways. I suffered no permanent brain damage as a result of my drug abuse or my gruesome suicide attempt. When I was hospitalized in Nashville, numerous CAT scans, MRIs, and PET scans were performed, and doctors could find nothing wrong with my brain. The swelling and trauma it endured when that massive bullet passed through my face should have damaged me beyond repair.

My seven-year love affair with methamphetamine should have

caused significant brain damage too. The parts of the brain that are impaired with methamphetamine use are the same ones that are associated with violent sociopaths, those who commit mindless violent crimes with no sense of remorse. Take a look at the horrific incidents of child abuse detailed in Appendix A at the end of this book. Meth addicts often turn into monsters who torture and murder their own children.

The brain damage caused by methamphetamine is devastating. Some of it is permanent; approximately 30 percent of recovered users are seriously disabled for their rest of their lives, unable to attend to personal hygiene or function in even the most menial jobs. Many of these burned-out addicts are in prison, mental institutions, or living homeless on the streets.

Medical professionals can't explain my amazing recovery. In fact, I haven't just been restored to the man I was before I started abusing methamphetamine, I am a new and improved David Parnell.

I kicked all of my addictions with the help of a number of godly people and my own deep faith. Healing can occur both physically and spiritually. The Bible is filled with examples of God's miraculous healings. He also heals us through the intervention of others, like medical and religious communities or trusted friends. James, Jesus' half brother and a leader in the Jerusalem church, writes this in James 5:13–16 (NKJV):

> Is anyone among you suffering? Let him pray. Is anyone cheerful? Let him sing psalms. Is anyone among you sick? Let him call for the elders of the church, and let them pray over him, anointing him with oil in the name of the Lord. And the prayer of faith will save the sick, and the Lord will raise him up. And if he has committed sins, he will be forgiven.

*Confess your trespasses to one another, and pray for one another, that
you may be healed. The effective, fervent prayer of a righteous man
avails much.*

When I woke up in the hospital after my near-death experience, I recommitted my life to Christ. The Lord put it on my
heart that He wanted me to share my story, and I want to do
what He wants me to do so that I might find favor and never
have to go back to that dark place again. I didn't have psycho-
therapy; I relied, instead, on the Great Physician:

*I waited patiently for the LORD;
And He inclined to me,
And heard my cry.
He also brought me up out of a horrible pit,
Out of the miry clay,
And set my feet upon a rock,
And established my steps.
He has put a new song in my mouth—
Praise to our God;
Many will see it and fear,
And will trust in the LORD.*

Psalm 40:1–3 (NKJV)

It's amazing what God has done. He saved me from the horrible pit and put a new song in my mouth. He has blessed me over
and over, and I will never stop singing His praises.

While I feel blessed in many ways, I've also felt cursed at times
by the things I've done. I have to walk around for the rest of my

life with a mark of disfigurement and tolerate people staring at me. I'll always look different.

Seven years later, I am still filled with regret every time I look in the mirror. That nice-looking high-school athlete is now just a distant memory found in old, faded snapshots. I have no feeling in my lips, so for the rest of my life I won't be able to feel the sensation of my wife's lips against mine when I kiss her. That's something I really miss. In fact, if my lips are touched with a hot spoon, I feel the sensation up near my eye because the nerves are all messed up. Doctors told me this is a common occurrence, similar to the phantom feelings an amputee has after an arm or leg is removed.

I don't have much feeling in my nose either. One day, I accidentally burned the tip of my nose and I didn't even know it until I smelled burning flesh. If I shut my eyes I don't know somebody is touching my nose at all unless they apply quite a bit of pressure. That's not surprising, I guess—after all, I blew the whole thing off and doctors had to build a new one from scratch. It's hard and inflexible, but I know the doctors did the best with what they had to work with. I'm thankful to have a nose at all. Oddly enough, my senses of smell and taste are better now than they have ever been.

One of my dreams is to be able to afford dental implants. The force of the blast blew out nearly all of my teeth; I only have a few on the top and bottom, and they are bent in and out. I can only chew on my left side, and it is more like gumming than chewing. My dentist used to have a very difficult time cleaning those few teeth because my mouth was so small and the corners would literally rip. Since then doctors have widened the opening and it's no longer a problem.

Having a mouthful of teeth will have a huge impact on my appearance because it will push my mouth out and make it a little curved like a normal person's. Right now, it sinks in like I am a very old man. Unfortunately, dental implants would cost me nearly twelve thousand dollars, and without insurance it will be a long time before that happens.

Beauty Is Only Skin-deep

All these years later I still cry about my circumstances at times. It doesn't help me on an emotional level that people constantly stare at me. When I go to a school, it's the little guys, kindergarten and first grade, who are the most mesmerized by the way I look. If I have lunch in the cafeteria, they can hardly eat because they are so busy turning around and staring at me.

Kids can be remarkably blunt. "Why is your nose so big?" Red-faced and horrified, their parents tell them to shut up when their children blurt out something like that, but I just laugh and tell them it is okay. I tell the kids I got shot in the face and doctors had to build me a new nose using the skin from my forehead. They are fascinated.

Unfortunately, it's not just the kids that gawk. The place I hate going most is the airport—people stare at me from the minute I walk into the terminal until I get on the plane. People simply treat me different wherever I go, even in church. We went to a new church a few months ago just to try it out, and when we walked in, there was a line at the front door about twenty people long waiting to shake hands with the greeter. I watched him smile and laugh as he shook hands with the visitors. When it was my turn, he looked up and saw me and his smile suddenly disappeared. The change in his expression was shocking. He simply stuck his hand out uncomfortably and turned his attention to the next person in line.

I know they don't mean anything by it, but people feel like they can ask me anything. I might be at a gas station and the guy behind the counter will say, "I've got to ask you this. What happened to your face? I know you would rather somebody ask you than just stare at you." I try not to let on that it bothers me, mostly because I don't want to give them the satisfaction of making me feel uncomfortable. I would never be that forward. I see people all the time who are disfigured or handicapped, and I don't say, "Man, how did you get in that wheelchair? Have you always been a cripple?"

To be brutally honest, I often feel like the Elephant Man. Standing in front of audiences of hundreds or thousands of people, there are times I feel like I'm in a freak show. To heighten the drama of my appearance, administrators at the schools where I speak often want me to stay behind the curtains until I am introduced so the kids will be shocked when I come out. I'm okay with that; I want to shock the kids. I want them to see what drug addiction could do to them.

Although they are initially pretty freaked out, almost every time the program is over, the students are smiling and laughing. They come up to me and thank me for sharing my story. Sometimes there will be dozens of kids surrounding me, shaking my hands and asking to have their pictures taken with me. Yes, people are shocked when they first see me, but when I share my heart, they look past my appearance.

If I didn't have a permanent reminder of what I did to myself, my story wouldn't have nearly the same impact. People may not always remember the details of my story, but for years they will remember the way my face was mutilated.

I'll always look like this, but I like myself better now. I would rather be around a bum with a good heart who lived on the streets than a man with a thousand-dollar suit on and an evil heart. I may be disfigured, but I'm such a different man in my heart that most people who meet me and get to know me would much rather be around me disfigured than the way I used to be. My kids often tell me they like the way I look now; before I shot myself I looked mean and ugly to them, like a monster. Now they see me as beautiful on the inside. Now they see me as Daddy.

Paying the Piper

Financially, the shooting has been devastating to my family. The only way we were able to make it during that first year was through the kindness of others. We had a lot of help from my mother and Amy's grandparents, and people from the church brought us food. A month after I got out of the hospital, our vehicle was repossessed. We didn't have a car to drive for a long time. If we had been living in a big city, public transportation would have been an option, but we lived out in the middle of the country and it was very difficult to get around. We were lucky my mother let us continue living in the house she owns, or we would have been homeless.

The total bill for my suicide attempt was mind-boggling. The first week alone cost more than $100,000. My medical insurance covered 90 percent of it, but the rest was my responsibility. I was technically on the payroll at General Tire for nearly a year after the shooting, but after that they were able to fire me for not being able to work. We were forced to go on public assistance, including Medicare and food stamps.

Taking handouts was hard on my pride; I'd been working steadily since I was only about thirteen years old. No matter how messed up I was on drugs, I always held down a job. We had seven growing kids, so we went to thrift stores and yard sales to buy their clothes. We couldn't even afford food; I often went without so the children could eat.

We still don't have much money, but we never go hungry, and I am grateful for that. We've come pretty far from the bottom. We're still paying off our medical debt; sometimes we can manage only twenty dollars a month, but we always do our best to send in something. I hope I live to a ripe old age so I can clean the slate and my kids aren't left with the financial burden of my mistake.

I understand some people believe their tax dollars shouldn't have gone to take care of a suicidal drug addict like me, and I regret that anybody would have to pay for something I did. I've been a taxpayer for more than a quarter of a century, and it doesn't bother me to pay for a mother's food stamps or a child's medical care. Personally, I would rather see the government spend my tax money on helping somebody who's messed up than on building a nuclear bomb to kill other human beings.

Blessing in Disguise

Much of my story is sad and depressing. There's little argument that my life has had more downs than ups—many of which were self-inflicted. Still, my life story is ultimately one of restoration and recovery.

I must be the luckiest man in the world. Numerous times I have been on death's door, only to inexplicably survive. I've been involved in several near-fatal car wrecks, been shot at close range, nearly beaten to death, overdosed more than once, hung myself, and tried to blow off my own head. Many of my friends lost their lives over far less.

I know now that I'm still here because I have a mission to fulfill. Every morning I wake up with a renewed sense of purpose: to warn others about the dangers of drugs. As a child I felt small and powerless, bullied by addicts all around me. I want to give parents who are using drugs encouragement to quit so they and their children can have better lives. I want the children in those homes to know they are not alone, that there are people who care about them. It is never a child's fault that someone else is making bad decisions. Prevention is the key, so it is critical to keep kids from using drugs in the first place. If you use drugs, get help. If you don't use them, don't start. Life is a precious gift—don't waste it.

I've worked hard to break the cycle of addiction and abuse in my own family. I broke that chain—that curse—by giving our kids a safe and healthy environment in which to grow and develop. They are involved in church activities and we keep a very close eye on them. We avoid spending time with family members who drink or use illicit drugs of any kind.

Our kids experienced firsthand what drugs and alcohol can do to a person, because their dad was a horrible person. On numerous occasions I've talked privately to each one of them about how my drug use caused me to become violent and selfish, losing my desire to achieve anything in my life but the next high. I make no excuses and accept all blame. They understand that abuse of any kind is wrong. Amy and I are very open with our kids, and they know we will talk about anything that happened in the past. Nothing is off limits. The material in this book won't surprise them.

I used to have a tight circle of druggies, drunks, and violent criminals surrounding me, but now my beautiful family is my gang. My children and my wife are my best friends; we do everything together. Whereas my first home was destructive and dysfunctional, our home is a sanctuary; a positive, nurturing environment. Our kids are busy with school, sports, and church activities rather than partying like Amy and I did.

The most important thing to a child is for a parent to spend time with them and that is my goal. I participate in my kids' activities; when I'm in town I go to their ball games and track meets. At least two or three times a month I go have lunch with my grade school kids. Unfortunately for me, that means I have to eat multiple meals of marginal chicken nuggets, but they are thrilled to have me there. I go fishing and hunting with my son David, and even though I don't particularly like to hunt, I do it because *he* likes it, and I want to support him and spend time with him.

My devotion to my wife and children is so complete that I don't hang around with other men my age at all; *all* of my free time is spent with my family. Amy and I missed out on so much with our kids when we were using that we would rather spend time with them over anything else. Our proactive steps are working: all of our kids either excel in school or are amazing athletes. God is good.

The scars on my face are ugly, but they are nothing like the ones on the inside. I shoulder guilt, shame, and regret because of my poor choices, and those are the wounds that hurt the most and may never fully heal. Still, I have hope in my heart. In Luke 7:47 (KJNV), Jesus blessed a sinful woman who had anointed his feet with oil by saying, "Therefore, I tell you, her many sins have been forgiven—for she loved much." My many sins have likewise been forgiven. For the first time I have a future full of promise. No matter what tomorrow brings, I know God loves me. It was brutal hand-to-hand combat, but good finally triumphed over evil and slew the dragon.

Appendix: Methamphetamine Abuse and the Impact on Children

Please be advised: Much of the content in this appendix is disturbing. Meth-addicted parents can inflict horrendous harm on innocent children.

IN 1995, FOUR-YEAR-OLD Genny Rojas was placed with her aunt and uncle in Chula Vista, California, while her father was in prison for child molestation and her mother was in drug rehabilitation.

For six months, Veronica and Ivan Gonzales, the parents of six young children, tortured the little girl. Genny was forced to stand on the edges of an open box suspended in the closet with a rope around her neck. She was also made to stand behind the door while enough pressure was put on the door to shove her head through the drywall. She lived in a box and was starved and burned on her face with a blow-dryer.

On July 21, 1995, Genny was repeatedly pushed into scalding bathwater until her skin peeled from her body and was then left to die on a urine-soaked rug. An autopsy found that she had been burned to death over a period of approximately two hours. Other injuries were also discovered—her lip was busted and pulled away from the gum, and her eye was black. She had been handcuffed around her biceps and both her ankles had been tied until they bled.

A jury convicted twenty-nine-year-old Veronica of first-degree murder with special circumstances of torture and mayhem. Her attorney argued for a sentence less than death, stating that she was a first-time offender who was battered by her husband. He also said that her judgment was impaired by the crystal methamphetamine she had been taking. The jury didn't buy it; Veronica and Ivan Gonzales became the first married couple in California to be put on death row for the same crime.

In a perfect world, all children would live in homes that are healthy and safe with parents who love, protect, and nurture them. Sadly, for increasing numbers of children, their formative years are miles away from that *Leave It to Beaver* ideal.

When I speak at schools, churches, jails, or other organizations, I make a special point to talk about the real victims of addiction: children. Kids are silent sufferers; they don't have the voice to speak for themselves, so I put them in my programs to be a voice for them and share what they are really going through. Users make conscious decisions to put poisons into their bodies, but little children never choose to live with a meth addict.

One in eight children in this country is living with someone who abuses drugs, and three-quarters of those in foster care are there because of parental substance abuse. Children of methamphetamine addicts grow up in especially chaotic homes. These blameless victims not only experience chronic neglect due to their parents' drug habits, they often must also endure harsh physical and sexual abuse.

Not only that, methamphetamine is poison—every day innocent children are exposed to toxic ingredients and noxious fumes when it is used or manufactured. I did a lot of bad things, but I never got high around my children. Because Amy and I never cooked meth, and we ate, rather than smoked it, we didn't expose our kids to this type of poison.

Over the last decade, methamphetamine has had a profound impact on the child welfare system. Unfortunately, there are no nationally representative data on the number of children in child welfare who are affected by parental substance abuse. Social services agencies do collect numbers on abuse, but they don't always collect drug information.

Studies do indicate, however, that there is a significant correlation between drug use and child abuse:

- More than 6 million children lived with at least one parent who abused or was dependent on alcohol or an illicit drug during the past year (U.S. Dept of Health & Human Services, Substance Abuse & Mental Health Services Administration).
- One-third to two-thirds of families in child welfare services are

affected by substance use disorders. In some states, the number is as high as 90 percent (National Center on Substance Abuse and Child Welfare; NCSACW)

- 5.5 million children were reported for abuse/neglect (2004) (NCSACW)
- 3.5 million children received an investigation (62.7 percent of referrals made to child protective services) (NCSACW)
- 872,000 children (47.8 percent of those receiving an investigation or assessment) were victims of neglect (64.5 percent); physical abuse (17.5 percent); sexual abuse (9.7 percent); emotional or psychological abuse (7 percent); and medical neglect (2.1 percent). (NCSACW)
- The National Child Abuse and Neglect Data System (NCANDS) reported that an estimated 1,760 children died in 2007 as a direct result of abuse or neglect. This translates to a rate of 2.35 children per 100,000 children in the general population. Children under four years of age accounted for more than 75 percent of the fatalities, because they are unable to defend themselves.

What statisticians tend to forget, however, is that behind these sobering statistics are the beautiful faces of voiceless little boys and girls who have been ignored, beaten, tortured, starved to death, raped, and murdered because their parents chose to get high. These are their stories.

Exposure in the Womb

Child abuse can start well before an infant takes its first breath. Despite the broadcasting of well-intentioned, "Say No to Drugs" and March of Dimes public service campaigns, drug abuse among pregnant women continues to rise. According to the U.S. Dept of Health and Human Services, an estimated 5.1 percent of pregnant women ages 15 to 44 used illegal drugs in 2008. Research from the University of Chicago reveals that the number of pregnant women seeking treatment for methamphetamine use tripled between 1994 and 2006. (see http://www.drugs.com/news/methamphetamine-triples-among-pregnant-rehab-patients-17892.html)

Research reveals that mothers who used methamphetamine were more likely to have a lower socioeconomic status, to live in a household earning less than $10,000 per year, and to be on Medicaid. They were less likely to finish high school. They also tended to be younger and to seek prenatal care later in pregnancy or not at all.

Sixty percent of women who use meth/cocaine during their pregnancies also use marijuana and alcohol, and nicotine use is nearly universal. Nearly half of pregnant meth users have no prenatal care at all—many young women have unprotected sex with multiple partners and don't even know they're carrying a child until they are in the advanced stages of pregnancy. Many miscarry, and more than a quarter give birth prematurely. Since the medical care for premature newborns can cost as much as one million dollars, the social services system is bogged down with expensive medical care for drug-exposed infants.

Babies who are born too early can have problems with many of the systems of their body because they have not finished developing. They are at increased risk for lifelong breathing, hearing, vision, and learning problems. Some evidence also suggests methamphetamines can increase the chance for sudden infant death syndrome (SIDS), even in babies not born early.

Methamphetamine exposure during pregnancy can have serious ramifications on a developing fetus. An ultrasound study of the brains of newborns who were exposed prenatally to methamphetamine or cocaine indicated higher rates of bleeding, decay, and lesions. A high dose of methamphetamine taken during pregnancy can cause a rapid rise in temperature and blood pressure in the brain of the fetus, which can lead to stroke or brain hemorrhage.

The drug also has adverse effects on the placenta, the organ that supplies blood and nourishment to the fetus through the umbilical cord. Methamphetamine restricts the flow of oxygen and nutrients from mother to child. Unfortunately, there is no treatment that can stop the placenta from detaching and there is no way to reattach it. In cases where severe placental abruption occurs, approximately 15 percent of pregnancies will end in fetal death.

Babies born to meth users are three and a half times more likely to be small for their gestational age, with low birth weights and reduced head circumferences. Low-birth-weight infants have an increased risk of mortality and childhood illness. They also have an increased risk of developing type 2 diabetes and metabolic syndrome later in life. In addition to potentially serious medical complications, children with decreased head circumference also have an increased incidence of developmental problems, including reading and problem-solving difficulties. Other common side effects to in utero meth exposure include cleft lip and/or palate and congenital heart defects. In a recent study published in the April 2009 online issue of *Neurology*, researchers found that prenatal meth exposure accelerates brain development in an abnormal pattern, which may explain why some meth-exposed children have delayed developmental milestones.

Newborns who are prenatally exposed to meth often experience dopamine depletion syndrome. Dopamine is a neurotransmitter that is linked to the brain's complex "feel good" system of motivation and reward. Dopamine also plays a key role in addiction. A meth baby's first four weeks of life is a time of recovery from the effects of the methamphetamine on his or her system.

While addicted mothers often think their babies are especially good because they sleep so much, the infants have measurable levels of sleep apnea during which they repeatedly stop breathing. Meth-exposed infants are difficult to wake and feed, and they struggle with very poor suck-swallow coordination. Some babies show abnormal neurological signs, including tremors and too much or too little muscle tone, for many months.

Tainted breast milk is also of great concern. If a mom didn't use during pregnancy, the first thing she is going to want to do as a reward is to get high. Meth-laced breast milk can cause seizures and even death, and if authorities don't test for it, the cause of death will likely appear to be sudden infant death syndrome (SIDS).

Meth-exposed babies often sleep a great deal after they are born, but after that initial thirty-day honeymoon period, meth-exposed babies become grumpy and colicky because their brain needs something it is unable to get. Addicted moms often recognize this fussing as a form of withdrawal and try to soothe their babies by giving them a little meth to ease the symptoms—they'll dip a pacifier in meth or put a little on the baby's gums. The result can be devastating, including seizures, overdose, and even death.

By the time they are ready to enter kindergarten at about age five, meth babies have already exhibited a number of telltale developmental indicators: delayed motor development, poor social interaction, problems processing information through the senses, distractibility, poor anger management, and aggressive outbursts. One of the biggest problems is that these children rarely get the medical care they need because parents hesitate to tell their pediatrician they are struggling; they won't do anything that could be a threat to their ability to use more drugs.

The heartbreaking consequences of using meth during pregnancy don't just apply to women who are habitual users. In 2005, researchers at the University of Toronto found that a single prenatal dose of methamphetamine is enough to cause long-term impairment of the growth and development of the brain or central nervous system. In other words, it's not just the babies of addicts that are at risk; the children of casual drug experimenters are damaged as well.

Caught in the Crosshairs: Health Implications of Meth Exposure

Methamphetamine abuse is not merely a selfish, destructive pastime; it leaves untold victims in its wake. Beyond the addicts themselves, defenseless children are the greatest casualties. Caregivers who use or manufacture the drug subject the most vulnerable to potentially fatal injuries.

Ingestion

Kayden Branhem was a beautiful child with bright blue eyes and curly blond hair. An angel who freely passed out kisses, he loved to play outside and splash in his small plastic wading pool.

At 11:00 PM on May, 2009, the twenty-two-month-old child took a sip from a coffee cup that had been left on a table. His fourteen-year-old mother screamed when she realized he had ingested liquid fire, a corrosive drain cleaner that is used in making methamphetamine.

She and the child's nineteen-year-old father rushed their son to the hospital. The chemical had caused burns around his mouth and on his chest and stomach when it spilled from his mouth; Kayden was wearing shorts but no shirt.

Medical personnel worked to save the boy, inserting a tube to help him breathe, but the toddler's airway was too badly burned and his heart rate plummeted. At 11:57 PM, little Kayden was pronounced dead. He had experienced an unimaginably excruciating death as the sulfuric acid burned him internally.

Authorities are alarmed by the sharp increase in the number of children brought to emergency rooms with burns on their lips, in their mouths, and on their chests because they unknowingly drink the chemicals used to produce methamphetamine.

The final step in the meth production process is called "gassing off." Cooks take the meth base, which is a highly acidic liquid, and neutralize it by mixing it with drain cleaner and salt to form crystals that can be used to get high. This is done by creating a hydrogen chloride (HCl) gas generator. One of the simplest generators is a soft drink bottle topped off with plastic tubing. Unfortunately, to kids it looks very similar to a drink with a straw in it, and they put it in their mouths and get burned.

Another popular method of gassing off is to use a baby bottle. Cooks simply squeeze the nipple, insert a piece of aquarium tubing and let the chemicals do their magic. Not only does it work well mechanically, but their activity is easy to camouflage—the chalky white residue looks like old milk.

When these toxic chemicals make contact with the esophagus, it usually dissolves. It's the same principle as spilling bleach on a delicate garment and watching it eat a hole in the fabric or feeling the burn if it is spilled on the skin. There are three possible outcomes from accidental ingestion. Even if a child spits out the toxic soup, he or she is still probably looking at fifteen to thirty surgeries in their lifetime to continue to stretch the esophagus so they can feed themselves. If damage is too extensive and surgery is not an option, a child faces a lifetime of feeding tubes.

Swallowing these noxious chemicals is usually fatal because there is no way to repair the damage caused by the acid burns traveling past the lips, across the tongue, down the esophagus, and into the stomach. More small children die from accidental ingestion because older ones realize what they've done sooner and spit out the poison.

According to the El Paso Intelligence Center's (EPIC) National Clandestine Laboratory Seizure System, there were an estimated 1,025 children injured at or affected by methamphetamine labs during calendar year 2008. Officials at the Drug Endangered Child Training Network, an organization that seeks to increase community and professional awareness of the impact of adult drug involvement on children, has seen a wide variety of injuries caused by direct exposure to methamphetamine. One of the most unusual incidents involved a young boy who came across an old HCl generator (a soda bottle with the tube in it) in a public park. The device had some meth residue on it, and when the boy put it on his mouth, he had a violent seizure.

It takes a very miniscule amount of methamphetamine to cause a seizure in a child. A starting dose of it is approximately one-tenth of a gram. To get an idea of how much that is, pour out the contents of a Sweet 'N Low packet and divide it into ten portions. Or wet your pinky and put it into the powdery sweetener. The amount of meth that sticks to your finger is more than enough to kill a small child.

Methamphetamine can also be ingested by eating food that has been tainted by the toxic residue that is created by smoking and the manufacturing process. Kidney, stomach, and intestinal problems are common—young children will have bouts of diarrhea or constipation because the meth strips away the good bacteria from the intestinal track. It's almost like they starve to death from the inside out because they aren't getting the proper nutrients.

Fire

On the day after Christmas in 1995, a deafening explosion rocked the tiny desert community of Aguanga, California, that could be felt for miles. Concerned neighbors along the dusty road came running toward the large mobile home that had burst into flames.

Kathy James, thirty-nine, her seven-year-old son Jimmy, and two men managed to escape, but trapped inside the inferno were James's three younger children: Deon, three, Jackson, two, and Megan, one. Seriously burned, the oblivious mother never tried to rescue her screaming children and told a neighbor she didn't want anyone to call for help. By the time firefighters found the charred bodies of the children, James, her son, and the two men had disappeared into the brush-covered hills.

Investigators later discovered why they sneaked off. Amid the burned-out remains of the trailer, they found heating units and containers of precursor chemicals that are used in the manufacture of methamphetamine. Traces of methamphetamine were also found in the mother's bloodstream after she was apprehended. The survivors of the fire, including the boy, later testified that cocaine and meth were being cooked at the time of the fire.

Kathy James was convicted of second-degree murder.

Police find meth labs in almost any location you can imagine. Cooks set them up on the side of the road, in barns and shacks, and in suitcases and car trunks. They are even operating in children's bedrooms.

Experts report that nearly one out of every six meth labs seized by authorities is discovered because of a fire or an explosion. In fact, one-third of meth cooks experience multiple lab fires. National Clandestine Laboratory Seizure System (NCLSS) 2003 data showed that there were 529 reported methamphetamine laboratory fires or explosions nationwide. That number is misleading, however, because it is believed that only about 20 percent of lab fires are actually reported.

The raw materials involved in manufacturing methamphetamine are extremely volatile, and all it takes is one mistake to cause an explosion. An experienced cook can have all the steps right, but something as simple as lighting a cigarette in a room that's not well ventilated can cause a deadly blast.

Lithium strips, which are used in the synthesis of methamphetamine, form highly flammable hydrogen gas when they come into contact with liquids. Even sweating on them during the cooking process may lead to spontaneous ignition.

Careless handling of highly volatile hazardous chemicals and waste—along with unsafe manufacturing methods—can cause materials to burst into flames or explode. Overheating also plays a huge role; many recipes call for heating the chemicals just short of when they will ignite. Improperly labeled and incompatible chemicals are often stored together. Left on easily accessible surfaces, these combustible materials can be torched by a careless spark or flick of a cigarette. HCl generators used during production are little more than bombs waiting to be detonated.

Meth lab fires are most common during the winter months as cooks struggle to stay warm. Labs are often set up in garages, sheds, or other buildings where there is no heat, and to keep the cold out, doors and windows are tightly sealed. As volatile solvents evaporate during the cooking process, they slowly make the air in a small, unventilated room flammable.

Sadly, many parents are willing to sacrifice innocent children to satisfy their cravings for methamphetamine. When the home of one couple exploded while they were cooking meth, they escaped, but they left their little girl inside to die. The flames burned the child's fingers off and burned most of her tiny body. She was in the hospital in constant agony for three weeks before she died, but her parents never bothered to visit. They didn't even attend her funeral. They didn't disappear altogether though—they were caught in a different state a few months later trying to buy chemicals to manufacture more methamphetamine.

Dangerous Living Conditions

The five children ranged in age from one to seven years old. They lived in a one-bedroom home that had no electricity or heat; the only way to keep the chill off was to prop open the door of the gas oven.

The kids had no beds; instead they shared blankets underneath a small card table in the living room. The bathtub was full of backed-up sewage, so it was impossible to bathe.

Used hypodermic needles and dog feces littered the floors where the children were found playing, and they had needle marks on their feet, legs, hands, and arms from accidental contact with syringes. All of them were infected with hepatitis C.

There isn't a word in the English language strong enough to describe the conditions so many children are forced to live in because of meth addiction. Unfortunately, the kinds of living conditions described above are not uncommon in the meth-using community. Ankle-deep garbage, including rotting food, used condoms, dirty laundry, unwashed dishes, and animal feces attract rodents and insects, including cockroaches, fleas, ticks, and lice. Vermin like this can actually survive exposure to meth. In one home, a two-year-old was found with what appeared to be burn marks all around his face. When properly diagnosed, however, the marks turned out to be untreated cockroach bites.

When people first start using meth, they seem to be full of boundless energy. They pour themselves into taking care of themselves and their homes. But once addiction takes hold, users no longer care about their appearance or the condition of their homes. All that matters is getting high.

Meth houses often become garbage houses. In most states it is perfectly legal for anyone, including law enforcement, to go through trash that is sitting on the curb, but they need a warrant to enter the dwelling. To keep what they are doing a secret, users allow trash to accumulate between the four walls of their homes. It's like walking through a maze of trash and debris. With that kind of tinder, house fires are a huge concern.

One of the worst homes I ever came across had layers of trash covering most of the floor space. At night the four children walked across the filth so they could lock themselves in the back room; it was the only place they were safe from the rats that came out after dark. To earn their keep, the kids' job was to dump the toxic meth waste in the backyard.

One day when they saw the police coming, the parents told the children to hide under the trailer—they didn't want police to see how starved the kids were. The crawl space was disgusting. The trailer had a broken sewer line, so every time the toilet was flushed, raw sewage poured on the ground beneath the trailer. The police found the four terrified kids crouched down in human excrement.

Living in a meth house can be hazardous for everyone, but especially for children. Because of paranoia associated with using meth, many addicts rig their homes with explosives to protect themselves. These booby traps can include trip wires, hidden sticks with nails or spikes, and appliances or light switches wired with bombs. Like I did, many addicts keep caches of firearms locked and loaded in case they are crossed by other users.

Another way addicts protect themselves is by keeping dangerous dogs in the home. Canines actually serve a dual purpose. First of all, they make great guinea pigs for manufacturers; they can try a drug out on unsuspecting animals to see if they are safe for human consumption.

Of course, the main reason a junkie has a dog like a pit bull is for protection. But without proper training and nurturing, animals can turn on the kids in the home. In 2001, a seventeen-month-old baby boy was attacked by a pit bull that was kept locked in the basement of the family home. The dog bit off and ate the little boy's genitalia. Reattachment by surgeons proved unsuccessful. The young mother, high on meth, slept through the attack.

Meth users often like to disassemble electronics so when you walk into a home it is in complete disarray. The parts of four televisions will be intermingled, and the electrical outlets and switch plates will be off the walls, allowing raw wires to hang out of the walls. It is a very dangerous environment for curious little ones.

Lambs to the Slaughter: The Child Abuse Epidemic

Little Kalab Lay didn't stand a chance. He and his twin sister Kayla arrived two weeks early on May 10, 2004, to parents Amanda Brooks and Terry Lay. Claiming she was unaware she was pregnant, Amanda admitted using methamphetamine and smoking cigarettes daily during the first half of her pregnancy. Her prenatal care was described as "late and scant."

As soon as he was born, physicians were very concerned about Kalab. Failing to thrive, he was unable to keep food down and was operated on to correct an intestinal blockage. Doctors believe that blockage was likely a result of prenatal exposure to methamphetamine.

Even though the Illinois Department of Child and Family Services was involved with the family for five months before the birth of the twins, they were released to their parents from the hospital. On July 9, 2004, police entered their apartment after smelling ether. They found three adults and four children sleeping in the presence of a methamphetamine lab. Officers recovered acid, ephedrine, communication radios, a police scanner, drug paraphernalia, and a towel containing suspected methamphetamine hidden in a toilet tank.

Malnourished and in poor physical condition, the children were removed from the home and placed in foster care. Parents Amanda Brooks, 29, and Terry Lay, 36, were arrested, charged and convicted of manufacturing methamphetamine and child endangerment.

Upon examination, all four children were found to be in poor physical condition and suffering from obvious maltreatment. Kalab had been especially neglected—he had a flat spot on the side of his head, most likely from being left lying in a crib for long periods of time. He suffered from dehydration, diarrhea, and a severe case of diaper rash. He was listless, painfully thin, and had difficulty taking formula. He also had an increased heart rate, a potential side effect of methamphetamine exposure.

The siblings were split into two separate foster homes. When Kalab's foster mother expressed concern about his small size, stiffness, constant diarrhea, and episodic tremors, he was diagnosed with muscle tetany, a permanent condition that can cause muscle cramps, twitching, or convulsions. The condition was believed to be the result of his mother's meth use during pregnancy.

He also showed at least a 30 percent delay in physical development, language, speech communication, social-emotional development, and adaptive self-help skills. At fourteen months, he was unable to walk alone.

After their parents were released from prison, the children were scheduled for brief visits. The Lays had another child and appeared to be cleaning up their act, but many care workers were against reunification. They felt raising five kids under the age of four years would be stressful for anyone, let alone two parents who were recovering meth addicts.

Despite thriving in foster care for more than two and a half years, however, Kalab and Kayla were returned to their parents on December 18, 2007, for extended thirty-day visits. That proved to be a fatal mistake. On March 31, 2008, emergency responders were called to the Lay home.

Kayla had been savagely beaten; her face and much of her body were covered in bruises in various stages of healing. There were contusions and bruises on her thighs, back, buttocks, and legs, as well as thick scabbing under her left eye.

Thin and frail, little Kalab lay lifeless near a bedroom door. Rescue workers tried frantically to resuscitate him before he was sent by ambulance to the local hospital. Neither of Kalab's parents accompanied him in the ambulance.

He was admitted to the pediatric intensive care unit at St. Mary's Hospital in critical condition shortly before 1:30 PM. Physicians described him as being extremely dehydrated and noted multiple scrapes and abrasions across his face and a large area of bruising over his right thigh that resembled a handprint. He had bruising, abrasions, and dried blood on his scrotum and the shaft of his penis, and swelling, discoloration, and broken tissue near his rectum.

By 2:10 PM Kalab was declared brain-dead. An autopsy determined the cause of death was blunt force trauma to the head, resulting from beatings that had occurred over a period of days. The bleeding and swelling in his brain had created enough pressure to damage the brain stem.

The report also noted that the three-year-old boy had suffered widespread bruising and abrasions at different stages of healing, retinal hemorrhage, had pneumonia, and thin, sparse, and missing hair. Yanking a child's hair can cause hemorrhaging under the skin. Posterior retinal hemorrhage is a classic sign of being shaken.

Of normal height for his age, Kalab was only in the fifth percentile for his weight. His mother admitted being frustrated with him for getting into the cabinets and eating food. Kalab's death was ruled a homicide.

So many times it's small children who pay the ultimate price. Anytime children live in a home where there is heavy meth use, like my children did, they're likely abused. The National Child Abuse and Neglect Data System (NCANDS) reported an estimated 1,760 child fatalities in 2007. This translates to a rate of 2.35 children per 100,000 children in the general population. The term "child fatality" is defined as the death of a child caused by an injury resulting from abuse or neglect, or where abuse or neglect was a contributing factor.

With the exception of 2005, the number and rate of fatalities have been increasing over the past five years, yet many experts believe child fatalities due to abuse and neglect are still underreported. Studies in Nevada and Colorado have estimated that as many as 50 to 60 percent of child deaths resulting from abuse or neglect are not recorded as such. Substantiated child abuse and neglect deaths outnumber those attributed to accidental falls, choking on food, suffocation, or fires in the home combined, according to the U.S. Department of Justice.

More than 80 percent of victimized children are abused or neglected by their own parents, according to the U.S. Administration for Children and Families. At least one-third of those victims grow up to abuse or neglect children of their own.

Absolute Power: The Prevalence of Sexual Abuse

Candice Alexander was first given methamphetamine when she was just twelve years old. That's also probably when the sexual abuse began. Candice reported the abuse to her school, but instead of calling social services, they called her mother, Rebecca Lee, who in turn removed her from school.

Candice was not the first child to be abused by her mother. Her older brother, Cody, was taken from his mother as an infant by child protective services in 1986. A bone scan at a local hospital revealed fractures to the right ulna and radius, the tibia and femur of both legs, and multiple rib fractures in varying stages of healing. He was also blind. Nearly six months old, Cody weighed only nine pounds.

While Cody was in foster care, his mother gave birth to two more children, Amanda and Candice. Amanda was the first of the two to be molested by her stepfather. When Rebecca caught the couple in a sex act when Amanda was fourteen, the girl was kicked out of the house and forced to live with older meth addicts. The parents then moved on to Candice.

Rebecca knew her husband was sexually attracted to her daughter, but didn't mind if he molested Candice as long as she was also present. But one day, Johnny took Candice fishing without inviting her mother. When Rebecca found out they'd had sex on the trip, she went berserk.

For the next ten days, Candice was violently beaten. Then on May 9, 2003, the 90-pound teenager was forcibly injected with enough methamphetamine to kill four 150-pound men. She had a wound on her arm where the drugs were injected and finger-shaped marks near the injection site that were consistent with her arm being forcibly held. Her mother and stepfather also injected her with saline to try to revive her, but it was too late. Candice, at fifteen, was dead.

The killers waited more than three hours to contact law enforcement. By the time they arrived, the meth lab had been disassembled and the bathroom scrubbed with the water hose that had been brought in from outside. The crime scene had also been cleaned.

In the autopsy, Candice's battered body revealed what had occurred during her nightmare. She had fingernail marks on her face from being held down. There were marks extending the length of her right arm from being struck multiple times with a hard, round, elongated object. There was a large abrasion on her nose and blood in her right nostril indicative of being struck in the face.

Candice's hands and chest were covered with motor oil and dirt that had come from the transmission of a truck; at some point during the savage beating she had run out of the house and sought refuge under the vehicle. There were bright red abrasions on her hips that had occurred when she was pulled away from the car by the back of her belt. There was also a prominent linear bruise on the midline of her abdomen, an imprint of the inseam of her pants, and fingernail marks and grass in her pubic area.

In 2005, Rebecca and Johnny Lee were found guilty of murder and sentenced to life in prison. Candice's younger sister, who was thirteen at the time of her death, spent time in a psychiatric hospital while her mother was on trial. She had witnessed part of her sister's murder and was forced to participate in the cleanup.

Tragically, the cycle of abuse continues. On September 5, 2008, Benjamin Terrance Rawls, the biological son of Rebecca Lee, was indicted for abandoning and endangering his ten-week-old son after he allegedly shook the infant. He was also accused of endangering his eighteen-month-old son by leaving him alone in the house with drugs, weapons, and a pit bull.

One of the most dangerous side effects of methamphetamine is an increase in sex drive. Methamphetamine not only triggers the release of powerful brain chemicals that enhance libido and reduce inhibitions, users become more aggressive during sex. They are also much more likely to engage in risky sexual behaviors, like having multiple and anonymous sexual partners or unprotected sex. Users can get so lost in sex that they participate in it for hours and hours, sometimes until they literally rub the skin off their bodies from the friction. When a user is coming down from an extended high, they can become frustrated, angry, and paranoid. If sex makes them feel better, that's what they'll do.

Because meth increases the sexual appetites of users, children of meth users are also at greater risk for sexual abuse, either by parents themselves or by their circle of drug friends. Children serve another purpose beyond being personal playthings for meth abusers: they can also be bargaining chips. If caregivers can't afford their drugs, they simply offer their children as payment. Pedophiles can become convenient babysitters for their meth-addicted friends. There often is no exchange of money or drugs for the sex; instead there is a "don't ask, don't tell" policy.

Penetrative sex with small children causes significant physical injury, especially with younger children. Unfortunately, it's also not uncommon to see sexually transmitted diseases in small children and toddlers.

No child is psychologically able to cope with repeated sexual stimulation. A two- or three-year-old will develop problems resulting from abuse, even though he or she can't possibly know that what is being done to them is wrong. Once they are school age and older, an abused child feels trapped between loyalty to the abusing parent and guilt and shame. The victims of meth-addicted parents also have a profound sense of fear from a parent who threatens them with physical harm if they speak up.

Prolonged sexual abuse also impacts a child's views on sex later in life. Some children who have been sexually abused have trouble relating to others except on sexual terms. Many become sex trade workers or child abusers themselves if the cycle isn't stopped.

Signs a child is being sexually abused include:
- Sleep disturbances or nightmares
- Depression
- Withdrawal from friends or family
- Seductive behavior
- Truancy or sudden changes in school performance
- Comes to school or other activities early, stays late, and does not want to go home
- Difficulty concentrating
- Misbehavior, criminal delinquency
- Secretiveness
- Games and drawings depicting sexual activities
- Aggressive behavior
- Overly compliant, passive, or withdrawn behavior

The Emotional Toll: Meth-Endangered Children and Post-Traumatic Stress

Children who grow up in an environment of drug-induced chaos, violence, abuse, and neglect experience trauma that will affect every aspect of their lives, in the present day and long into the future. Their overall safety and health are compromised, particularly their mental health. Behavioral, emotional, and cognitive functioning are greatly impacted.

These are the most common emotional consequences of living among methamphetamine addicts:

Poor self-esteem: Confused and frightened, meth children often demonstrate low self-esteem and an overall sense of shame. One of the most devastating side effects is that children of meth-addicted parents often have very poor social skills and have difficulty relating to their peers on a normal basis. They become sexually promiscuous, troubled, and isolated.

School Performance: Meth kids often become delinquent and perform poorly in school—if they attend at all. This lack of education and achievement sets them up for unemployment, poverty, and drug and alcohol abuse as adults.

Attachment Disorder: When caregivers fail to respond appropriately to an infant's basic needs, children often develop an attachment disorder. Attachment disorders place children at greater risk for subsequent criminal behavior and substance abuse. Symptoms of attachment disorder include the inability to trust, form relationships, and adapt.

Depression and Anxiety: When emotional trauma occurs during developmentally critical times, there can be damage to the hippocampus region of the brain, which is crucial for memory transfer, learning, and emotional responsiveness. This can ultimately lead to depression and anxiety.

Addiction: As the cycle of drug abuse continues to spiral, more than 60 percent of abused and neglected children will one day land in rehab themselves. Research indicates that as many as two-thirds of all people in treatment for drug abuse report that they were physically, sexually, or emotionally abused during childhood.

Why Kids Don't Want to Tell You

- If they tell, everyone will know the secret.
- Their parents may go to jail—you cannot promise they will not.
- They may be forced to enter a foster home. Perhaps the only thing more painful than the neglect and abuse of a drug home is experiencing safety and silence in an unfamiliar place.
- There is nothing scarier than the unknown.
- The worst thing abused children can imagine is the terrible thing that may happen—that they are sure will happen if they use words to describe what has happened to them and what they have witnessed.
- They are not sure you will understand.
- They are not sure you can fix it.
- They are not sure you care.

—*DrugEndangeredChild.org*

Resources

Educational Resources

United States Department
of Health & Human Services/
Substance Abuse & Mental Health
Services Administration (SAMHSA)
www.samhsa.gov
(877) 726-4727

National Center on Substance
Abuse and Child Welfare
www.ncsacw.samhsa.gov/
default.aspx
(866) 493-2758

National Institutes of Health/
National Institute on Drug Abuse
www.nida.nih.gov
(301) 443-1124

United States Department of
Justice/U.S. Drug Enforcement
Agency
www.justice.gov/dea/index.htm
(202) 307-1000

PBS *Frontline*:
"The Meth Epidemic"
www.pbs.org/wgbh/pages/
frontline/meth

Addiction Resources

Meth Addiction Helpline
www.methhelpline.com
(866) 535-7922

CrystalRecovery.com
www.crystalrecovery.com
(800) 559-9503

MethResources.gov
www.methresources.gov

Partnership for a
Drug Free America
www.drugfree.org
(212) 922-1560

Mothers Against Methamphetamine
www.mamasite.net
(866) 293-8901

Substance Abuse
Treatment Locator
(from the Substance Abuse & Mental
Health Services Administration)
http://findtreatment.samhsa.gov/

Alcoholics Anonymous
www.aa.org
(212) 870-3400